Going
Green

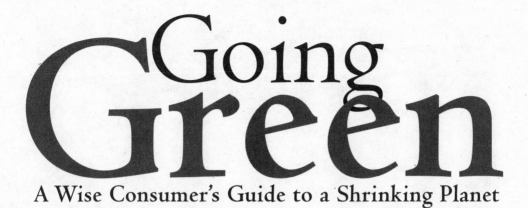

Going Green

A Wise Consumer's Guide to a Shrinking Planet

Sally Kneidel, PhD, and Sadie Kneidel

FULCRUM
GOLDEN, COLORADO

Library of Congress Cataloging-in-Publication Data

Kneidel, Sally Stenhouse.
  The wise consumer's guide to a shrinking planet / Sally Kneidel, and Sadie Kneidel.
    p. cm.
  Includes bibliographical references and index.
  ISBN 978-1-55591-598-8 (pbk.)
  1. Environmental responsibility. 2. Alternative lifestyles. 3. Sustainable living. I. Kneidel, Sadie. II. Title.
  GE195.7.K64 2008
  640--dc22

                          2007052785

Printed in Canada by Friesens Corporation
0 9 8 7 6 5 4 3 2 1

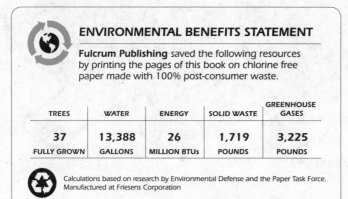

ENVIRONMENTAL BENEFITS STATEMENT

Fulcrum Publishing saved the following resources by printing the pages of this book on chlorine free paper made with 100% post-consumer waste.

TREES	WATER	ENERGY	SOLID WASTE	GREENHOUSE GASES
37	13,388	26	1,719	3,225
FULLY GROWN	GALLONS	MILLION BTUs	POUNDS	POUNDS

Calculations based on research by Environmental Defense and the Paper Task Force.
Manufactured at Friesens Corporation

Design by Jack Lenzo

Fulcrum Publishing
4690 Table Mountain Drive, Suite 100
Golden, Colorado 80403
800-992-2908 • 303-277-1623
www.fulcrumbooks.com

Contents

Introduction

Listening to the news these days can be pretty discouraging. Global warming, over-population, habitat destruction, the Middle East conflict ... Two minutes of this litany is enough to make anyone turn the radio off. Most of us are worried about the future—but what can we do about it?

This dilemma is precisely what motivated us to write this book. Americans are more aware now than ever before of the major challenges facing our planet, but many of us feel powerless to make changes or we don't know where to begin. If you've ever said, "Yeah, I'd *like* to save gas, but I can't live without my car," this book is for you. If you've ever thrown a soda can in the trash and said, "Does recycling make any difference?" this book is for you. If you've ever said, "Hemp clothes are for hippies!" or "Solar panels are for rich people!" this book is for you.

We've said all those things and believed them because we had no idea how much our everyday choices really do matter. We had no idea how to make wise consumer selections—how to choose products that save our money, our health, our resources, and the planet all at the same time.

If these are the kinds of choices you're interested in making, then read on.

Today is not a good time for American consumers to tune out with indifference. With the dollars we spend so abundantly on consumer goods, we unwittingly support industries that are warming the planet, destroying habitat, and degrading our own health. Most of us spend casually and blindly, trusting somehow that the providers of our goods are people with integrity.

But most corporations don't merit such trust. The goal of almost all businesses is to make a profit, regardless of the means or the consequences. Corporations commonly use methods we'd rather not support, such as factory farming, sweatshop labor, and destroying forests, and conceal their methods as much as they are legally allowed to. These cheaper methods allow CEOs to maximize profits for their shareholders, leaving taxpayers to pay the price for environmental repairs and health costs later on.

Not only are corporate methods short-sighted and damaging, but products such as luxury cars that gulp fuel, foods that are laden with mercury, and clothes that leave heavy-metal dyes on your skin continue to damage the environment and consumers.

The purpose of this book is to guide you as a conscientious consumer. As we become informed, we wield enormous power for change. Corporations scramble to produce what we want and spend billions of dollars on marketing research to target our desires. If we demand healthy, safe, and ethical products—if we spend our money only on products that we deem sustainable—then such products will come to predominate the shelves of our neighborhood stores.

We wrote this book because we are

concerned about wild things and green places. We care about human health—our own, and the health of workers laboring on our behalf. We care about the well-being of animals involved in the food industry, and wildlife displaced to make room for factories, stores, and industry.

Perhaps most of all, we care about the future. We who inhabit the planet today are just a gateway for the hundreds or thousands of generations that will follow us.

If you care too, then this book is for you.

Our quest to become informed, activist consumers, we decided, was twofold. First, we had to learn about the systems we don't want to support. Second, we had to discover practical and sustainable alternatives.

Thus we set out to discover some of the true costs of the products we commonly partake of—the cars, the clothes, the food, the fuel for our homes, and so on. We made phone calls, interviewed, and took notes. Then we looked for progressive thinkers in the fields of green housing and transportation, in sustainable forestry and clothing. We looked for people raising Earth-friendly foods and for experts in energy efficiency. We interviewed them too. Then we researched and pulled together solutions and recommendations.

Here's what we found out.

Chapter One

Choosing Energy-Efficient and Clean Transportation

CARS

Petroleum-Powered Cars
The Environmentalist's Driving Dilemma

How should you get around? Ideally, you should walk, bike, and ride public transportation. But quite likely, you live in a town too small to use mass transit and yet too big to walk. Or maybe your job is located on a busy street where you don't feel comfortable biking. Unfortunately, there are a whole host of reasons why you probably feel the need for a car in order to get around in modern-day America. In all but a few cities, our public transportation system is sadly lacking, and in all but the smallest towns, stores and homes are spread too far apart for easy foot access.

Depending on a car can be frustrating when you know that our gas-guzzling ways have contributed to our international woes as well as to our environmental problems. However much you may wish for change, the reality remains the same: our country is built for cars. Yes, in Europe, you can hop on a train and get anywhere on time in (relatively) clean comfort. Even in many developing countries, you can make fine time on a city bus—albeit with a chicken in your lap. But in the United States, we have invested very few resources in developing these sorts of systems.

This is not to say the situation has to stay this way. With an energy crunch looming on the horizon, more and more Americans are ready for change.

"But there's no way I can get by without my car!" you say. Well, you might not have to. Even with an ordinary gasoline-powered car, you have choices. As discussed later in this chapter, *how* you drive can significantly impact your consumption of fuel.

If you are in a position to change your vehicle or transportation habits, you have myriad choices. Some of them aren't worth your time. But others are surprisingly simple and highly effective. Quite a few of them have yet to receive the publicity they deserve. We'll explore them all here. We'll talk to a biodiesel co-op cofounder, another man who makes his own biodiesel, a couple of folks who run their cars on free vegetable oil, a couple of hybrid owners, a biker who cycles, and students who rely on mass transit. They're all mavericks in their own way, unencumbered by conformity. If the prospect of joining their ranks excites you, read on. We'll figure out how to make it work for you.

Petroleum Products Pollute

Whatever your situation may be—whether you are a driver, rider, walker, or biker—your transportation choices are more complex and far-reaching than you could ever imagine. According to the Environmental Protection Agency (EPA), driving is, for most of us, the most polluting action we ever make.[1]

The Enemy Is Us

The greenhouse gases that flow from our tailpipes are the most damaging aspect of our driving. Carbon dioxide is the gas most responsible for global warming. Scientists agree that global warming is and will continue to change life in profound ways for all generations to come. Like a blanket over the Earth, carbon dioxide and other greenhouse gases in the atmosphere trap solar heat close to the planet, preventing it from radiating back into space. This heat retention is already melting polar ice caps, raising sea levels, changing oceanic currents, altering wildlife habitats, and changing our weather—and this is just the beginning.

Unfortunately, Americans are largely responsible for the accumulation of carbon dioxide in the atmosphere—and, hence, for global warming. Although we comprise only 5 percent of the world's population, we own 30 percent of the Earth's cars. More than 204 million cars and trucks are registered in the United States at present.[2] And worse—we're responsible for almost half of the world's existing greenhouse gases. That's because we travel longer distances with weaker fuel-economy standards than drivers in most other countries do. In fact, in 2004, we in the United States drove our cars and light trucks 2.6 trillion miles, equal to driving back and forth to Pluto more than 470 times.[3]

Tailpipe Emissions

In one year, an average driver in the United States emits a staggering 10,000 pounds of carbon dioxide into the atmosphere—that's in addition to 300 pounds of carbon monoxide and 10 pounds each of hydrocarbons and nitrogen oxides.[4] These secondary pollutants are dangerous to our health as well as to the environment. Carbon monoxide impairs breathing by interfering with the blood's ability to carry oxygen. Hydrocarbons react with nitrogen oxides to form ground-level ozone, or smog, which causes respiratory problems such as asthma—a serious ailment that's on the increase. Nitrogen oxides cause acid rain and water-quality problems that threaten the survival of entire ecosystems.

Cars Affect Water Quality Too

About 4 percent of toxic chemicals in our water comes from the manufacturing of batteries for personal vehicles. Other sources of car-related water pollution stem from the manufacturing of paints, plastics, fluids, and steel, and the runoff from salt and other chemicals applied to roads.[5]

What's the Difference between Gasoline and Diesel?

Both gasoline and diesel fuel are refined from petroleum oil. The extraction and refining of oil into these and other various petro-fuels is hazardous in a variety of ways, from oil spills and wastewater seepage to habitat destruction and potential fires and explosions near refineries.

Although they are similar, gasoline and diesel do have some differences that are worth noting. Diesel has more energy per volume than gas, so a diesel engine is 30 to 35 percent more fuel efficient than a gasoline engine of the same size.[6] However, diesel emits more pollutants than gasoline, particularly in the United States where emissions standards are lax. In addition to the array of compounds emitted by gasoline, diesel combustion also produces sulfur oxides, which, like nitrogen oxides, cause acid rain. For this reason, some people feel that gasoline is the lesser evil of the two.[7]

Notes

1. National Safety Council, "What You Can Do about Car Emissions," www.nsc.org/ehc/mobile/mse_fs.htm.
2. Ibid.
3. Janet Wilson, "U.S. Emits Half of Car-Caused Greenhouse Gas, Study Says," *Los Angeles Times*, June 28, 2006, www.commondreams.org/headlines06/0628-07.htm.
4. Michael Brower and Warren Leon, *The Consumer's Guide to Effective Environmental Choices: Practical Advice from the Union of Concerned Scientists* (New York: Three Rivers Press, 1999).
5. Ibid.
6. Environmental Protection Agency, Fuel Economy, "Diesel Vehicles," www.fueleconomy.gov/feg/di_diesels.shtml (accessed December 16, 2007).
7. "Ask Umbra," Grist magazine, www.grist.org/advice/ask/2005/03/14/umbra-svo/index.html?source=daily.

Additional Resources

Environmental Working Group, "Asthma and Automobiles," www.ewg.org/sites/asthmaindex/about/.
John Rockhold, "Green Means Go," *Mother Earth News*, October/November 2005.

The Politics of Pollution

Ice caps are melting, the ocean is rising, and fossil fuels are the main culprit. The fastest solution is to burn less fuel—a feat that could easily be accomplished. We have the technology to manufacture all new personal vehicles to get at least 35 to 40 miles per gallon; Japan currently boasts an average of 45 miles per gallon. If we're the richest nation in the world, and we're generating more greenhouse-gas emissions than any other nation except for China, then why doesn't the government require all new personal vehicles to get 35 miles per gallon right now? If tailpipe emissions and global warming are not sufficient motivators, what about our military entanglements in the Middle East? Strife with oil-rich nations has become an all-too-familiar and persistent centerpiece to our international affairs.

Federal fuel-economy standards, known as Corporate Average Fuel Economy, or CAFE, do exist for new vehicles. These standards dictate the minimum number of miles per gallon an automobile must get. Automakers are fined for cars that don't meet the standard, which is currently 27.5.[1]

What about trucks? CAFE standards were created during an oil embargo in the 1970s when oil was temporarily in short supply. Lawmakers wanted to give farmers a break on farm vehicles so the standards mandated for trucks were much weaker than those for cars. At that time, trucks constituted relatively inconsequential highway traffic.[2]

The new standards for cars had the desired effect of decreasing the number of Cadillacs and other big gas-guzzling cars on the road, which helped the country conserve oil. But after the oil crisis was over and prices declined, the standards remained the same and continued to give trucks a break. During the 1980s, when neither President Ronald Reagan nor the American public was concerned about energy conservation, Detroit created sport-utility vehicles (SUVs), sexy and powerful new gas-guzzlers that could be classified as light trucks and thus evade the stricter car standards. Today, nearly half the personal vehicles sold in the United States are big enough to elude the restrictions for cars. Current CAFE standards for new SUVs and light trucks under 8,500 pounds is a very permissive 22.2 miles per gallon.[3]

The standards are even more permissive for really big personal vehicles weighing more than 8,500 pounds, such as Hummers and Ford Excursions, which are at present completely exempt from any fuel-economy standards at all.[4]

But things are looking up ... sort of. In December of 2007, legislation was passed to raise CAFE standards for the first time in more than three decades. The Energy Independence and Security Act will increase fuel-economy standards to 35 miles per gallon by the year 2020 for new cars and trucks. The law has been hailed by many scientists and others as an important move—or at least an important step—toward saving oil and curbing global warming. Union of Concerned Scientists (UCS) president Kevin Knobloch called the new law "a very significant, concrete, and long-overdue step forward."[5]

Although many people are encouraged by the enactment of this law, critics maintain that the new legislation lags far behind already existing standards in Europe and Asia, and that upon closer scrutiny, it is not as favorable as it might sound initially. The new standards will require a corporate *average* of 35 miles per gallon, rather than a per-vehicle standard. This provision will allow Detroit automakers to continue manufacturing oversized SUVs and light trucks. In the political wrangling that preceded passage of the legislation in Congress, Detroit automakers were granted this measure because SUVs and light trucks generate most of their income and have for some time.[6]

Consumer Choices

A drive across town will tell you that SUVs are still immensely popular in the United States. In fact, after a temporary slump during 2006, sales increased during 2007.[7] And yet sales of fuel-efficient cars are increasing too. As Americans grow more energy conscious and feel the pinch of rising gas prices, they are turning their attention to Asian automakers who have been making fuel-efficient cars for decades. The availability of inexpensive Asian cars is expected to surge, especially as the Chinese move toward capitalism and suddenly ramp up auto production in an unprecedented frenzy for more and more cars. Car sales in China increased 54 percent during 2005 alone. According to *The New York Times*, cheap Chinese cars, starting at around $10,000, will be available here in the next few years.[8] A conversation with our local car dealer told us that Korean cars are on the way as well.

In an effort to appeal to newly fuel-conscious shoppers but avoid the costs of retooling factories, in June of 2006 Ford announced plans to turn its focus to flexible-fuel cars that can burn E85, a fuel that's 85 percent ethanol and 15 percent gasoline. General Motors and Chrysler have expressed an interest in flex-fuel models as well. Flex-fuel cars can be manufactured using technology that Detroit factories already have in place, meaning that the cars can be made at a much cheaper cost than hybrids, which would involve the costs of revamping factories for production. Japanese automakers' grasp on the hybrid market is insurmountable, but the two largest Japanese carmakers, Toyota and Honda, do not at present market flex-fuel cars in the United States. Although U.S. automakers won't for the foreseeable future be competing with Asian companies in the market for flex-fuel cars, they will be competing with each other.[9]

Staking out the flex-fuel market is a way for Detroit to appear green, although E85 fuel is not widely available and won't be for some time. As of January 2008, only 1,400 of 180,000 service stations in the United States sell E85 fuel.[10]

Despite the current limitations of ethanol as a fuel (see pages 11–14), the new fuel-emissions legislation has been crafted to assist Detroit automakers in their development of flex-fuel vehicles. In fact, the loophole that scientists most object to in the new law is the provision for flex-fuel vehicles. The law will allow automakers to calculate the average fuel economy of their fleet based on an assumption that all of their flex-fuel vehicles are burning no more than 50 percent gasoline, whereas in reality most flex-fuel vehicles use higher blends of gasoline, or straight gasoline. To take advantage of this wink and nod from Congress, Detroit automakers plan to concentrate their flex-fuel development plans on their large and heavy models—the SUVs and trucks. Since these vehicles use the most fuel, this plan will allow auto manufacturers to gain the most benefit from the flex-fuel loophole. Thanks to this new legislation, auto corporations will be held accountable for only a fraction of the gasoline that is actually burned by their large and fuel-inefficient vehicles.

Detroit automakers will continue to develop some hybrids—but not to the extent they had previously indicated. The changing strategies of American automakers are a bit confusing, but the reality seems to be that Detroit finds itself up a creek with no green paddle in sight. At present, Japanese automakers appear to be better positioned to meet the needs of new-car shoppers seeking maximum fuel economy.

Window Stickers Lie

The gas mileage touted on the window sticker for a new car is always more favorable than its true mileage. These official estimates, which come from the EPA, are based on driving at a constant speed on level ground and without air-conditioning, idling, stop-and-go traffic, and so on. The Environmental Working Group (EWG), a nonprofit scientific research center, made their own estimates of "real-world miles per gallon" for new cars, trucks, and SUVs using federal reports and data.[1] According to the EWG, the real-world miles per gallon for new cars is closer to 21.7 instead of the 27.5 currently mandated by the federal government. The true miles per gallon for new SUVs and trucks is closer to 16.3 rather than 22.2. The true figures are 21 percent and 26 percent lower for cars and SUVs/trucks respectively than current federal CAFE standards.

The EPA's system of estimating miles per gallon for window stickers has recently been revamped to be somewhat more realistic, and the change will be reflected on 2008 stickers. The new EPA estimates for each car and SUV/truck model are expected to show 10 to 20 percent less fuel efficiency than the current EPA estimates—which will be closer to reality, but still not accurate.

Note
1. David Goldstein, "Realistic Gas Mileage Is Urged," *Charlotte Observer*, July 13, 2006.

Oil Companies Soar

Because SUVs and other "light trucks" have been promoted so heavily and have been so popular, the United States' fuel economy actually declined between 1985 and 2000.[11] Oil companies have reaped big benefits from keeping gas-guzzlers on the road. In 2003, the United States was the global oil industry's biggest customer, gulping a quarter of the world's production of gas and oil[12]—even though we have only 5 percent of the world's population. (China is a close competitor for oil consumption, but has more than four times as many people.) Oil and gas companies go to great lengths to keep Americans addicted. According to a report by the Center for Public Integrity, between 1998 and 2004 the oil industry spent more than $420 million on politicians, political parties, and lobbyists in order to protect its interests in Washington.[13] The oil industry's influence on the government is enormous, as one might infer based on the limited attention paid to auto emissions and the aggressive postures toward Persian Gulf suppliers.

Indicative of oil companies' gluttony and greed, ExxonMobil reported $36 billion in profits in 2005, a record for an American company.[14]

Chopped Up by Highways

Cars' major impact on wildlife is through habitat loss—due to the extraction and transporting of oil, as well as greenhouse gases and other pollutants. But collisions with vehicles are also a major source of wildlife mortality, even for protected populations within national parks. In addition, highways fragment breeding populations. Roads are often permanent barriers to animals' migration and to breeding and foraging movements. The number of individuals in a small population isolated by roads may be too low to sustain the group. Your community may not have any bobcats, wolves, or elk remaining, but even small animals have home ranges that cover long distances in order for them to find mates or adequate food. Box turtles may travel a distance of two thousand feet in their usual meanderings, and a five-inch-long dusky salamander has a normal home range of forty-eight square miles! But every time either one crosses a road, they're likely to be killed. Although we may feel we don't have much control over the building of roads, our tremendous reliance on personal vehicles is the major impetus behind road construction.

Where to Turn?

The good news is that because we have more resources than most of the world, we also have more choices. In the coming sections, we'll introduce you to a number of people who are finding different ways to get around some of these problems. The more we demand alternatives such as mass transit, cleaner fuels, and cars with better fuel economy, the sooner we'll get them. We can hasten the process by rewarding companies that are already providing them.

Notes

1. Maria Godoy, "CAFE Standards: Gas-Sipping Etiquette for Cars," *All Things Considered*, National Public Radio, June 7, 2006, www.npr.org/templates/story/story

.php?storyId=5458404.

2. Angela Bradbery, "The SUV Phenomenon: Ducking Regulations for More Than a Decade," *Public Citizen News*, www.citizen.org/autosafety/suvsafety/articles .cfm?ID=5445.

3. Godoy, "CAFE Standards."

4. Ibid.

5. Union of Concerned Scientists, "House Vote Sends Landmark Energy Bill to President Bush," December 18, 2007, www.ucsusa.org/news/press_release/house-passes-land mark-energy-bill-0092.html (accessed January 8, 2008).

6. Jeremy W. Peters, "Car Sales in the U.S. Show SUVs Lose Appeal," *The Herald Tribune*, May 5, 2005, www.iht .com/articles/2005/05/04/business/auto.php.

7. Michael Taylor, "High Gas Cost Won't Drive Away Buyers of Big SUVs: After 2-Year Slump, Demand Rebounds," *San Francisco Chronicle*, May 20, 2007, www .sfgate.com/cgi-bin/article.cgi?f=/c/a/2007/05/20/ MNG2NPU9FD1.DTL (accessed January 8, 2008).

8. Ted Conover, "Capitalist Roaders," *The New York Times Magazine*, July 6, 2006.

9. Micheline Maynard, "Ford Plans Shift in Focus away from Hybrids," *The New York Times*, June 30, 2006.

10. National Ethanol Vehicle Coalition, www.e85refueling .com/ (accessed January 8, 2008).

11. Godoy, "CAFE Standards."

12. Aron Pilhofer and Bob Williams, "Big Oil Protects its Interests: Industry Spends Hundreds of Millions on Lobbying, Elections," Center for Public Integrity, July 15, 2004, www.publicintegrity.org/oil/report.aspx?aid=345.

13. Ibid.

14. Jim Snyder, "Gas-Price Surge Strains Oil-Auto Pact," *The Hill*, May 2, 2006.

The Real Cost of Sport-Utility Vehicles

An interview with Mike Stenhouse, PhD, engineer, publisher, and consultant on automotive performance

Sally (S): Considering alternative-engine technologies and alternative fuels, which do you think is the most likely to reduce our dependence on foreign oil in the next two or three decades?

Dr. Stenhouse (DS): Currently, pickup trucks and SUVs are not included in the Corporate Average Fuel Economy goals, which limit the sizes of cars. So if you want a huge, conspicuous-consumption, "mine is bigger than yours" gas-guzzling ride, you have to buy a pickup or an SUV. This is why we have these monstrous luxury pickups and SUVs

that never carry anything and never even go off road. Nobody wants to fix this loophole. The auto manufacturers use it to sell high-profit luxo-barges. Consumers use it to get the in-your-face big rides that no longer exist in the car market. The government uses the loophole to keep the consumers (voters) and car companies (contributors) happy while giving the pretense of doing something about fuel consumption.

The first step is to close this loophole and get the gas hogs off the road. It will take years for all these aberrations to wear out and disappear from the road.

S: What advice would you give to a consumer who wants to reduce his own contribution to harmful tailpipe emissions and reduce his own consumption of petroleum for transportation?

DS: First, cut down on unnecessary driving, and second, make his next car purchase based on fuel economy.

S: Why are Americans responsible for 25 percent of the world's energy consumption when we have only 5 percent of the world's population? What's the solution to that problem?

DS: Because we have a lot of money and a lot of energy and we believe that more is better and bigger is better. We need a real attitude adjustment.

S: Although biofuels were mentioned in the 2006 State of the Union address, the government is currently funding only a pilot program for the development of cellulosic ethanol. There's no funding for any commercial application. What's holding the government back from simply saying, "Starting in 2008, all new cars must get 35 miles per gallon"?

DS: Keeping consumers (voters) and car companies (contributors) happy, as I mentioned earlier.

S: Do SUVs keep our kids safe?

DS: I have a neighbor who purchased a monstrous SUV for his kids to drive to school. His explanation: that they would be safer. This I have a problem with, first, because I *doubt* that it is safer for his kids, and second, because I *know* it is not safer for other people's children.

Safer? Studies for antilock brakes have shown that they do not reduce accident rates. They, in fact, may increase them. The apparent reason is that drivers who feel more protected by their vehicles drive more recklessly. My misguided neighbor may have made it more likely that his kids would be involved in an accident.

Safer for whom? Even if his kids are safer, the people his kids run into are not safer. Studies show that [people in] small cars hit by large SUVs and pickup trucks are four times more likely to be injured. Sounds a bit selfish to me. All parents have the right and the responsibility to protect their children, but not at the expense of the lives of other people's children.

More to the point, we are sending someone else's sons and daughters to foreign lands to fight and die for our oil supply—oil needed to feed the voracious appetite of my neighbor's SUV. This is not only selfish, it is sinful.

Community Voice

Emily, Age 23: Living without a Car

"I don't have a car because I don't have my license. It's just never been convenient to get. Ideally, I'd like to live somewhere with good public transportation and never need a car. I guess I should get my license so I could help drive on road trips, or drive friends' cars occasionally, but I don't really want a car of my own. Even if I could afford it, I don't want the responsibility. Or the guilt!

"Not having a car isn't too difficult. In Washington, DC, it was really easy; I took the bus and metro everywhere. And in my hometown, which is a very small town, I rode my bike everywhere. It was actually good for me; I rode my bike a lot more in high school than I would have if I'd have had a car. What's tough is living in a midsize city like Greensboro [North Carolina]. It's not too hard to catch a ride to school with a friend, but Greensboro's public transportation system is pretty mediocre. Actually, it's awful. If I want to do anything on my own, like go to a concert nobody else wants to go to, I'm out of luck."

Quick, Let's Do Something!

So now you know the facts. You've seen the car-induced haze over your city, and you've emptied your wallet far too often at the pump. You're tired of feeling enslaved to a system that's so obviously flawed. Yet no matter how dismayed you may feel about your current transportation habits, you probably can't change them overnight. But you have more control than you think you do. Even in your very same vehicle, you can make changes that will significantly affect your environmental impact.

Driving Style

Following are a few fuel-saving tips you can easily use right now to reduce the environmental impact of your driving:

- Don't warm up your engine before driving. Engines emit the most pollutants when cold and heat up faster while driving than while idling.

- Combine outings. Even if you have to turn the car on and off at each parking lot, using the car for many errands at once reduces the number of cold starts.

- Drive steadily. The most fuel-efficient speed is between 35 and 45 miles per hour.[1] It's much more efficient to chug along steadily at 45 miles per hour than to race to a stoplight only to slow down, idle, and accelerate again.

- Don't idle. Leaving the car running for thirty seconds uses just as much gas as it would to restart the engine.

- Maintain your car. A faulty or poorly serviced engine can release up to ten times the emissions of a well-maintained one.[2] This includes all parts of the car; old tires, for example, impede the car's movement and decrease its fuel efficiency.

- Share rides. It costs you about 25¢ a mile to drive your car, figuring in all the operating costs as well as fuel. By carpooling on the daily commute to work, you can save as much as $3,000 a year on gas, insurance, parking, and maintenance.[3]

- Drive at nonpeak times. This is the best way to avoid idling, stop-and-go traffic, and non–fuel-efficient speeds on the road.

If you think all this is insignificant, think again. Nationwide, the amount of gasoline and money wasted by inefficient driving is tremendous, adding up to 753 million gallons of gas per year, or $1,194 per driver in wasted fuel and time.[4]

Notes

1. National Safety Council, "What You Can Do About Car Emissions: Better Car Maintenance Can Save Money, Improve Safety, and Reduce Pollution," www.nsc .org/ehc/mobile/mse_fs.htm.
2. Ibid.
3. Ibid.
4. Ibid.

Alternatives to Gasoline
Biofuels for Gasoline Engines
Ethanol and Flex-Fuel Cars

Right now, good or bad, our family has cars with gasoline engines. That means we don't have many biofuel choices. An ethanol-gasoline blend is the only biofuel currently being developed for gasoline engines. Ethanol is alcohol—the same kind as in beer and wine. Currently, the gasoline we use in the United States is on average 2 percent ethanol.[1] Standard gasoline engines can handle a blend that's up to 10 percent ethanol.

Ethanol contains high amounts of oxygen; this allows the gasoline to burn more completely and emit less pollutants. A blend of just 10 percent ethanol releases a quarter less carbon monoxide and 10 percent less carbon dioxide than straight gasoline. When ethanol is mixed with diesel fuel, the amount of sulfur oxides and particulates in tailpipe emissions is much lower.

But for ethanol to make a significant difference in our fossil fuel consumption, we'll have to use blends with more than 10 percent ethanol. New flexible-fuel cars are able to burn blends of up to 85 percent. But few of us own flex-fuel vehicles, and, as mentioned earlier, only 1,400 gas stations nationwide offer E85, the 85 percent ethanol blend.[2] Most of these stations are in the Midwest, but not all. The U.S. Department of Energy offers an interactive map at www.fueleconomy .gov that will tell you the address of gas stations in your area that sell E85.

The Rush to Produce More Ethanol

As gas prices rise, the enthusiasm for ethanol blossoms.

The vast majority of ethanol produced in the United States is made from corn. Corn ethanol has its supporters and its detractors, but the overall consensus among scientists and engineers is that corn ethanol won't solve our fuel problems in the long run. Making ethanol from corn is easy; the problem is

Can corn ethanol save us? Courtesy of Harlan Weikle

growing enough corn. It's not an ideal crop, from many perspectives. Corn is relatively expensive to grow and is heavily subsidized, meaning that the federal government pays farmers to grow it to ensure that they'll keep growing it regardless of the market price. It requires more-intensive management than most crops—more water, more chemical fertilizers, more pesticides. Irrigating corn depletes underground aquifers in the Midwest, and the fertilizers and pesticides pollute air and water, and compact soil.

Another difficulty with getting ethanol from corn is the availability of agricultural land. In order to replace 75 percent of Persian Gulf oil with ethanol by the year 2025, as proposed in the 2006 State of the Union address, we would need to devote at least half of the nation's farmland to growing corn *just for fuel*.[3] That's not going to happen. Corn is already our biggest crop nationally, and the meat industry has staked out a hefty portion of it—56 percent—for livestock feed.[4] Agricultural experts such as Dan Basse, president of Ag-Resources, are predicting imminent wars between the livestock and ethanol industries for our nation's corn.[5] With the global demand for food expected to double in the next few decades, we need a biofuel that doesn't interfere with our food supply.

Yet another serious drawback for corn ethanol is the fuel required to produce and transport it. David Pimentel of Cornell University and many other scientists assert that corn uses more fossil fuels than the ethanol can replace. How so? Producing nitrogen fertilizers for corn requires fossil fuels. The

manufacturing of farm machinery such as plows and combines requires energy, and while they're in use, these machines guzzle fuel. After the corn is grown, harvested, and fermented, yet more energy and fuel are needed to extract the ethanol from the 8 percent ethanol solution that forms during fermentation.[6] Some disagree with Pimentel in his calculations of a net energy loss, but more-optimistic calculations—that corn ethanol could yield up to 25 percent more energy than is used in its production—still aren't particularly encouraging.

In spite of these problems, there is at present a mad dash to produce corn ethanol in the midwestern states where most corn is grown. Archer Daniel Midlands Company and a host of smaller companies are investing heavily in the cultivation of corn and its conversion to ethanol. That's largely because a federal subsidy of 51¢ per gallon makes ethanol production a very profitable business at present.[7]

But the infatuation with corn ethanol won't last long. Reality will settle in sooner or later. What then? Ethanol from sugarcane? Brazil is the world's leading exporter of ethanol, all made from sugarcane, and is looking to North American, Japanese, and Indian markets to boost exports.[8] But Brazil is also the heart of the rain-forested basin of the Amazon river and all of its tributaries. Fifty percent of the world's species are from tropical rain forests, and already the world is losing a patch of rain forest the size of Great Britain each year. So we might think twice about encouraging the conversion of Brazilian forests to sugarcane fields.

A Solution That Could Really Work

Although government and corporate honchos profess enthusiasm for corn ethanol, scientists and engineers are investigating another source: cellulosic ethanol, which requires much less land and energy for production than does ethanol.

Cellulosic ethanol can be derived from waste plant matter—from both agricultural and suburban land, so land use is not an issue. The United States accumulates nearly a billion tons a year of agricultural detritus, such as corn husks, waste straw, and wood chips, all of which could be used to make cellulosic ethanol.[9] This simple alcohol can also be made from perennial grasses, such as switchgrass, which will grow in marginal lands unsuitable for agriculture. In either case, there's no competition with food producers. Even on marginal lands, the yields per acre of usable material are much higher for cellulose than for corn: ten to fifteen dry tons per acre[10] as opposed to four to five tons for the best grain crops, including corn. That is because the entire plant is used to make cellulosic ethanol, whereas only the kernels are used for corn ethanol.

Also, much less fossil fuels are used to produce cellulose than to produce corn ethanol. Because cellulose is generated from plant waste or weeds, it requires little to no added energy to create. Switchgrass, for example, requires little energy input to cultivate; it thrives without irrigation, fertilizers, or pesticides. Because the plants resprout on their own after harvest, they don't require the use of gas-guzzling farm machinery that is needed to replant corn every year.[11]

The U.S. Department of Energy confirms that cellulosic ethanol outshines both gasoline and corn ethanol in terms of energy used in its production. According to their analysis, for every one unit of energy available at the fuel pump, 1.23 units of fossil energy are used to produce gasoline, 0.74 units of fossil energy are used to produce corn ethanol, and only 0.2 units of fossil energy are used to produce cellulosic ethanol.[12]

These advantages in land use and energy efficiency are huge and obviously tip the scales in favor of cellulosic ethanol—if we can work out the kinks.

The main kink is the molecular nature of cellulose—it's harder to break down than corn or sugarcane. The enzymes required to break down cellulose are currently far too expensive for cellulose technology to be competitive with corn or sugarcane fermentation. According to the U.S. Department of Energy, scientists hope to eventually reduce the cost of the enzymes by as much as 98 percent.[13] In 2006, the research company Novozymes, working with the National Renewable Energy Laboratory, achieved a thirtyfold reduction in enzyme costs, from $5 per gallon of ethanol to between 10 and 20¢.[14]

Alternatively, scientists have developed a completely different method of attacking cellulose, a process called thermal gasification. Instead of breaking cellulose into sugar molecules, the carbon in the cellulose is converted into carbon monoxide. A microorganism, a species of *Clostridium*, ingests the carbon monoxide to produce ethanol, hydrogen, and water. Or, alternatively, the carbon monoxide can be converted to ethanol with a catalytic converter. Thermal gasification presents its own challenges and is under investigation at pilot plants. But at present, the method using enzymes (called enzymatic hydrolysis) seems to be picking up steam faster. Agrivida, working on genetically modified plants that have enzymes to break down their own cellulose, and Mascoma, working on genetically modified bacteria, are among the companies making headway with enzymes. Novozymes and Genencor have both made advances supported by the Department of Energy.[15]

But eyes are on Iogen Corporation at present. The Rocky Mountain Institute, an energy think tank, reports that the first commercial-scale plant for producing ethanol from cellulose with the use of enzymes is scheduled to be built by Iogen by 2008. They expect production costs of only $1.30 per gallon (to which distribution costs must be added).[16] With a $45 million investment from Shell, they seem poised to get the cellulosic ball rolling for real.[17]

Notes

1. Nathan Glasgow and Lena Hansen, "Focusing on the Nexus of Agriculture and Energy Value Chains," Rocky Mountain Institute, 2006, http://ncaltfuels.blogspot.com/2005/10/energy-value-of-ethanol-article-in-rmi.html (accessed December 16, 2007).
2. National Ethanol Vehicle Coalition, www.e85refueling.com/ (accessed January 8, 2008).
3. Alex Barrionuevo, Simon Romero, and Michael Janofsky, "Ethanol Bonanza Is Reshaping America's Heartland Economies," *The New York Times*, June 25, 2006.
4. Ibid.
5. Ibid.
6. "Growing Expectations: New Technology Could Turn Fuel into a Bumper Crop," *Science News* 168: 218–220.
7. Alex Barrionuevo, "It's Corn vs. Soybeans in a Biofuels Debate," *The New York Times*, July 13, 2006.
8. Reese Ewing, "Brazil Races to Keep Ahead of World Ethanol Demand," *Reuters*, June 15, 2005, www.planetark.com/dailynewsstory.cfm/newsid/31249/story.htm (accessed December 16, 2007).
9. "Growing Expectations," *Science News*.
10. Glasgow and Hansen, "Focusing on the Nexus."
11. Ibid.
12. Ibid.
13. U.S. Department of Energy, Energy Efficiency and Renewable Energy, Biomass Program, Technologies, "Enzymatic Hydrolysis," www1.eere.energy.gov/biomass/enzymatic_hydrolysis.html.
14. Glasgow and Hansen, "Focusing on the Nexus."
15. Gareth Cook, "Drive to Make Fuel from Plants Gets a Boost," *The Boston Globe*, July 4, 2006, www.boston.com/news/science/articles/2006/07/04/drive_to_make_fuel_from_plants_gets_a_boost/.
16. Glasgow and Hansen, "Focusing on the Nexus."
17. Stuart Brown, "Biorefinery Breakthrough," *Fortune* magazine, CNNMoney.com, February 8, 2006, http://money.cnn.com/magazines/fortune/fortune_archive/2006/02/06/8367962/index.htm.

Hybrid Cars

You may be one of the lucky for whom buying a new car is an option. Have you considered a hybrid? You may find yourself wondering what all the fuss is about. Is it worth paying the extra money? Will it really make a difference—to your wallet or to the planet? Let's talk to a few hybrid owners and find out.

Who's Driving Them?

Shirley is a friend and neighbor, a spunky southern hairstylist. Teresa is a banker turned Methodist minister, married to an English teacher. Liz is a retired county commissioner and role model for a generation of green activists in our community. Brenton is a high school student. They all drive hybrids, and they all rave about their cars.

"I just sing its praises," said Liz. "It gets great mileage. The 2005 is supposed to get 50 miles per gallon; I'm sure it gets close to that. And it's so quiet. I talk about my Prius every chance I get. It's just a darn good car."

Shirley agrees. "I knew the price of gas would be going up. Bob gets *Consumer Reports* magazine, and it said the Prius has the best gas mileage plus the best frequency-of-repair record. And it really is a good car. I love it. If I don't do a whole lot of running around, other than going to work and back, I go five to six weeks without filling it up!"

We've met quite a few people in the last year who are committed to driving eco-friendly cars (*eco-friendly* meaning that they have low tailpipe emissions). While some have opted for hybrids, others have jumped whole hog into the biodiesel or waste-vegetable-oil camp. And some are just driving Japanese cars that have been getting great mileage, with the resulting low tailpipe emissions, for years. Among our own acquaintances, biodiesel and waste-veg users seem to be entrepreneurs or artists who are still building their careers and may have limited funds or are just independent do-it-yourselfers. Hybrid owners are more likely to be well-established in their careers—people who can afford brand-new cars. If you're willing to spend the money on a new car, some hybrids are excellent choices for the environment. In his monumental movie on global warming, *An Inconvenient Truth*, Al Gore advised us all to drive hybrids if we can.

What Are the Costs?

There are several hybrids already on the market, including the popular Toyota Prius, Toyota Camry, Nissan Altima, Honda Civic, Honda Accord, and Ford Escape, with promises from virtually every automaker to make more models soon. The purchase price of a hybrid is higher than corresponding conventional models, often several thousand dollars more, but much of the extra cost of the purchase price will be made up in fuel savings.

How Does a Hybrid Work?

A hybrid vehicle combines a conventional, but small, gasoline engine with an electric motor and battery. But unlike a battery-electric vehicle, the hybrid's battery does not require being plugged in for long hours of recharging. Instead, the car is designed to recharge its battery while being driven in a process called regenerative braking—the car captures the energy that's given up during braking and returns this energy to the battery.

Basically, a hybrid-electric vehicle merges the best features of gasoline-engine and electric cars. The electric motor and battery help the gasoline engine operate more efficiently, cutting down on fuel use and emissions. Meanwhile, the gasoline engine overcomes the limited acceleration capacity and driving range of an electric vehicle. A hybrid can travel 500 miles or more before it needs to be refueled. The Honda Insight, the first mass-produced hybrid, could go 700 miles between fueling stops. This little hybrid played an important pioneering role, but had a number of shortcomings that limited its consumer appeal. It had only two seats, and, as a hatchback, had a small cargo area. Its batteries drained quickly, and consumers reported inadequate acceleration for passing, especially on uphill grades. Over time, higher-performing hybrids displaced the Insight, and Honda discontinued it at the end of 2006.[1]

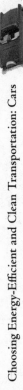

Great Fuel Economy

The best hybrids get dramatically better fuel economy than the American average of 25 miles per gallon.[2] Hybrid automakers advertise 36 to 60 miles per gallon or more, but like all window-sticker estimates, that's an exaggeration. Owners of hybrids typically report gas mileage in the low 40s in town and mid-40s on the highway—still fantastic figures. If a mandatory national fuel economy of 40 miles per gallon were imposed right now, our fuel consumption for personal vehicles would be cut by nearly 38 percent. That's how good 40 miles per gallon is.

Low Emissions

The low level of tailpipe emissions is a huge plus for all of us who enjoy breathing clean air and hope for a stable climate. According to the UCS, the Toyota Prius generates 90 percent fewer smog-producing pollutants than the current national average.[3] Smog is associated with multiple respiratory ailments, including emphysema, asthma, and lung cancer. "It's the clean air that's important to me," said hybrid-owner Teresa. "That's why I bought a Prius. I invite my neighbors with little kids to come drive it, but they never do. They're all driving these big SUVs. Apparently, they've never given a thought to clean air." Teresa thinks about it—her grandson has asthma. With her car choice, she feels like she's doing something about it.

Are all hybrid models as clean as the Prius? We weren't sure, so we contacted Jim Kliesch, the green-car expert at the American Council for Energy Efficient Economy (ACEEE, greenercar.com). The ACEEE is a great resource for assessing environmentally friendly cars and home-energy savings. We asked Kliesch if all hybrids cause less smog than conventional cars. He said not necessarily. "The level of smog-forming emissions will depend largely on the vehicle's design, and especially the design of its after-treatment system. While most hybrids to date meet relatively clean emission standards, not all of them do."[4]

We also asked Kliesch if all hybrids emit fewer greenhouse gases than conventional cars. He said *only* if they're designed for fuel efficiency. The better the fuel economy, the greener a car will be with respect to global-warming emissions. "Some hybrids, such as the Lexus sports car, are not very fuel efficient. In other words," said Kliesch, "the common perception that all hybrid vehicles equal green vehicles isn't necessarily true."[5]

Fuel-efficient hybrids do contribute less to global warming than conventional vehicles do—30 to 50 percent less, according to the UCS. And that figure is expected to improve as hybrid technology improves.[6]

In addition to these health and environmental merits, hybrids accelerate well and earn high ratings for overall performance. Owners often comment on the quiet, smooth ride, and find the cars responsive and fun.

Five Components of Hybrid Technology

Kliesch also pointed out that not all cars that are called hybrids make use of the greenest hybrid technology. The UCS concurs and has found that a car can have some hybrid components without having much improvement over conventional cars in terms of tailpipe emissions and fuel economy. The UCS identifies five aspects of hybrid technology that a vehicle can have. In order to be considered a true hybrid, a car must have at least the first three.

1. The first is *idle off*, which means that the gasoline engine turns off when the car is stopped in order to save fuel. The electric motor is still on, though, and the car is ready to roll when the accelerator is depressed.
2. The second essential feature for a true hybrid is the use of regenerative braking operating above 60 volts. This technology captures the energy of forward motion that would normally be lost to heating up the brake pads as the car slows and uses that energy to recharge the battery.
3. The third attribute that qualifies a vehicle as a true hybrid is having a big enough electric motor to assist the small gasoline engine when accelerating, thus saving fuel and cutting down on tailpipe emissions.[7]

The UCS refers to a vehicle with only these three features as a "mild hybrid." The Civic and Accord hybrids from Honda have all three of the above features and thus are considered by UCS to be mild hybrids. Although the UCS uses the word *mild*, the 2007 Honda Civic hybrid shows substantial improvements over the emissions and fuel economy of conventional cars, with 49 city and 51 highway miles per gallon.

The UCS identifies two additional features that can bump a car from their mild-hybrid category to a full hybrid, or, best of all environmentally, a plug-in hybrid. Each feature has its trade-offs.

4. The fourth hybrid feature is called electric-only drive. As of September 2007, the only hybrids mentioned by the USC to have this feature are the Toyota Prius and the Ford Escape. As such, they are considered by USC to be "full hybrids." Electric-only drive allows a car to draw power from only the battery and electric motor when starting off and at low speeds. This means that when pulling out of the driveway, for example, the Prius and Escape have no engine noise whatsoever—a startling discovery to new owners. When we test-drove a Prius, the silence was the most novel and enjoyable feature, making the car seem like an oversized golf cart. "I have to be careful when backing up," said one friend. "Because you can't hear the car, people don't know to get out of the way if they aren't looking."
5. The fifth hybrid feature is a bigger battery pack that can be recharged at any 120-volt outlet. A vehicle with this is called a "plug-in hybrid" and is the most fuel efficient of all. A plug-in can operate as a 100 percent electric, zero-emission car for local travel of up to sixty miles. On a longer trip, a plug-in can work as a typical full hybrid, supplemented with gasoline. All-electric travel is quite cheap—only 2 to 4¢ per mile for the cost of the electricity. This is equivalent to a gasoline price of less than $1 per gallon, whereas conventional car travel costs approximately $3 per gallon of gas, or 8 to 20¢ per mile, depending on the car's fuel efficiency.[8]

The biggest challenge with plug-in technology is cost. Cars with this feature are expensive because they use larger electric motors and battery packs to provide sufficient all-electric range. Currently, plug-in hybrids are not readily available as passenger vehicles. But conversion kits or instructions for conversion may soon be available.[9] Many passionate supporters of plug-in hybrid electric vehicles believe that they may soon become a major piece of our transportation solution. Supporting this perspective, the Electric Power Research Institute and the National Resources Defense Council, in July of 2007, published a study concluding that plug-ins may get environmentally greener as they get older *if* the power grid that charges the batteries gets cleaner. Moreover, they conclude, plug-ins could result in reductions in the use of our national electrical grid by providing power from parked plug-ins during the day.

For more details about how this scenario would hypothetically work, see the California Cars Initiative's All About Plug-In Hybrids website, www.calcars.org/vehicles.html.

Another useful resource to help consumers evaluate hybrid cars can be found at a UCS website, www.hybridcenter.org.

Muscle Hybrids and Hollow Hybrids

Some automakers are guilty of greenwashing—labeling vehicles as hybrids when they actually have little or no improvements in fuel economy over regular cars. Consider the so-called muscle hybrids. Such cars have idle off and may have regenerative braking, but they don't have smaller gasoline engines and thus have only slightly improved fuel economy, if any. Rather, they have improved horsepower and acceleration—more muscle. Some consider the Honda Accord hybrid, with its six-cylinder engine, a muscle hybrid.

Hollow hybrids have even fewer hybrid characteristics, and include the Chevy Silverado hybrid and GMC Sierra hybrid. These pickups use 10 percent *more* fuel than their conventional counterparts,[10] and thus have higher tailpipe emissions as well. For more about hollow hybrids, see the UCS Hybrid Watchdog website, www.hybridcenter.org/ hybrid-watchdog-whats-in-a-name.html.

Which Hybrid Is Greenest?

For an expert opinion, we consulted the ACEEE. They rate the Honda Civic GX, a car that runs on natural gas but has limited availability, as the greenest vehicle of 2007. Second is the Prius.[11] Since all the hybrid owners we personally know have chosen a Prius, we asked Kliesch how his organization rates cars and why some are more popular than others.

According to Kliesch, ACEEE considers fuel economy and tailpipe emissions, as well as "upstream" emissions resulting from the extraction, refining, and transporting of fuels between the head of the oil well and the fuel pump. ACEEE also incorporates a vehicle's manufacturing impacts. We noticed on ACEEE's Greenest Vehicles chart that the cars listed meet differing emissions standards. We asked Kliesch about the ULEV II (ultra-low-emission vehicle) emissions standard met by Toyota Corolla and Honda Civic. He replied that this particular standard indicates an extremely low level of smog-forming tailpipe emissions, but the partial-zero emission standard met by the Prius is even more stringent, at near-zero levels. He referred us to ACEEE's How to Buy Green website, www.greenercars.org/guide.htm, for a further explanation of these and other federal and California low-emission standards used in ACEEE's ratings.

We asked Kliesch why the Prius is so much more popular than the Honda Insight, which was discontinued in 2006. He thought about it for a moment, then replied that although both can be considered environmentally friendly, the Prius may have more mass appeal because it seats four. The Prius has also been in production globally for nearly a decade and has been through a number of refinements. In a sense, he stated, the Prius has become the gold standard for hybrids.

All in All …

For consumers who want a car and can afford to buy a new vehicle, a true hybrid may be the best choice. A highly rated hybrid has twice the fuel economy of an average American car. The best hybrids produce at least 90 percent fewer air pollutants contributing to smog, and 30 to 50 percent fewer emissions contributing to global warming. Plus, they have the acceleration and distance capacity of a conventional car. The hybrid owners we talked with were all delighted with their cars, their fuel economy, their low emissions, and had no complaints about their green automobiles.

Notes

1. "'Honda Insight Review," Edmunds.com, www.edmunds.com/honda/insight/review.html.
2. The California Cars Initiative, www.calcars.org/vehicles.html#5 (accessed September 16, 2007).
3. Union of Concerned Scientists, Clean Vehicles, Hybrid-Electric Vehicles, www.ucsusa.org/clean_vehicles/cars_pickups_suvs/hybridelectric-vehicles.html (accessed September 17, 2007).
4. Jim Kliesch, personal communication.
5. Ibid.
6. Union of Concerned Scientists, Hybrid-Electric Vehicles.
7. Union of Concerned Scientists, "Hybrids under the Hood (part I)," www.hybridcenter.org/hybrid-center-how-hybrid-cars-work-under-the-hood.html (accessed September 16, 2007).
8. The California Cars Initiative, All About Plug-In Hybrids (PHEVs), www.calcars.org/vehicles.html (accessed September 15, 2007).
9. The California Cars Initiative, "How to Get a Plug-in Hybrid (Bottom Line: Individuals Can't Easily Get Them Yet)," www.calcars.org/howtoget.html (accessed September 15, 2007).
10. John Rockhold, "Green Means Go," *Mother Earth News*, October/November 2005.
11. American Council for Energy Efficient Economy, "Greenest Vehicles of 2007," www.greenercars.org/highlights_greenest.htm (accessed September 16, 2007).

Battery-Electric Cars

There are a couple of other green car options out there besides hybrids, such as battery-electric cars and fuel-cell cars. Will these be the wave of the future? Probably not, but they're interesting to contemplate nonetheless.

Battery-electric vehicles are the only cars on the road today that emit no tailpipe emissions at all without requiring an emissions-control device such as a catalytic converter. They're emissions-free because their power comes from a battery rather than from fuel of any kind. Sounds great! Yet, in spite of this strong environmental asset, battery-electric cars are not currently in production by any of the major automakers.

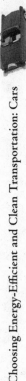

Crushed by General Motors

They were at one time, though. In 1996, General Motors launched the first commercially available electric car, the EV1. The company produced a little more than a thousand EV1s that were offered for lease to consumers. Other Detroit automakers subsequently developed their own models. The electric cars developed a loyal and enthusiastic following, still represented today in the Electric Auto Association.[1] Many owners of electric cars claim the cars perform very well and have good acceleration and maneuverability. But by 2003, the cars were discontinued. The leased autos were recalled and crushed by the automakers! They claimed they couldn't sell enough of the electric cars to make them profitable.

Accusations and Denials

Today, some people claim that GM never really wanted the electric cars to succeed and accuse GM of intentionally undermining their own marketing efforts out of fear of displacing their gasoline-based business. The close alliance of Detroit automakers and the oil industry raises questions about a possible role of oil interests in the sabotage of the electric car.[2] Of course, GM disputes all of these claims. A recent documentary, *Who Killed the Electric Car?*, explores these accusations and denials (www.sonyclassics.com/whokilledthe-electriccar/). Said director Chris Paine, "The film is about why the only kind of cars that we can drive run on oil. And for a while there was a terrific alternative, a pure electric car."[3]

But in spite of all this, as many as 10,000 electric cars still cruise our American highways today. Most of these were created by people who converted other cars to electrics, but several hundred were commercially produced—most of these are Toyota RAV4 EVs.

Coal-Fired Electricity Isn't Green

Critics point out that the ultimate source of an electric car's power is the power plant generating the electricity to recharge the battery. Most power plants in the United States burn coal, which generates carbon dioxide, the biggest culprit in global warming, as well as sulfur dioxide, a major contributor to acid rain. In the southeastern states, 61 percent of electricity is from coal-fired power plants. But even if you factor in the power-plant emissions, battery-electrics are still up to 99 percent cleaner than conventional vehicles. If they can be recharged using renewable and eco-friendly sources such as wind or solar power, then they generate no air pollution or heat-trapping gases at all.[4]

Electric Cars Are Pricey

Although these cars have an almost cultlike following of enthusiasts, they have at least one indisputable disadvantage: the price. The battery packs are costly, making the cars significantly more expensive than gasoline vehicles. The battery packs are heavy, too, and some electric models are said to be a bit sluggish due to the extra weight.

The limited range of miles from one recharging to the next could be a negative factor as well, particularly for people who do a lot of highway driving. However, with new battery technologies, the range has improved from fifty or sixty up to one hundred miles,[5] which is an adequate daily range for most people's needs. The car can be easily plugged in every night for recharging.

Even though the cars are not currently being promoted by any major Detroit automaker, smaller companies continue to produce battery-electrics for use in self-contained areas such as airports, retirement communities, planned neighborhoods, and vacation destinations.[6]

Battery-electrics seem to have come and gone for the present—before most of us had much chance to notice. But their development was important. They paved the way for hybrids and fuel-cell electrics, which use a lot of the same technology.

Notes

1. www.eaaev.org/.
2. Jim Snyder, "Gas-Price Surge Strains Oil-Auto Pact," *The Hill*, May 2, 2006, www.hillnews.com/thehill/export/TheHill/Business/050206_gas.html.
3. "Who Killed the Electric Car?" PBS *Now*, www.pbs.org/now/shows/223/index.html#here.
4. Union of Concerned Scientists, Clean Vehicles, Battery-Electric Vehicles, www.ucsusa.org/clean_vehicles/cars_pickups_suvs/batteryelectric-vehicles.html.
5. Union of Concerned Scientists, Clean Vehicles.
6. Union of Concerned Scientists, Transportation, Frequently Asked Questions, www.ucsusa.org/clean_vehicles/cars_pickups_suvs/transportation-faq.html.

Fuel-Cell Cars

Fuel-cell cars are not commercially available at present, and some say they never will be. The primary obstacles are high costs and low energy efficiency compared to the energy required to produce the fuel.

Others believe fuel-cell vehicles to be among the most promising technologies for the future. Jason Mark of the UCS has estimated that each fuel-cell car could save the dirtiest U.S. cities $4,300 to $8,300 in costs associated with air pollution.[1]

Only Water-Vapor Emissions

Fuel-cell vehicles don't burn gasoline or diesel, and the cars themselves have zero emissions. Most model fuel-cell cars run on hydrogen. The hydrogen reacts with oxygen to generate electricity in an electrochemical reaction that produces no greenhouse gases, only water vapor.* The electricity powers electric motors at the vehicles' wheels. Fuel-cell demonstration cars have onboard fuel tanks that carry hydrogen. In the future, fuel tanks could be filled at hydrogen refilling stations—although creating a new kind of filling station to deliver hydrogen would be costly.

Toyota has a demonstration model based on the Highlander SUV. The demo has four torpedo-shaped tanks that together hold 3.5 kilograms of compressed hydrogen. The car gets about 60 miles per kilogram, with a range of about 200 miles. Ford and Volkswagen have similar fuel-cell demos, both of which max out at about 80 miles per hour. In the Ford Focus model, the hydrogen tanks consume most of the trunk space.[3]

---

* The electrochemical reactions of a fuel cell begin when hydrogen enters one side of the fuel cell (the anode), where it is separated into an electron and a hydrogen ion. In the case of one type of fuel cell, the proton exchange membrane, the ions move through a membrane (the cathode) to combine with oxygen on the other side, making water. Meanwhile, since electrons cannot pass through the membrane, they are forced to take an external route through the cathode, creating an electrical circuit that carries them through the electric motor. As they pass through the motor, the electrons transfer power from the fuel cell to the motor. The motor, in turn, drives the wheels of the car.[2]

Stabbing the Accelerator

Because they are electric, fuel-cell cars are often compared to battery-electric cars, but fuel-cell cars have some advantages over battery-operated cars. For example, they don't require plugging in overnight or onboard heavy battery packs, and they may perform better. Said Mike Stenhouse, an automotive-performance consultant, "Americans want to stab the accelerator, and that doesn't work with a battery-electric car, or with some hybrids."[4] It will work with the fuel-cell car of the future, though. The industry projects a fuel-cell car that will accelerate from 0 to 60 miles per hour in less than twelve seconds.[5]

Fuel-cell vehicles are extremely efficient compared to other kinds of cars that run on fuel, according to Stenhouse. In a conventional gasoline-powered car, only 40 percent of the fuel goes toward moving the vehicle forward. The other 60 percent of the energy produced by burning the fuel is released into the atmosphere as heat. In a fuel-cell vehicle, by contrast, 90 percent of the energy derived from the fuel produces forward motion in the car, while only 10 percent dissipates into the air as wasted heat. This fuel efficiency means that future fuel-cell cars will achieve 70 to 80 miles per gallon of fuel and will be able to travel 250 to 400 miles before needing to be refueled.[6]

Ardor Wanes

Fuel-cell cars do sound promising in some respects. But the initial optimism that these cars could deliver the country from fossil-fuel dependency has waned as the snags may be insurmountable.

Coming up with pure hydrogen is one problem—it doesn't occur in nature in significant amounts. Hydrogen can be extracted from water, coal, natural gas, biomass, and other sources. But the extraction processes use energy, and some of the processes generate greenhouse gases. The extraction is also expensive.

One way around that is to develop fuel-cell vehicles that run on hydrocarbons from natural gas, or even gasoline, instead of pure hydrogen. These hydrocarbons can provide a source of hydrogen atoms for the fuel cell. Fuel-cell vehicles that use hydrocarbons are not as clean as those that run on pure hydrogen, but they are much cleaner than conventional cars. A fuel-cell car running on hydrocarbons from natural gas creates 60 to 70 percent fewer emissions than a conventional gasoline-powered car.

Stand Back …

Any other problems? According to Stenhouse, hydrogen is so explosive that a collision with a hydrogen-filled tank would cause an explosion that could be seen fifteen miles away. Well, then. … We trust someone is working on an uncrushable fuel tank.

Notes

1. Union of Concerned Scientists, Clean Vehicles, "The Promise of the Fuel-Cell Vehicles," www.ucsusa.org/clean_vehicles/cars_pickups_suvs/the-promise-of-the-fuel-cell-vehicles.html.
2. Ibid.
3. Michael Kanellos, "Hydrogen Cars to Hit the Road by 2015?," ZDNet News, July 13, 2006, http://news.zdnet.com/2100-9595_22-6093817.html.
4. Michael Stenhouse, PhD, personal communication.
5. Union of Concerned Scientists, Clean Vehicles, "The Promise of the Fuel-Cell Vehicles."
6. Ibid.

Diesel Alternatives

Europeans are crazy about diesel cars—at least 50 percent of all new cars sold in Europe these days have diesel engines, up from 17 percent in 1992.[1] But that's not the case here in the United States—only about 3 percent of American cars are powered by diesel engines.[2]

Europeans prefer diesel partly because of the high gasoline prices in Europe, at present around $6 per gallon.[3] Diesel fuel is cheaper for Europeans than gasoline, averaging less than $5 per gallon.[4]

Better Mileage from Diesel

Diesel cars also get about 30 percent better mileage than comparable gasoline-powered cars. They are most efficient in steady highway driving. In fact, passing power is greater than with gasoline engines. When pressed to accelerate from 50 to 70 miles per hour, a diesel car "takes off like nothing on Earth," said David Champion, head of auto testing for *Consumer Reports*.[5]

Another advantage is that diesel engines typically last longer than gasoline-powered engines because they're built stronger. They have to be: the way diesel fuel is ignited creates more pressure inside the cylinders.[6]

Diesel is so unpopular in the United States because Americans associate it with noisy buses and choking exhaust from semis. Those foul fumes can result from low-grade fuel. Historically, diesel fuel sold in the United States and Canada has been among the poorest quality diesel in the world. That's been improving, though. Modern diesel engines are engineered better too—they no longer emit black smoke.

Diesel Fuel

Diesel-powered cars cost $1,000 to $2,000 more than a comparable car with a gasoline engine. Given the greater expense of the cars and our relatively low gasoline prices, Americans have had little incentive to buy diesel cars. But as gas prices continue to escalate, this may change.

Petroleum diesel, the type of diesel sold at most gas stations, is refined from petroleum, just like gasoline, but created specifically for use in diesel engines. Like gasoline, it produces carbon dioxide, particulates, and sulfur emissions, and increases our reliance on foreign oil sources.[7] And, of course, petroleum is a nonrenewable source of energy and its availability will continue to wane in coming decades.

In short, there's no real advantage to a diesel vehicle unless it runs on a cleaner alternative fuel. Although we may think of vegetable fuels as progressive and perhaps faddish, they're not really new. The diesel engine debuted at the World's Fair in 1900 running on peanut oil.[8] Rudolph Diesel, the inventor of the engine, used a variety of fuels ranging from coal to various vegetable oils. Unfortunately, over the years the cheap availability of petroleum products has eclipsed the other options.

But today, many diesel drivers are returning to alternative fuels. Biodiesel, which is chemically modified vegetable oil, and straight vegetable oil, or SVO, are two practical choices. In the following sections, we'll discuss the pros and cons of each.

Notes

1. Mike Hudson, "Diesel, Gas or Hybrid? The Auto Industry Is Pushing All Three, but Americans Aren't Sure," Edmunds, www.edmunds.com/ownership/techcenter/articles/106216/article.html (accessed June 28, 2006).
2. Associated Press, "US Diesel Sales Expected to Rise: Fuel Economy May Drive US Market Share up from 3 Percent," *Boston Globe*, Jan 13, 2006, www.boston.com/business/articles/2006/01/13/us_diesel_sales_expected_to_rise/.
3. James Martin, "Gas Prices in Europe—European Gasoline and Diesel Prices," About.com: Europe Travel, October 6, 2005, http://goeurope.about.com/od/transportation/a/gas_prices.htm.
4. Ibid.
5. Peter Valdes-Dapena, "With Gas High, It May Be Time for Diesel. Diesel Cars Have Been Slow to Catch On in the States. With Gas Prices Rising, That Might Change," CNNMoney.com, September 1, 2005, http://money.cnn.com/2005/08/29/Autos/tipsandadvice/diesels/index.htm.
6. Ibid.
7. Lyle Pearl, Caleb John Clark, and Paul Vachier, "Biodiesel Benz: Case Study in Converting a Diesel Auto to Run on Vegetable Oil," *No End Press*, April 2005, www.noendpress.com/caleb/biodiesel/index.php.
8. James Croonenberghs, personal communication.

Biodiesel

Biodiesel, which works in any diesel engine, is a clean-burning and renewable fuel derived from vegetable oils. About 90 percent of the biodiesel in the United States is made from soybean oil.[1] Roughly seven pounds of soybean oil are needed to make one gallon of biodiesel.[2] Other plant sources include peanuts, canola/rapeseed, hemp seeds, and some grains. Pure biodiesel from plant sources produces zero sulfur emissions and significantly lower emissions overall than petroleum diesel or blends of the two.[3]

Biodiesel is created when vegetable oil is subjected to transesterification, a chemical process that brings the oil to industry standards for diesel engines and keeps it from thickening at colder temperatures. Sometimes biodiesel is mixed with petroleum diesel in different proportions and retailers may misleadingly use the name *biodiesel* even when the biodiesel content is as low as only 5 percent. Biodiesel and petroleum diesel mix easily, and providers often label the blends as B5, B20, B50, or B100 to reflect the percentage of biodiesel in the blend. For example, B90 is 90 percent biodiesel and 10 percent petroleum diesel.

In the United States, which is the second largest biofuel producer (after Brazil), hundreds of major truck fleets use biodiesel or blends, including all branches of the U.S. military, NASA, several state departments of transportation, and public utility fleets.[4]

Environmental Impact

How polluting is pure biodiesel? After all, it is a carbon-based fuel, like gasoline and diesel, that is burned to release energy. Burning any carbon-based fuel releases pollutants to some degree. But burning biodiesel releases 50 to 70 percent less hydrocarbons than burning petrofuels, and about 65 percent less particulate matter. Burning biodiesel emits no sulfur oxides at all, 50 percent less carbon monoxide, and 78 percent less carbon dioxide than burning petroleum-based fuels.

Many scientists point out that burning fossil fuels such as petroleum releases carbon into the atmosphere that was previously trapped harmlessly underground, while biodiesel releases only the same carbon that was removed from the atmosphere by the present-day soy or crops it came from. (All plants remove carbon dioxide from the atmosphere in order to manufacture sugars.) So the net release of carbon from biodiesel is zero; it is carbon dioxide-neutral (as long as it contains no methanol).

Although biodiesel does emit nitrogen oxides, this can be tempered with catalytic converters.

Biodiesel is a renewable and sustainable fuel because soybean and rapeseed crops, unlike fossil-fuel deposits, can be resown and reharvested indefinitely—if managed correctly, that is. However, as the soy industry in the United States becomes increasingly genetically modified and chemical-dependent, the sustainability of large-scale biodiesel production becomes questionable.

Researchers are also investigating algae as a highly prolific source of biodiesel fuel.

How to Get It

There are three ways to get biodiesel. The simplest way is to buy it at a biodiesel station, just as you buy petro-diesel at a gas station. An interactive map of hundreds of retail fueling stations across the country can be found at www.biodiesel.org. Biodiesel from a gas station costs around $3.50 a gallon.

Joining a biodiesel co-op is a way to save some money on fuel. The co-op produces and sells biodiesel to the community and also provides space, supplies, and equipment for members to make their own biodiesel for their personal use. As Leif Forer of Piedmont Biofuels explained, "Members pay the co-op for supplies, and the co-op pays road taxes on the fuel. Then the members use our setup to make their fuel. The members provide labor

for other co-op jobs too."[5] Those who work get fuel at cost, but they are trading their labor for the monetary savings. You can find a co-op near you at www.biodieselamerica .org/biodiesel_coop_guide.

A third option is to produce biodiesel on your own, but it's a complex and tricky process. The necessary equipment is also expensive for just one person. On our visit to Piedmont Biofuels, Forer described the biodiesel process: "You start with straight vegetable oil," he told us, "but then you add some methanol and catalyst, either potassium hydroxide or sodium hydroxide. You have to heat and mix it all just right so as to carefully control the reaction and push it to completion. The process creates biodiesel molecules and gets rid of glycerol, which is a thick

Leif Forer of Piedmont Biofuels, one of the nation's largest biodiesel co-ops. Courtesy of Leif Forer

nonvolatile substance that makes for poor fuel. We do it in stainless steel, conical bottom, jacketed reactor vessels under low pressure."[6]

To us, the process sounds a bit complicated to try on our own. "Only a handful of our several hundred members are making their own biodiesel right now," Forer told us. "The easiest solution of all is to stop driving. Walk to work. Ride your bike."[7]

An excellent point, but many entrepreneurs do manage to produce biodiesel successfully.

Notes

1. Reuters, "Key Points about Bush's Energy Plan," February 1, 2006, www.planetark.org/dailynewsstory.cfm/newsid/34820/story.htm.
2. Al Kurki, Amanda Hill, and Mike Morris, "Biodiesel: The Sustainability Dimensions," The National Sustainable Agriculture Information Service, 2006, www.attra.ncat.org/attra-pub/biodiesel_sustainable.html.
3. Lyle Pearl, Caleb John Clark, and Paul Vachier, "Biodiesel Benz: Case Study in Converting a Diesel Auto to Run on Vegetable Oil," *No End Press*, April 2005, www.noendpress.com/caleb/biodiesel/index.php.
4. Reuters, "FACTBOX: Key Facts on Biodiesel, Ethanol," February 3, 2006, www.planetark.com/dailynewsstory.cfm/newsid/34849/story.htm.
5. Leif Forer, personal communication.
6. Ibid.
7. Ibid.

Leif Forer leads public tours of the co-op's biodiesel refinery. Courtesy of Leif Forer

Straight Vegetable Oil

A thriftier alternative, meanwhile, is straight vegetable oil, or SVO. Straight vegetable oil is plain vegetable oil—just like the stuff you cook with. Straight vegetable oil users can buy cooking oil and use it straight from the bottle (relatively expensive), or can get used oil from restaurants, which is sometimes called greasel, straight veg, or waste vegetable oil. Waste vegetable oil, or WVO, must be filtered to remove food particles.

Environmental Impact

No matter the supplier, SVO is derived from plants such as peanuts, soy, rapeseeds, and other grains, which are, of course, renewable. The major drawback of SVO is that it thickens at cool temperatures and can clog fuel systems unless it's heated before reaching the engine. Vegetable-oil conversion kits include a heating system and usually a second gas tank to circumvent the cold-weather issues. Straight vegetable oil produces extremely low emissions.[1]

Few studies have been done on emissions of SVO because it's not recognized as a fuel by the EPA, but preliminary research suggests that its emissions are similar to those of biodiesel. Straight vegetable oil is also carbon-dioxide-neutral. And because waste vegetable oil would otherwise be thrown away, using vegetable oil as fuel doesn't affect the supply and demand of genetically modified crops as biodiesel does.[2]

Straight vegetable oil can be a controversial topic. There is some tension between SVO users and the National Biodiesel Board and the American Soybean Association because SVO users are using waste oil and therefore not paying taxes on their fuel. According to the soybean industry, SVO undermines the industry by stepping outside the trackable, taxable channels. However, that's one reason SVO appeals to many of its users.

How To Get It

Unlike biodiesel, you cannot buy SVO at a gas station. While this means you have to make it yourself, it also means it's free. Most SVO users ask a local restaurant to set aside their waste vegetable oil that would otherwise be thrown away. The SVO user then filters the oil to remove food particles and impurities before putting it in his or her diesel engine.

The very simplest filtering method is to pour the oil into a cloth bag, which costs about $10, and wait for it to drip through. However, this is a laborious and time-consuming process. According to Forer, "A more typical cost for a filtering system is about $500. And the most expensive ones involve motorized pumps and stainless-steel canisters. Those can cost thousands."[3] Eventually, though, if the oil itself is free, an SVO user will recoup that cost in fuel savings.

There are an equally diverse number of ways to make the engine modifications necessary to use SVO. Because there are so many different methods to filter fuel and convert engines, we visited two different SVO users to learn more about their systems. (See sidebars on pages 28 and 31.)

Notes

1. Lyle Pearl, Caleb John Clark, and Paul Vachier, "Biodiesel Benz: Case Study in Converting a Diesel Auto to Run on Vegetable Oil," *No End Press*, April 2005, www.noend press.com/caleb/biodiesel/index.php.

2. "Ask Umbra," *Grist* magazine, www.grist.org/advice/ ask/2005/03/14/umbra-svo/index.html?source=daily.

3. Leif Forer, personal communication.

Free Fuel— with Taco-Scented Exhaust

To find out more about SVO, we met up with two industrious drivers who are doing exactly what the soybean, biodiesel, and diesel industries fear the most: running their cars off waste veggie oil.

The first of these was political activist Kim Calhoun, whom we met through the network of sustainable farmers and builders that we've tapped into through our research. A massage and polarity therapist and an aspiring herbalist, Calhoun lives in an intentional community established three decades ago by folks trying to make sustainable lifestyle choices.

Kim Calhoun with one of the carboys that she uses to transport used vegetable oil from a restaurant to her filtration system at home.

When I pulled into her drive to interview her, I saw Calhoun's car right away. She drives a 2003 diesel Volkswagen Golf—a sensible, compact choice. I smiled at the colorful hand-lettered sign on the back of her car that reads "This Vehicle Powered by USED VEGETABLE OIL. www.biofuels.coop."

Making the Choice

Calhoun came out to greet me in the greasy pants she wears for fueling and wearing a bright orange knit cap to hold her hair up. As we strolled toward her car, Calhoun explained that she got interested in SVO through her search for a more fuel-efficient car. "I was thinking about what made the most ecological and economic sense, considering a Honda Civic hatchback, which gets great gas mileage. I learned about running cars on waste vegetable oil from my friends who work at Piedmont Biofuels. I took the alternative-fuels class they teach at the community college and decided to get a diesel car. There's a lot of interest in biofuels in this area—those classes are full every semester. More and more people and groups I know are making their own biodiesel now."

After taking the class, Calhoun decided to get a one-tank Elsbett conversion system because of its fuel flexibility, compactness, and low maintenance needs. One-tank conversion kits can include injector components, glow plugs, fuel-heating components, temperature controls, and additional fuel filters, all designed to enable the engine to handle vegetable oil, which is thicker or more viscous than diesel fuel at cool temperatures. "The folks at Piedmont Biofuels have had a technician from Elsbett come over annually to do conversion workshops at Central Carolina Community College. I had their kit installed during [the] workshop in 2003," she said.

One Tank

In Calhoun's one-tank system, the veggie-oil fuel is heated by a sleeve that fits around the fuel filter, like a small cylindrical heating pad. "This is a 'high-end' conversion; it costs close to $2000," Calhoun told me. "But it'll pay for itself in a year and a half or two, because my fuel is free. My system works with the car's original fuel tank. I can use any combination of petroleum diesel, biodiesel, or straight vegetable oil in the tank. So if I'm out of town and I didn't bring enough filtered used vegetable oil, I can buy diesel anywhere, or biodiesel at certain pumps, or even five gallons of virgin cooking oil at Costco for about $2.60 per gallon."

Calhoun usually gets her used oil from Carrburritos, a Mexican restaurant in nearby Carrboro. "A lot of people who use donated oil have to pull the used grease out of the restaurant's grease traps that are outside. But the staff at Carrburritos is really supportive. Whenever they empty out their fryer, about once a week, they put the grease back into the 5-gallon carboy containers that it comes in. The carboys are waiting for me to pick up when I stop by. It's really helpful, and it's also good grease. When I run the car, it smells like tortilla chips!"

Filtering

Before Calhoun can run Carrburritos' oil through her engine, she has to filter it. She chuckled recalling her first efforts. "The first eight or so months, I had a tedious process that I had to set up and break down every time I filtered. It was hilarious-looking, I'm sure! It involved climbing up onto my picnic table and attempting to slowly pour a heavy five-gallon carboy into sock filters suspended by a bamboo pole stuck through my stepladder, which was counterbalanced by cinder blocks. I'd catch the filtered grease in two buckets. The really comical part was trying to hurriedly pour the contents of the first bucket into my car's fuel tank, with a funnel that didn't fit right, before the second bucket got full. Not very sustainable for my back—or my peace of mind!

"So as a Christmas present, I requested—actually, begged—Leif Forer to help me design and build a more streamlined system. The result was a portable system with a 12-volt pump and a filter that I would often use on-site in the Carrburritos parking lot, educating customers as they came to eat the tortilla chips that fueled me down the road. That lasted over a year but was not filtering the grease finely enough and caused me to have to change my car's fuel filter too frequently, which is expensive.

My current filtering system, based at home, is much better, although it's still evolving—I still find things that need tweaking."

With that, we wandered over to the roofed but open-sided shed where Calhoun keeps her filtering setup. There's not much for her to show me, because it's a pretty simple arrangement. The most conspicuous piece is the single big drum.

"I got my fifty-five-gallon drum for storing my filtered oil for free," Calhoun explained. "It was clean and in good condition. My dad helped me cut a hole in the top of it that is just big enough to hold the sock filters, which have a metal ring around the top.

"After I pick up the carboys of oil from the restaurant, I let them settle out for a few weeks so the food particles fall to the bottom. Then I use my pump to pull the oil out of the carboys and into the filters."

Her pump is about the size of a big flashlight, with two blue tubes attached. To transfer the oil, she puts one tube into a carboy, the other into the drum.

The pump is powered by a cable that attaches to the battery in her car.

"Pumping the oil out of the carboys is easier than pouring it because they're so heavy," said Calhoun. "Plus, pumping is less messy, and gets less sediment into the filters, so they last longer."

To let me see the oil clearly, Kim picked up a carboy that was only partly full and poured a little into the nested filters in the top of the fifty-five-gallon drum. I was surprised that the oil looked clean and golden—it hardly looked used at all.

This 12-volt portable diesel pump transfers filtered vegetable oil from the fifty-five-gallon drum on the left into Kim Calhoun's VW Golf's fuel tank.

Fueling Up

Now, after patiently answering our questions, the moment of truth had arrived. Calhoun was ready to fill the fuel tank in her car. She backed her car up to the shed. She put one blue tube from the pump into her drum of clean oil through a small opening in the top. The other blue tube went to her car's fuel tank. This second tube ends in a nozzle that can be opened by squeezing a handle, exactly like the nozzle for a gas station pump, only a bit smaller. After putting the tubes in place, she hooked up the battery cables, turned the pump on, and filled her tank in about five minutes—with sweet, pure, golden vegetable oil. Freedom! She is free from rising fuel prices, free from guilt over greenhouse gases and air pollution, free from responsibility for foreign wars. Free and independent. Wow. I was jealous.

Why Bother?

To wrap things up, I asked Calhoun to give me the quick and dirty on why her fuel choice is important to her.

"It's worth all the greasy mess and processing time to be running my car on vegetable oil that's a waste product and to be educating the community about sustainable energy sources," she said with conviction. "Our current use of fossil fuels is not environmentally, politically, or economically sustainable. It causes so much suffering and oppression around the world that affects all of us—families in the Middle East as well as my brother Matt, my uncles, and several friends who serve in the U.S. military. For me, running on veggie oil is another way of resisting a foreign policy that is influenced by our country's dependence on foreign oil. It's another way of resisting the greed, violence, and isolation of capitalism. And in a bigger sense, I see my commitment to using vegetable oil as a part of my spiritual path of being love and spreading love, not harm—of building and healing communities.

"What if we all reduced our use of petroleum products? Imagine the effect on world events. Imagine the difference we could make for all beings now and for the generations to come."

Calhoun has done much more than imagine. She's put principles into action, like many of the other mavericks and trailblazers profiled in this book.

Kim Calhoun fills her fuel tank with filtered straight vegetable oil.

Straight Vegetable Oil—Parts and Process

Following is a list of the equipment Calhoun currently uses to filter her oil and her simplified step-by-step process.

Parts

1. One 55-gallon barrel with lid. I got my barrel used, free, and in good, clean condition.
2. One 12-volt portable diesel pump from Northern Tool and Equipment Company in South Carolina (800-222-5381) that cost $147.15. It has cables that attach to a car battery as a source of power for the pump.
3. Jumper cables to connect my pump cables to my car battery because the pump cables are too short.
4. Two filters from McMaster-Carr in Atlanta (404-346-7000). One is a two-in-one polyester felt filter bag, 5/1 micron, model #5726K71, for $16.94. (This filter is two bags in one—the inner bag is 5 microns, the outer one is 1 micron.) The other filter I get is a 50-micron polyester microfiber bag, model #9844K76, for $16.94. I put the 50-micron filter bag inside the other filter to remove the biggest pieces of sediment first. This makes the two-in-one filter last longer.

Process

1. I pick up two 5-gallon carboys of oil weekly from Carrburritos, a local Mexican restaurant.
2. I let the oil in the carboys settle out for a few weeks (sediment falls to the bottom).
3. I use my pump to pull used oil out of the carboys and into the filters resting in the top of the 55-gallon drum. It's less messy, and less sediment gets into the filters, so they'll last longer.
4. I run clean grease through the pump to clear it out, feeding that oil back into the filters.
5. When needed, I fill my car by pumping oil from the 55-gallon drum into my tank using the 12-volt diesel pump.
6. I rinse out and recycle the carboys. And sometimes I wash my greasy jeans!

Additional Resource

Keith Addison, "Straight Vegetable Oil as Diesel Fuel," *Journey to Forever*, http://journeytoforever.org/biodiesel_svo.html.

Little Red Switch:
My Ride in a Greasel Car

Oh Where, Oh Where …

Kim's economical, environmentally motivated SVO system is just one of many ways to set up your own efficient system. For a different perspective on these do-it-yourself methods, I tracked down another SVO user.

With a couple of phone calls, I located Jim Efird just outside of town. A few days later, I was pulling up his long gravel driveway through a field of rambling goats, my eyes trained on the 1983 Mercedes in the carport.

Efird, clad in a Panthers sweatshirt, bounded out the back door of his house. Eager to plunge into an enthusiastic tour of his fuel adventures, he wasted no time leading me over to his car and filtration system.

Although he likes the idea that he's helping the planet, Efird's switch to SVO was motivated mostly by efficiency and monetary savings, and by the mechanical challenges of hauling and filtering his own fuel—challenges he seemed to enjoy.

Jim Efird saves about $140 a month by using vegetable oil as his car's primary fuel.

"I Thought, I'm Gonna Save Money."

"I liked the economics," he told me. "I work 19 miles away, so I'm driving almost 40 miles a day, 200 miles a week to work and back. My car gets about 25 miles a gallon—whether diesel or vegetable oil, the mpg is the same. So I'm using 8 gallons every week just to [get to] work and back. With whatever driving I do, I was using 12 to 15 gallons a week, $2.50 a gallon, you're talking roughly $35 a week, so $140 a month for diesel fuel. That's $1,680 a year. So my savings on diesel fuel in just one year has paid for my total investment for the conversion kit, the labor, and the two pumps, which came to $1,450. The savings were my original reason for making the change."

Efird grinned at the memory. "My wife thought I was crazy. Some of my friends thought I was crazy. The guys at work … about half of them thought it was pretty cool, about half thought I was gonna ruin my car."

"But I did it anyway. And after Hurricane Katrina, when the cost of fuel in Charlotte went past $3 a gallon and it was hard to find stations that were even open, I just kept rolling along. It didn't affect me at all, and I was saving even more money. That was a good feeling."

Just Plain Vegetable Oil

I was eager to compare Efird's setup with what I'd seen at Kim Calhoun's. Like Calhoun, Efird has made an arrangement with a local restaurant—he picks up waste frying oil from two nearby Italian restaurants. While biodiesel can be made from almost any quality of oil, SVO requires high-quality oil that hasn't been fried too many times. As a result, a town can only support as many SVO drivers as there are restaurants with decent oil to give away.

The Conversion Kit

Unlike Calhoun, Efird chose a two-tank system for his car. Instead of fortifying the engine with stronger parts, as a one-tank system does, a two-tank system protects the engine from SVO's corrosive effects by heating the oil before using it. At outdoor temperatures below 60 degrees Fahrenheit, vegetable oil is thick and sluggish. When the oil is too thick, it clogs the fuel lines. A two-tank system eliminates this problem by starting the car and warming the engine on a small tank of regular diesel fuel. A second, larger tank holds SVO. When the car has warmed up, the driver flips a switch to draw warm oil from the SVO tank.

Efird spent $700 on his engine-conversion kit, which he bought from www.greasel.com. (The kits are also available from www.greasecar.com and www.elsbett.com.) In addition to the two tanks, the kit also includes a heat exchanger to warm the vegetable oil, hoses and hardware for routing hot water between the radiator and heat exchanger, and an enticing little red dashboard switch.

When Jim Efird hits the switch on his car's dashboard, the engine draws fuel from the vegetable oil tank instead of the diesel tank.

Let's See the Goods

Efird eagerly popped the trunk to show me how his trunk has been transformed to accommodate his new fuel arrangement. The big black fuel tank the car came with is still there, at the back of his trunk, lodged just behind the backseat. It now holds SVO and is accompanied by a small red plastic six-and-a-half gallon tank of diesel nestled on one side of his trunk. "It's really a marine tank you would use on a boat!" said Efird happily.

In addition to the $700 purchase price, Efird paid a mechanic $450 to install the heat exchanger, the small red tank, all the hoses, and a small fuel filter up under the hood, which filters the veggie oil coming from the black tank in the trunk just before it enters the engine. Another small heater, in the form of a little sleeve, was wrapped around the filter.

Fuel

After getting the conversion kit, Efird's next step was to find a source of fuel. He said he visited about twenty restaurants before he selected two with high-quality oil—not too dark and relatively clean. "At first, I was getting it from a Chinese restaurant, and they fry pretty much everything. The oil was a lot dirtier; it was blacker and had more food particles. And McDonald's? No way. Their oil is lardy, fatty, white, and creamy.

"The Italian restaurants I get oil from now are just using their oil for chicken fingers and a few things, so it's cleaner. You can see a restaurant's waste oil if you look in their bin out back."

Each week, Efird picks up two full five-gallon buckets from each of his two restaurants, leaving empty buckets for the coming week's oil. He built a bracket in his trunk to keep the buckets from turning over during the trip home. When he gets home, he unloads the buckets—and then it's time for filtering.

Jim Efird built a bracket in his trunk to transport two five-gallon buckets of used vegetable oil from the restaurant to his home.

The Filtering Gizmo in the Workshop

For Efird, filtering is no big deal. "I've come up with a filtering system that works for me. It doesn't take much time now, but I spent a lot of weekends out there in the shed getting it worked out. My wife said, 'Good gracious, is that all you're gonna do from now on?'"

As it turns out, no. Now that he's fine-tuned his system, Efird spends just ninety minutes a month filtering his oil, which is essentially the only labor still required. At the time I interviewed him, he had close to 100 gallons already filtered and stored. Completely free.

Efird's filtering system is set up in his workshop. He has three fifty-gallon drums—two for dirty oil, and one for oil he's already filtered. He got the used drums for free from Jiffy Lube. He also has nine five-gallon buckets. As we looked around, the lid was off one of the big drums; I could see that it was full of dark brown oil.

Efird explained the filtering process to me. He begins by pouring his buckets of unfiltered oil into one of his drums for dirty oil. When the drum is full or close to full and most of the food particles have settled to the bottom, he uses a 115-volt alternating current electric pump he bought for $250 to suck the cleanest oil off the top. The oil moves through the pump and out another hose, into a 5-micron filter that he has suspended over another fifty-gallon drum. The filter is like a big tube sock, about three feet long and seven inches across. (These filters are available from www.mcmastercar.com for $6 apiece.) Oil drips through the filter into a bucket that rests on top of the drum for filtered oil. Efird has put a small faucet from Home Depot into the side of the bucket near the bottom. As the oil drains from the filter into the bucket, he opens the faucet so the filtered oil can flow into the drum under the bucket.

This 115-volt pump sucks oil from the top of the settling drum into a 5-micron filter that finishes cleaning the oil.

The last step is to transfer the filtered oil back out of the drum and into the car. Efird has a manual pump with a long vertical shaft for that, for which he paid about $50. He lowers the shaft into the drum, and in sixty seconds he can pump out enough oil by hand to fill a five-gallon bucket. He carries the bucket outside (it was heavy!) and sets it on a stool he made expressly for that purpose. The stool is exactly the right height to position the bucket's faucet at the opening to his gas tank.

"Once a week, I'll carry three of these five-gallon buckets of filtered oil out to the car," explained Efird. "They're pretty heavy; it's a good workout. I set a bucket up on the stool, put a regular funnel into my tank, just open up [the faucet] and fill up the car. Gravity feeds the [contents] into my fuel tank."

The Magical Red Switch

Now that I'd seen the system, I was eager to experience SVO in action. "Wanna go for a ride?" said Efird with a grin.

I was excited—I'd never ridden in a veggie-powered car. As we settled in our seats, Efird showed me the little switch on his dashboard that was installed as part of the conversion kit. I felt like the switch might send us airborne, like in *Harry Potter*, or off on a magic carpet ride into some alternate universe. It would do something extraordinary, surely.

Efird set the switch to draw from the diesel tank. He turned the key and the car rumbled to life. We set off down the gravel drive and then onto the country highway near his home. After a couple of minutes of tooling smoothly along, Efird flipped the red switch. There was no magical blast off, but the transition *was* remarkable. The wonder for me was that the transition was completely seamless, undetectable, just as he had said it would be. The car's performance was exactly the same before and after. He gunned it a couple of times to demonstrate its consistent pickup, then we headed back to his house.

"I would say there's no difference whatsoever between diesel and vegetable oil in the way the car operates. You flip that switch, you go back and forth—it's the same. Except for what comes out of the tailpipe."

Vegetable oil passes through the 5-micron filter into a five-gallon bucket. When Jim Efird opens the faucet on the bucket, clean oil flows into the storage drum.

When we pulled into the carport, he left the car running for a moment so I could go around back and catch the smell from the tailpipe. Crouching down behind the car, I detected the faint scent of very hot vegetable oil, the same smell as a pan of frying oil on a hot stove. But what struck me most of all was the *absence* of smell. Standing two feet from the tailpipe of a running car, there was no noxious odor—no smoke or clouds, nothing visible, nothing stinky, nothing that burned my throat or nose or eyes, nothing polluting. *That* was a strange sensation.

Like many of the other users of alternative technologies we've talked to, Efird has a healthy dose of self-reliance and independence. I believe he's enjoyed choosing a route that others thought was risky and having it prove to be a sound investment for his bank account as well as for the planet's future. "It's worked well," he said. "It's just a good feeling. It's all good from my perspective."

As we lingered, looking over the goats and smelling the veggie oil, I imagined a city of cars with no sickening emissions, no pollution at all. Now that would be a mystical carpet ride, indeed, into a hopeful future. Maybe the little red switch is magic after all.

Additional Resources

American Council for an Energy-Efficient Economy (guide to buying cars), www.greencar.com.

Biodiesel (the official site of the National Biodiesel Board), www.biodiesel.org/buyingbiodiesel/retailfuelingsites/.

Elsbett (sells conversion kits), www.elsbett.com/engl/.

Environmental Protection Agency, www.epa.gov/greenvehicles.

EV World (information on electric, hybrid, and alternative-fuel vehicles), www.evworld.com.

Golden Fuel Systems (formerly Greasel Conversions), www.goldenfuelsystems.com/.

Greasecar Vegetable Fuel Systems, www.greasecar.com.

Green Car Journal (quarterly magazine with car reviews and technology features), www.greenercars.com.

Hybrid Cars (comprehensive information on hybrids), www.hybridcars.com.

Hybrid Center (consumer guide to hybrids from the Union of Concerned Scientists), www.hybridcenter.org.

McMaster-Carr (sells filters), www.mcmaster.com/.

Mother Earth News (information on alternative transportation), www.motherearthnews.com/alternative-transportation.

Mother Earth News, Hybrid Blueprints (information on converting a car into a hybrid), www.motherearthshopping.com.

Northern Tool and Equipment (sells electric and manual pumps that can be used to move oil from one container to another), www.northerntool.com.

Union of Concerned Scientists, Clean Vehicles program (learn more about UCS research and take action to improve fuel-economy standards), www.ucsusa.org/clean_vehicles.

U.S. Department of Energy, Energy Efficiency and Renewable Energy (guide to buying cars), www.fueleconomy.gov.

Zipcar (the leading provider of car-sharing services), www.zipcar.com.

BEYOND CARS

Community Voice

Jim Cameron, Green Builder

Hybrids are good, but are they the best solution? Long before hybrids, Honda and Toyota were already making simple cars that got great mileage, had fewer parts, and weighed less. They still are.

Then along came the hybrids. They get a few more miles to the gallon, but they have a lot more parts. To produce all those parts, you have to get all the raw materials and transport it all. That uses a lot of energy. Is it worth the trade-off? It might not be. I think trains and mass transit are a better way to go. … Reduce our dependence on cars. I mean, the car is the problem. Period. …

Advantages of Biking

If all of our cars suddenly turned into bikes, the impact on our nation's energy consumption would be profound. About 35 percent of the nation's energy supply, mostly fossil fuels, is devoted to vehicles. This percentage includes not only vehicle fuel, but also the energy required to manufacture and transport parts and new models, and the energy required to create and maintain roads.[1]

We all know biking is better exercise than riding in a car and offers significant benefits to cardiovascular health. Think about the fact that the stationary bike has been the standard in-home exercise equipment for decades. The weight-management potential of cycling is considerable. A 150-pound person who rides half an hour to work burns 250 calories on the morning commute alone.[2]

Biking can benefit your budget too. Author David Lamb calculates that if 10 percent of car commuters began biking to work, collectively they would save more than $1 billion on gasoline annually. Currently, each bike commuter saves as much as 400 gallons of gas per year. Even those who bike just as far as the nearest bus or train station save as much as 150 gallons per year.[3]

Cyclists save money on more than just fuel. Ken Kifer analyzed how much of his income was invested in his car. Using 2002 figures, he estimated the cost of driving a car to be about 63¢ per mile. This takes into account the purchase price of the car; insurance; license fees, tags, and yearly taxes; financial charges and loan interest; gas and oil; repairs and maintenance; and parking fees, tolls, fines, and tickets. Gas, the most obvious car expenditure, ends up being only about 12 percent of this total figure.[4]

Kifer's figures don't take into account the more hidden costs associated with a car-based society. In the report "The Real Price of Gasoline," The International Center for Technology Assessment adds on the complicated tax subsidies that keep the price of gasoline low; money spent protecting access to foreign oil sources; money spent addressing damage to human health and the environment; and the cost of urban sprawl.[5]

Bikes, meanwhile, are relatively cheap. A cyclist with a new bike and up-to-date accessories spends about 12¢ per mile; someone riding an older bike might average as low as 3 or 4¢ per mile.[6] To put it another way, it costs about $300 a year to keep a bike up and running. A car, meanwhile, costs around $3,000.[7] In terms of community costs and allocation of tax funds, building a car parking deck costs up to $30,000 per car, while a bike locker costs $200 per bike.[8]

Bikes also save time. Transportation experts calculate that the average American drives about 7,500 miles annually and spends about 1,600 hours per year interacting with his or her car, including driving, buying gas, or maintaining the car. This comes to an average of less than 5 miles per hour.[9] Not surprising when government analysts estimate that the average urban motorist spends seven hours a week idling in traffic jams.[10]

For a closer look at comparisons between bikes and cars, see Ken Kifer's detailed investigation at Ken Kifer's Bike Pages (www.kenkifer .com/bikepages/advocacy/autocost.htm).

Read on for a more subjective look at the world of cycling.

Notes

1. "Bicycling to Work: Swift, Silent, and Efficient," *The Greensboro News & Record*, May 14, 2006.
2. Ibid.
3. David Lamb, *Over the Hills: A Midlife Escape across America by Bicycle* (New York: Crown Publishers, 1996), www.chatt bike.com/bikechat/didyouknow.htm.
4. Ken Kifer, "Auto Costs versus Bike Costs," Ken Kifer's Bike Pages, www.kenkifer.com/bikepages/advocacy/auto cost.htm.
5. The International Center for Technology Assessment, "The Real Price of Gasoline," Washington, DC, November 1998, www.icta.org/doc/Real%20Price%20of%20 Gasoline.pdf.
6. Ken Kifer, "Auto Costs versus Bike Costs."
7. "Bicycling to Work," *The Greensboro News & Record*.
8. Lamb, *Over the Hills*.
9. Ivan Illich, "Energy and Equity," *Toward a History of Needs* (New York: Pantheon, 1978).
10. Lamb, *Over the Hills*.

Community Voice

Kathleen Jardine: I Grieve for Momo and My Lost Bike World

Summer solstice in 1977, I got off the *Southern Crescent* in Charlotte, North Carolina. It was 2:00 A.M., and I was twenty-four years old. I had about $200, my backpack, my border collie—and my bike. I felt pretty well equipped for adult life.

I had not driven a car much since starting college. I didn't need a car, and I sure didn't want one. This car-less state largely accounted for my pleasant, carefree, and well-exercised young adulthood. My bike was my transportation. I got to school and work in all weather by bicycle, and to any recreation too.

The thing is, I wasn't the only one. During college and my first few years in Charlotte, my idyllic biking life was shared by many people. Even people who owned cars commonly used their bicycles to get around. Biking was easy. There were one-third fewer people in this country then, and maybe half the cars. In my quiet little college town, I worked twenty hours per week at a work-study job in the botany department greenhouse. I was paid minimum wage and could actually live on that pittance because I didn't have to support a car.

Biking was fun. My dog heeled to my bike, attending my classes in addition to going to my work-study job with me. Momo ran twelve miles almost every day, sprinting along beside me. I bicycled wearing flip-flops, and I quickly trained her to heel by inserting a vanilla wafer between my toes. "Momo, see this cookie?" I asked her. "Follow it closely and it's yours."

All of my friends used bikes. Many of them lived nearby, and we often took off in massive bike flotillas to go to a movie or to an ice cream parlor across town. These wacky trips were especially splendid on summer nights.

I was unwilling to give up this freedom when I got my first real adult job in Charlotte—although I did have to leave Momo at home. It wasn't hard to keep biking because there were so many fewer cars. I taught third through fifth grades in a school about seven miles from my house. Charlotte was delectable by bike. I had never lived anywhere so fragrant, so leafy. She was a big sleepy town in 1977, with cheap housing downtown and lots of people my age riding bikes. We rode through the wide, car-sparse boulevards laughing and racing one another like we owned the place. I was healthy and fit. I rarely biked more than twenty miles a day, but it was enough to make me strong. Such regular outdoor workouts were good for my soul too.

Eventually, I married my bike mechanic. Jim and I courted on bikes. We had a lot in common, starting with our refusal to own cars.

Then Charlotte changed. It seemed to happen almost overnight. All the other folks who moved there brought their cars with them, and in just a few years, it became really scary to get around by bicycle.

I did something I hoped I would never do: I got off my bike and bought a stupid car.

I still grieve for that lost bike world, and for my Momo running beside me.

Public Transportation

Every day, Americans use more energy for transportation than for any other single activity. In fact, almost half of the energy we consume—a whopping 43 percent—is devoted solely to moving ourselves from one place to another. Most of those 26,580 British thermal units of energy are used in our personal vehicles. Certainly, this is convenient, but it shouldn't come as a great surprise that a private vehicle for each of our nation's 300,000 residents is not the most energy-efficient solution to our transportation woes.

But does sharing vehicles make any difference? After all, most buses, trains, subways, and carpools run on the same dirty fuels. In terms of fuel economy, most buses lag behind cars. And most buses use diesel fuel, which is in general dirtier than gasoline.

Trains, meanwhile, require unexpected amounts of energy due to the relative heaviness of the rail cars (twice the weight per seat as an automobile), high travel speeds punctuated by long, slow braking in which much energy is lost, and the interior lights and air-conditioning, which operate even when the train is stopped.[1]

All of these points are valid. However, they can be conquered with one single factor: ridership. The average vehicle occupancy for commuters to work is a pitiful 1.1 riders per car.[2] That's pretty sad when you think about how many of those commutes start and end very near each other, if not in exactly the same place.

Attempts to encourage carpooling and ridesharing have, for the most part, failed. In fact, vehicle occupancy has fallen in the past few decades (down from 1.2 in 1970).[3]

This is where public transportation has a huge advantage. Just a handful of passengers on a bus or train rapidly multiply the efficiency of the vehicle. Per passenger mile traveled, mass transit uses half the amount of fuel that cars do, and less than a third the amount used by SUVs and light trucks. Robert J. Shapiro, Kevin A. Hassett, and Frank S. Arnold, writing for The American Public Transportation Association, estimate that mass transit produces less than 50 percent of the carbon dioxide and nitrogen oxides that the same number of passengers traveling the same distance in private vehicles would create.[4] As a result, public transportation already in use reduces carbon dioxide emissions by 7.4 million tons a year. In addition, the 27,000 tons of nitrogen oxides currently saved through mass transit are equal to more than a third of the total emitted by all domestic sources combined.[5]

These emissions benefits already exist, and we barely use public transportation at all. If Americans increased their use of mass transit to 10 percent of our transportation needs (the European average), the benefits would be even greater. This small increase would reduce our dependence on imported oil by 40 percent—the amount we import from Saudi Arabia each year.[6] Using mass transit for 10 percent of our travel would save as much energy as is used by the entire American food industry per year. Our carbon dioxide emissions would fall to 25 percent less than the minimum outlined in the Kyoto Protocol.

Notes

1. David S. Lawyer, "Does Mass Transit Save Energy?," www.lafn.org/~dave/trans/energy/does_mt_saveE.html.
2. Ibid.
3. Ibid.
4. Robert J. Shapiro, Kevin A. Hassett, and Frank S. Arnold, "Conserving Energy and Preserving the Environment: The Role of Public Transportation," American Public Transportation Association, July 2002, www.fypower.org/pdf/RES171664_shapiro.pdf.
5. Ibid.
6. Ibid.

Buses Win

What kind of mass transit is the best environmental choice? The Union of Concerned Scientists calculated that intercity bus travel is the least polluting mode of personal travel when you factor in the number of people served and the number of miles traveled. Passenger rail and air travel generate somewhat more greenhouse gases per passenger mile than intercity buses, but they are still far better than cars, trucks, and motorcycles.[1]

Many of our transportation issues relate to the layout of our cities and towns. The best way to reduce our fuel consumption is simply to travel less, and that's hard to do when urban centers and suburbia are separated by long commutes. So designing self-contained communities will have to be part of our future solutions.

For now, we could make huge inroads into our use of fuel by making better use of mass transit, especially in cities. Half of the nation's twenty-six largest urban areas currently fall short of the EPA's minimum air-quality standards. Increasing ridership on the thirty-five public transportation systems serving these cities would improve air quality, congestion, and the financial strain of building new highways and widening roads.[2]

However, municipal dollars will not be funneled into mass transit unless consumers demand it. So start demanding. If you live near a functioning mass transit system, consider picking up a schedule and seeing what your options are. How could you arrange your schedule to make it work? You might be surprised at how easy it is to leave your car home on your next trip.

Notes

1. Michael Brower and Warren Leon, *The Consumer's Guide to Effective Environmental Choices: Practical Advice from the Union of Concerned Scientists* (New York: Three Rivers Press, 1999).
2. Robert J. Shapiro, Kevin A. Hassett, and Frank S. Arnold, "Conserving Energy and Preserving the Environment: The Role of Public Transportation," American Public Transportation Association, July 2002, www.fypower.org/pdf/RES171664_shapiro.pdf.

Rocking, Rolling, Romantic Trains

My first train ride began on a sweaty June night. The air outside the train station was heavy and steamy, even at 2:00 A.M. The wooden bench where I slumped after an hour of patient waiting stuck like a hot car seat to my sweaty legs. I was eleven years old, and thus far I'd never ridden in any vehicle other than a car, unless you counted the school bus or my granddad's pontoon boat.

Amtrak's northbound Carolinian came screeching into the station only an hour and a half behind schedule. The cement platform offered no shelter from the squeal of breaks, the acrid scent of hot metal, or the blast of heavy air against my face. I don't remember a conductor helping us on board, or the frenzied transfer of suitcases to luggage racks and the search for four seats together, but those things must have happened. My mother must have anxiously shepherded us up the silver steps, calling to my father to count the bags and get the tickets out, please. I know my brother and I must have held each other's hands, exchanging nervous and excited glances, because I *do* remember the thrilled knot in my stomach, boarding that metal monster. I do remember the magic of that first nighttime train.

The other passengers were sleeping, or trying to. The car was dark, and its dimensions were impossible to judge. I could see a long aisle stretching before me and neat rows of seats on either side swimming in murky blackness. Behind me was the shining silver compartment where the two cars joined together. In the gaps between the metal, I could see the gleam of moonlight on the tracks and the coupler holding the cars together. It was just like my train set, but big. Really big.

We were barely settled in our seats when the train gave a violent shudder and lurched forward. It seized once, then lurched again and began, oh so slowly, to roll forward.

Scrunched down in my seat, the ceiling seemed impossibly far away. We swayed smoothly over the tracks, the wheels churning sleekly like roller skates flying over asphalt. The car seemed to loll and pitch, leaning out impossibly as we rounded curves. Shadows swirled and flickered as we rolled past the streetlamps and dim porch lights of slumbering Mecklenburg County. I watched the lights play garishly over the faces of the people sleeping around me. How could they be sleeping? We were riding a roller coaster!

More than a decade later, train riding has lost some of its magic. Since that first mysterious venture, I've crossed the country four times on the train, zigzagged across the West, and lumbered dutifully back and forth across my home state. I've been stranded in Chicago, laid over in Albuquerque, and free to wander the streets of Washington and Flagstaff while waiting for connecting trains. As a carless adult, I've come to know the Piedmont Crescent intimately, as it has ferried me from friends to family, school to home.

The train is useful, unarguably. It gets me where I need to go—not always on time, exactly, but for less money than Greyhound and certainly less than owning a car of my own. The seats are more spacious than an airplane, you can stroll around the aisles and visit the café and observation cars—and, hey, sometimes there are even free snacks!

But I'll admit, none of those are the reasons why I really like trains. Trains, like cowboys, are part of American lore—they capture a magical and romantic link with our past that grungy buses, sterile planes, and automobiles simply do not offer. They are immortalized in popular art and song, a bittersweet image of a disappearing past.

A train trip is also a cultural immersion, a panorama of humanity that can hardly fail to fascinate. Unlike airplanes, which are prohibitively expensive to many, almost anyone can afford to ride a train. I can travel the 100 miles between Greensboro and Charlotte for only $13, far less than the cost of gas for a car ride. The resulting array of passengers on a cross-country train is mesmerizing, from Mennonite families juggling babies and bonnets to inner-city sweethearts hugging goodbye on the platform.

The route of the train takes you on a no-holds-barred tour of the back side of our country, the part you never see in travel brochures. Rail lines cut through side yards and main streets; they run alongside country roads and rivers. Often while riding the train, I forget to knit or read my book and get lost watching the sights out the window like a show on the Discovery Channel. I discover the country I live in: children jumping on trampolines in overgrown yards, miles of quiet pine forest, ramshackle brick storefronts and tidy town streets that flash by before my eyes can focus on them. I often forget my own presence, that I am part of a snorting, rattling, chugging beast roaring through these quiet scenes. I feel more like a ghost ephemerally slipping past unseen.

Perhaps the nostalgic beauty of these intimate landscapes, and of the whole train experience, is heightened by its disappearance. While Amtrak, the federally subsidized for-profit corporation that in 1971 replaced the private railroad industry, reports increasing ridership, it's obvious that most travelers these days "think no more of trains than of horses."[1] Just five of Amtrak's forty-four routes account for over 50 percent of all riders. Outside of the Northeast and Southern California, the number of train riders is so small—just 24 million in 2003[2]—that if the railways were to close, not a single flight would be added to the country's air system in compensation.

A few years ago, after getting stranded in Chicago for a maddening twenty-three hours and forty-five minutes, I vowed never to ride the train again. It was too slow, too imprecise, too disheartening. But to my surprise, I've already broken that vow too many times to count.

Riding the train may not deliver me to my doorstep at the exact moment I want to arrive, but it is strangely addicting. I always clamber off with a slightly dazzled sense of sorrow and splendor that comes with so many glimpses into other people's lives. I guess an occasional hour in a station waiting room is a small price to pay for the chance to teach a random six-year-old to crochet as we wait for our belated ride. I'll still choose a thoughtful train journey over a tedious car trip spent searching for interstate exits and cheap gas prices. And I wonder if one day I'll gaze down a deserted railroad track and say to my grandchild, "When I was a girl … "

—Sadie

Notes

1. Joseph Vranich, "Replacing Amtrak: A Blueprint for a Sustainable Passenger Rail Service," Reason Foundation, October 1997, www.reason.org/ps235.html.
2. "Long Distance Trains Lead 2.7% Amtrak Ridership Growth Rate," *Light Rail Now!*, December 2003, www.lightrailnow.org/facts/fa_amtrak-003.htm.

Airplanes

If you take an ecological footprint quiz,[1] you may be startled by the questions about your flying habits. Most of us fly so rarely that we forget to factor aviation into our transportation usage.

However, the magnitude of energy consumed by aviation is massive enough to make even the occasional flight significant. A transcontinental plane, such as a 747, uses tens of thousands of pounds of fuel on takeoff alone.[2]

While pollution controls have improved a bit since the mid 1990s, a single older jet—many of which are still in operation—produces as much nitrogen oxides just in taking off, idling, and landing as a car driven 26,500 miles.[3] As a result, it's not too surprising that many airports are among the biggest polluters in their city.[4]

Jet-fuel emissions are hard to quantify once the aircraft reaches its cruising altitude because at that height the emissions are dispersed out of the Earth's atmosphere. Although carbon dioxide has the same climate effects no matter where it is released, the impact of other pollutants increases at high altitude. Nitrogen oxides in particular have more than double the effects of carbon dioxide when released at high elevations.[5]

The white vapor trails that airplanes leave behind, which are formed when water vapor freezes around particles of engine exhaust, are also an issue at high altitudes.[6] In the three days after the terrorist attacks on September 11, when all American aircraft were grounded, the difference between daytime and nighttime temperatures increased by an entire degree Celsius compared with the average temperatures of the last three decades. This confirmed scientists' suspicion that vapor trails hinder natural temperature variations.[7]

Consumers who are concerned about the environmental impact of their air travel may want to compensate for their travel emissions by purchasing carbon offsets. A traveler can calculate the amount of carbon he or she is personally responsible for on the flight (companies provide calculators) and then purchase an offset for that amount. The funds the offset company receives are used to finance projects that avoid, reduce, or absorb greenhouse gases through renewable energy, energy efficiency, or forest projects that biosequester carbon.

The Tufts Climate Initiative has published a well-researched paper online that evaluates and compares the effectiveness and costs of purchasing carbon offsets for airline travel from thirteen different companies.[8] Of the thirteen, they recommend four without reservation: Atmosfair, Climate Friendly, MyClimate, and NativeEnergy. The Tufts Climate Initiative has also published online a user-friendly pamphlet on this subject.[9]

For information about other ways to offset the greenhouse gases you generate, see "A Consumer's Guide to Retail Carbon Offset Providers."[10]

Notes

1. Redefining Progress: The Nature of Economics, "About the Ecological Footprint," www.rprogress.org/ecological _footprint/about_ecological_footprint.htm.
2. Alliance of Residents Concerning O'Hare, Inc., "Pollution," www.areco.org/pollute.htm#AIRINTRO.
3. Elisa Murray, "Air Travel Heats Up the Planet," *Sightline Institute*, www.sightline.org/research/energy/res_pubs/ rel_air_travel_aug04.
4. Natural Resources Defense Council, "Flying Off Course: Environmental Impacts of America's Airports," 1995, http://rcaanews.org/nrdc_FOC.pdf.
5. Intergovernmental Panel on Climate Change, "Aviation and the Global Atmosphere," 1999, http://grida.no/ climate/ipcc/aviation/index.htm.
6. Murray, "Air Travel Heats Up the Planet."
7. Ibid.
8. Anja Kollmuss and Benjamin Bowell, "Voluntary Offsets for Air-Travel Carbon Emissions: Evaluations and Recommendations of Voluntary Offset Companies," Tufts Climate Initiative, December 2006, www.aceee.org/ consumerguide/TCI_06Report.pdf (accessed December 21, 2007).
9. "Flying Green: How to Protect the Climate and Travel Responsibly," Tufts Climate Initiative, Voluntary Offset Information Portal, A Consumer Handout, "Flying Green: How to Protect the Climate and Travel Responsibly," www.tufts.edu/tie/tci/carbonoffsets/TCI-offset-handout.htm (accessed December 21, 2007).
10. Clean Air—Cool Planet, "A Consumer's Guide to Retail Carbon Offset Providers," December 2006, www .cleanair-coolplanet.org/ConsumersGuidetoCarbon Offsets.pdf (accessed December 21, 2007).

Travel Solutions Depend on Where You Are

The sprawling midsize cities of America present a special brand of limbo. Few were designed with housing or essential services downtown. Instead, they fill miles upon miles with the endless lawns of suburbia centered loosely around a downtown of office buildings that close like tired eyes at 5:00 P.M.

Charlotte, the setting of my youth, is not much different. Although I can see the skyscrapers of downtown from the yard of my childhood home, there is little hint of bustling center-city life in our neighborhood. Instead, we have a shopping mall, which at least I can walk to in ten minutes. Friends who live farther out in the suburbs are less fortunate. One friend lives deep within a newer subdivision, fifteen miles from downtown and miles from the city limit. Four miles deep in purely residential streets, even the smallest errand from her house demands the use of a car.

Even in my relatively advantageous location, trying to avoid the car means taking my life in my hands. There's no room for my bike in the narrow city lanes and often no sidewalk for pedestrians. The bus costs $1.10 per ride and comes once an hour. The bus lines are so few that even a short trip requires going to the central station and transferring. No wonder everyone drives!

For twenty years, I accepted this setup as an annoying but unavoidable way of life. I'd never known anything different. So when I left home for the big city, I was in for a surprise.

My new home of Guadalajara, Mexico, was a city of 7 million people—not much smaller than New York City. I was entranced by this urban wonderland. When I called my family back home, I sounded like an annoying radio ad: "The public transportation here is *amazing*! I can go anywhere I want in the whole city or country on the bus. Six different bus lines go past my house, and buses are constantly going by. It costs only 30¢ to ride, and you can just get off and switch to a different bus if you need to, no transfers. Long-distance buses are half off for students and leave all day long going everywhere from Tijuana to Tabasco.

Seriously, I would *never* need a car here!" And I didn't. I walked to school, rode the bus to work, and took the metro, bus, or a taxi downtown or to visit friends.

When my friend Amanda joined me there, I was eager to introduce her to my dear, beloved buses. But her welcome to the wild world of bus riding didn't go as smoothly as planned. "Why aren't the bus stops marked?" she wailed. "I don't know where to wait! And how do I know where this bus even *goes*, or where to get off, or how to get back?! Don't make me go by myself!"

After all, public transportation takes a little getting used to. No matter where you are, you may have to wait a while for a bus to arrive. Sometimes it rains while you're waiting. Sometimes you have to sit next to stinky people and hear about their ex-wives. Sometimes you forget to pay attention and miss your stop. Nonetheless, you never have to buy gas. You never have car payments or insurance payments. You're never responsible for a wreck. You never have to deal with road rage, crazy drivers, or someone keying your new paint job. And you have the satisfaction of knowing that you're not generating globe-warming tailpipe emissions and you're not increasing our dependence on foreign oil.

It's easy to see how I fell in love with riding the bus. But the affair was all too brief. When I returned to the States, I moved to a small town in the southern Appalachians and became acquainted with the other end of the spectrum.

Hot Springs, population 639, had one main street. The Smoky Mountain Diner and Ricker's Grocery both closed at 7:00. But when they were open, they, as well as the post office, the library, and the café, were within a few minutes' walk of any house in town. It was so simple and so satisfying to set off down the street on foot and come back from the store carrying what I needed. I was getting exercise, a nice evening walk, and emitting zero exhaust, to boot. Why would I ever use a car here? By the time the engine warmed up, I'd be turning it off again.

After these two pleasing solutions, I hit a streak of bad transportation luck. A summer on a farm located deep in a national forest was maddening. I was ten miles and one huge mountain from the nearest store of any kind. Biking was treacherous; walking absurd. When my boyfriend's car broke down, I realized how utterly dependent on it I was. As much as I loved my beautiful, wild surroundings, the isolation was intense, and I wasn't sorry when the farming stint was over.

In striking contrast, after that I moved to one of those infuriating midsize cities—it offered no efficient public transportation, yet was too big for walking and too dangerous to rely on biking. And there I am today. Every bone in my body resists getting a car, yet what can I do? Car-less, I depend on rides from coworkers to get to work. I use my bike for errands on sunny days, but in the cold and rainy winter I'm forced to choose between bumming a ride from a friend or waiting for a bus that may never come. Even if I don't own a car, I still depend on them. And worse yet, my friends and family are forced to bear the financial and ethical responsibility of car ownership while I hitch

free rides. It doesn't make me feel good, and it's not a permanent solution.

No One-Size-Fits-All Answer

As I've learned from living in a variety of settings, my transportation needs depend upon the size and layout of my community. The hardest places to live without cars are cities with suburban sprawl where urban centers lack residential space. Such cities seldom have effective mass transit, and they're too spread out and congested for consistent biking or walking.

For me, as a current resident of a midsize city, one solution is to look for a job close to home, or a home close to work. If I have to get a car, I hope I can afford a fuel-efficient car that doesn't pollute. Meanwhile, I'll rely on the goodwill of my car-owning friends. For trips to visit my family, I'll continue to take the train.

For our culture as a whole, our solutions for the future must include city planning based on conservation principles and energy efficiency, as we've said before. That means designing urban centers to include residential space above street-level businesses. Outside the city center, it means planning small, self-sufficient neighborhoods and communities that provide essential services such as grocery stores, post offices, and libraries, where residents can walk and bike to most of their destinations.

What Can You Do?

If you're willing to move, you have the most options. The greenest choice is an urban area with homes, offices, and retail shops in close proximity. Second best is a residential community that includes your most common stops. Many cities are beginning to develop such pedestrian-friendly communities in areas that would otherwise be pure suburban sprawl. A third option is to relocate within walking distance of a mass transit system that can take you to work or shopping areas, or to live in an area with bike lanes.

If you can't live within walking or biking distance of what you need, and mass transit is not an option, then buy the most energy-efficient and nonpolluting car you can afford, or one that uses biofuels, and try to share rides with other car users.

Motorcycles might seem like good options, but they're not really. They do get twice the gas mileage per person of single-occupant cars, but their engines have few pollution controls and thus have high emissions. Motorcycle travel has twice the impact on air pollution as the average car.

Even if you find yourself unable to implement any of these recommendations, you can still make a difference by raising the consciousness of those around you. When you talk to friends and acquaintances who are real estate agents, developers, or government workers, encourage them to consider dwindling fuel supplies and growing greenhouse gases when evaluating transportation and development choices.

City within a City

City within a City (CWAC) is a great example of how struggling urban neighborhoods can become self-sustaining communities.[1] The program lends money to small-business owners, particularly minorities and women, who are trying to make a living in faltering urban areas. These loans are deferrable for ten years, allowing disadvantaged business owners to get on their feet while drawing commerce and life into self-contained neighborhood centers—like small villages within a big city.

Ninety percent of CWAC's loans, supported by the Self-Help Credit Union,[2] have financed the movement of services and retail businesses into distressed neighborhoods, from restaurants and groceries to child-care centers and dry cleaners. These loans improve economic assets for the residents, and improve the livability of the neighborhoods as well.

Although not the primary goal of the loans, the development of services in urban areas has environmental advantages too. Every additional neighborhood service or store means one less car trip for neighborhood residents. These new businesses also create jobs within walking distance of urban homes.

Change is possible! Similar initiatives are being pioneered in cities across the nation, such as Phoenix's EXPAND program, and results seem promising. As our population continues to grow, we must design self-sufficient communities that use energy and land efficiently. Ideally, that means planning residences in close proximity to work, shopping, and recreation. Lively, walkable, efficient communities include sidewalks, shops with apartments or condos upstairs, bike lanes, slow car traffic, if any, narrower streets, pedestrian right-of-ways, safety, and high connectivity between streets. With a little foresight, these features are easy to plan.

For more information about mixed-use villages, or developments that cluster homes to preserve green space, see What Conservationists Are Doing on a Larger Scale (page 97).

Notes

1. Anne Scorza, "Charlotte's Equity Loan Program: A Model for Financing Inner City Development," UNC-Chapel Hill Masters Thesis, 2001.
2. Self-Help Credit Union, www.self-help.org/.

Chapter Two

Green Housing

Making Changes in Your Home

A life-size gray hand stands upright on the kitchen table, stark and eerie in the shadows. It's another of my son's wax-candle creations illuminating our cold, powerless house. Living in an area prone to both ice storms and hurricanes, we have power outages on a fairly regular basis—and life comes to a complete standstill. Can't work on the computer, can't open the fridge, can't watch television, can't even see to read. I am humbled every time by my complete dependence on electricity. Sitting in the dark, I have plenty of time to ponder, uncomfortably, my total reliance on something that is so damaging to our health and our natural resources. Then suddenly, the refrigerator motor begins to hum, the lights come on, and life resumes.

Do you know where this electricity comes from? I find that a little knowledge about how energy is produced motivates me to use less of it.

—Sally

Conventional Energy Sources

Coal

Perhaps the most detrimental source of energy is coal. Nationwide, 23 percent of the energy used in this country comes from coal.[1] It's popular because it's cheap, but the environmental costs are huge, from strip-mining and mountaintop removal, to acid rain, smog, and global warming, to methyl mercury poisoning,

to name a few. Although it is dirty, some economists foresee an increasing reliance on coal as we run out of oil. But we have already taken most of the best quality coal that was closest to the surface and easiest to get to. At some point in the near future, the energy costs of extracting coal will exceed the energy provided by burning it.

Petroleum Oil

Oil supplies close to 40 percent of our country's power needs, mostly in homes and vehicles.[2] As you know if you've ever breathed car exhaust, burning petroleum releases a noxious brew of the same oxides, particulates, heavy metals, and greenhouse gases emitted by coal-fired plants, though not always in the same proportions. Like coal, oil contributes heavily to global warming and smog. Drilling, spilling, and transporting oil also causes major habitat destruction.

Natural Gas

About a quarter of our energy consumption is fueled by natural gas.[3] Like oil and coal, natural gas is also a nonrenewable fossil fuel. It, too, pollutes the air, but burning it releases only half as much carbon dioxide as coal, few particulates, and very little sulfur dioxide or other toxic emissions.[4] Energy experts see natural gas as a piece of the energy puzzle, but not a large-scale solution. Half the carbon dioxide of coal is still more pollution than we can afford.

Nuclear Power

Nuclear power is not a fossil fuel. Providing 8 percent of our energy,[5] it's touted as a miracle power source because it has no emissions. It's true that nuclear power doesn't release the pollutants we associate with oil, coal, and natural gas, but it does create enormous amounts of radioactive waste. In 2001, there was enough plutonium waste in the world to make 34,000 nuclear bombs. By now, there's much more.[6]

Hydroelectric Power

Power from hydroelectric dams currently supplies 3 percent of the nation's electricity,[7] and 80 percent of the electricity now produced from renewable resources.[8] Hydroelectric power converts the kinetic energy of water flowing downhill, in rivers, into electrical

Although hydroelectric power usually involves the use of dams, it is possible to generate it without disrupting the flow of natural waterways.

power. Although hydroelectric power is renewable, dams cause unpredictable surges that flood land and wreak havoc with aquatic organisms attuned to natural flow patterns. In spite of this, hydroelectric plants that operate without a dam can be one of the most benign ways to make electricity.

In short, virtually all of our most common sources of energy leave a wake of destruction behind them. Fortunately, we also have a lot of alternatives—if we are willing to use them.

One step is to demand that our power companies utilize green sources of energy, like wind and solar. You can do this by buying green power blocks through your local power company. A single green power block, also called a renewable energy certificate, costs about $4 per month in addition to your regular power bill. The money covers the higher costs to the utility company of getting energy from renewable resources rather than conventional sources. We would rather the utility company footed this cost, but we don't suppose that will happen until customers demand it. For the present, buying a green power block is a way of showing the power company that you prioritize green energy, and you want them to too.

In our house, our energy consumption dropped from 685 kilowatt hours last September to 363 kilowatt hours this September. This saves us $22.55 per month, which is enough to buy four green power blocks to cover 400 kilowatt hours and still save $7 per month.

If this green power option is not available through your utility, you may still be able to participate in this program. The U.S. Department of Energy offers an interactive map for locating green power programs.[9]

Green Grid: An Oxymoron?

If you do buy green power through the grid, where is it coming from? Some of it is generated by solar panels. Some utilities buy solar energy from private homes generating excess energy from their solar panels and redirect this energy to other homes.

Wind is another common source of green power. It is endorsed by conservationists and planners as sustainable and environmentally sound. It's captured by wind turbines, which generate no greenhouse gases, no acid rain, and no waste products.

Capturing Wind, the Invisible Energy

In addition to being nonpolluting, a major advantage of wind energy is the revenue it generates for rural communities. When energy companies build a wind park (multiple wind turbines in a single rural community), they are required to pay thousands of dollars to the government. According to our friend Daniel, who works for an alternative energy company, a large portion of the $9,000 per turbine and $6,000 per megawatt paid by the company goes to the local city or county government. One town, Daniel said, was able to buy a new truck for the county's highway supervisor. It replaced a truck that had to be pushed downhill to start. Other towns are able to pave roads or improve their water supplies, septic systems, or schools.

The landowners who host the turbines also receive an average of $7,500 per year *per turbine*; with as many as eight or nine turbines on one property, that money can add up quickly. Daniel said that turbines make it possible for many struggling family farms to survive. Many of the families he approaches about locating turbines on their property "live in deplorable conditions—dilapidated trailers or crumbling houses, with no plumbing. One man was getting his drinking water from a culvert behind his house." With the income from the turbines, rural families are often able to improve their living conditions and maintain a way of living that has been in the family for generations.

The main limitation of wind energy is that you can't put a wind park just anywhere. It must be an area with an average wind speed of at least 17 miles per hour and out of the path of migratory birds. A turbine must be at least 1,000 feet from the nearest home or other turbine, and 400 feet from a road. Once installed, however, farmers can plant crops or graze livestock right up to the base of the turbine.

Wind power faces a surprising amount of prejudice. Daniel said he's heard every objection in the book. "Most often, the real objection is the look of the turbines on their land. But for some reason people are reluctant to say that. One farmer said no because 'wind turbines cause mad cow disease!'"

But Wind Isn't Everything

Despite the many benefits of wind power, it isn't *the* solution to the energy crisis. It's only part of the solution. A future of sustainable energy use will involve several renewable and nonpolluting methods of generating power, and wind will be one of them.

Hearing Daniel talk about a form of energy that *improves* communities, we think back to the towns that have been degraded by blasting for coal, rivers ruined by sludge and mine tailings, and mountaintops reduced to rubble. We reflect on wildlife habitat destroyed by drilling for oil, and by oil spills. And we contemplate our global climate change from burning these fuels. The contrast is all too extreme. But with wind and solar, and people like Daniel working for change, we feel hope for the future.

Notes

1. Climate Change Global Dilemma, "Energy Consumption by Fuel Type for World's Largest 20 GHG Emitters," www.eenews.net/special_reports/climate_change _global/consumption_detail.
2. Ibid.
3. Ibid.
4. Electricity from Natural Gas, Pace Law School Energy Project, Power Scorecard, http://powerscorecard.org/ tech_detail.cfm?resource_id=6.
5. Climate Change Global Dilema, "Energy Consumption."
6. Allison Macfarlane, Frank von Hippel, Jungmin Kang, and Robert Nelson, "Plutonium Disposal: The Third Way," *The Bulletin of the Atomic Scientists* 57, no. 3 (May/June 2001): 53–57.
7. Climate Change Global Dilema, "Energy Consumption."
8. Electricity from Hydro, Pace Law School Energy Project, Power Scorecard, www.powerscorecard.org/tech_detail .cfm?resource_id=4.
9. U.S. Department of Energy, Energy Efficiency and Renewable Energy, The Green Power Network, Buying Green Power, "Can I Buy Green Power in My State?" www.eere .energy.gov/greenpower/buying/buying_power.shtml.

Reducing Your Consumption

Buying green power blocks is a powerful way to encourage your utility company to develop sustainable energy sources. But to have maximum impact on energy-related environmental problems, we all need to reduce our household energy consumption too. According to the U.S. Department of Energy, the average American household uses more than 900 kilowatt hours of electricity per month.[1] You'll read in the next few sections about how you can reduce this number by more than 50 percent with just a few adjustments and no reduction in quality of life. Many of these steps are unbelievably simple, such as changing lightbulbs. Some of the greatest energy wasters in homes, such as leaky insulation or inefficient appliances, can be rectified so easily, you'll wonder why you didn't make the changes years ago. Read on to learn more about quick and effective steps you can take today to change the energy efficiency of your current home.

Home construction choices have a huge effect on energy consumption, too, from materials used to home design and orientation. According to the U.S. Department of Energy, 70 percent of the energy invested in a building is in the production of the materials themselves.[2] Long before heating and air-conditioning run through your ducts, the metal to make those ducts was mined from mountainsides. Long before studs ever held up your walls, they were cut from forests near someone's home. Fossil fuels operated the mining equipment, the chain saws, and the logging trucks.

However, innovative builders are now incorporating many progressive and alternative construction materials and methods. If you've ever dreamed of building a new home or adding on to the one you have, you may be interested in reading about energy-efficient homes made of unconventional materials such as straw, AAC blocks, and earth. Others use more conventional materials, but strategically orient the house to make the most of solar energy. Positioning windows, overhangs, and trees to reduce or enhance the effects of wind or shading can affect your energy use too.

Many people feel that the ultimate step toward green power is to liberate themselves from the fossil fuel–burning utility company by generating their own power. If you can reduce your household's energy needs to 400 kilowatt hours, you may be an ideal candidate for a photovoltaic system that will end your family's dependence on dirty and climate-changing fuels used by utility companies.

Whether you're able to spend a few dollars on a lightbulb or ten grand on a down payment for a new home, you have a variety of options for changing your home's energy consumption.

Notes

1. Energy Basics 101, Department of Energy, Energy Information Administration, Official Energy Statistics from the U.S. Government, www.eia.doe.gov/basics/energy basics101.html (accessed May 6, 2006).
2. *Green Building Guidelines: Meeting the Demand for Low-Energy, Resource-Efficient Homes, Fifth Edition* (Washington, DC: Sustainable Buildings Industry Council, 2007).

Greedy Lightbulbs

We used to like to leave several lamps on in our house at night because it made the house seem cozier and more cheerful. If we left the living room to go make a snack, we'd leave the light on, not imagining one tiny lightbulb

could make much of a difference. Lightbulbs are so small, after all. But if you leave ten bulbs burning for just one hour—which most people do, every night—you've consumed one kilowatt hour of electricity.[1] And if you live in an area fueled by coal power plants, such as the southeastern United States, you've burned an entire pound of coal.

But what's one pound of coal in the scheme of things? Well, the pounds add up quickly. The average house in the coal-burning Southeast burns 36 kilowatt hours per day, or 1,100 per month. Nationwide, the monthly average is 850. When you consider that 8 pounds of West Virginia mountain terrain are blasted and removed to obtain each kilowatt of coal-fueled energy, those numbers start looking pretty ugly.[2]

Certainly, much of this can be attributed to heavy energy users such as air-conditioners (2 kilowatts per hour) and water heaters (4 kilowatts per hour).[3] But collectively, lights are heavy drawers too. Even though a single incandescent bulb uses only 0.1 kilowatt hour per hour, altogether lights use as much as 40 percent of the electricity in many homes.

The good news is, by switching to compact-fluorescent bulbs, you can leave your lights on just as much and burn only a fifth of the energy. A 20-watt compact fluorescent bulb emits the same light as a 100-watt incandescent bulb because it wastes less heat energy.

Fluorescent bulbs also last much longer than incandescent bulbs. Replacing just *one* incandescent bulb with a compact fluorescent will save you as much as $75 in replacement bulbs and energy bills. In the course of its lifetime, each compact fluorescent bulb will prevent more than 450 pounds of emissions from a power plant. If every American home replaced just one incandescent lightbulb with a compact fluorescent bulb, it would save enough energy to light more than 2.5 million homes for an entire year, and reduce greenhouse-gas emissions equivalent to those of nearly 800,000 cars.[4]

This seems incredible, but *you* do the math. Engineer Mike Stenhouse was doubtful as well, until he crunched the numbers for his own house. "We have six 65-watt spotlights in our kitchen, which burn around six hours a day," he calculates. "In the course of a year, it will cost me $24 for replacement bulbs, and $66 for the 280 pounds of coal to power them. I replaced them with 15-watt compact fluorescent spotlights with exactly the same light output. (My wife, Pat, said they give more.) They cost 50 percent more per bulb than incandescent, but last three times longer. In the course of a year, it will cost me $12 to replace them and $15 to power them, $27 total. So I will save $63. And it will use only 65 pounds of coal to power them, a savings of 225 pounds. That is an 80 percent reduction in power, heat, and emissions. Not bad."

Not bad at all. In fact, what's to lose? Some people complain that compact fluorescent bulbs take about thirty seconds to come up to full light output, and that the color of the light is slightly different. But after having them in our house for several months now, we don't notice that anymore.

Changing your lightbulbs is so ridiculously easy, it's hard to believe what a big difference it makes. This is one change you can make right here, right now, and feel good about right away.

Compact fluorescent bulbs are available at most home supply and hardware stores. Many grocery stores and drugstores carry them too.

Notes

1. *Kilowatt Ours: A Plan to Re-Energize America*, film (www.kilowattours.org/).
2. Ibid.
3. Ibid.
4. Energy Star, "Compact Fluorescent Light Bulbs," www.energystar.gov/index.cfm?c=cfls.pr_cfls.

Compact Fluorescent Disposal

Compact fluorescent lightbulbs contain a mercury vapor that is energized by electrodes to create light. While this is fundamental to fluorescent lighting, mercury cannot be thrown in the trash. To find out where you can dispose of fluorescent lightbulbs in your area, go to www.earth911.org and enter your zip code. You will be referred to a recycling center or other facility in your area that accepts mercury.

Energy-Efficient and Eco-Friendly Appliances

It's a slightly bigger investment than a $5 lightbulb, but switching over to energy-efficient appliances is another way to dramatically reduce your home's energy use. The EPA and Department of Energy have a program called Energy Star that identifies products and appliances that meet federal energy-efficiency standards. Energy Star appliances can reduce household energy consumption and greenhouse-gas emissions by one-third. In 2005 alone, use of Energy Star products reduced Americans' greenhouse-gas emissions by an amount equivalent to 23 million cars—the same as if one car in ten were retired. In turn, this saved $12 million in electricity bills.[1]

Energy Star is not a brand, it's a qualification. Appliances by many major brands qualify and are indicated by the blue Energy Star logo. The Energy Star website, www .energystar.gov, offers search engines for different products and stores where theses products can be found.

Dishwashers

Eco-friendly dishwashers use at least 25 percent less water and energy than those that simply meet the minimum federal standards. The most water-efficient models use 6.5 gallons or less per cycle.[2] You can maximize your dishwasher's efficicency by loading it fully before running it so that those 6.5 gallons of hot water wash as many dishes as possible. Also, skip the prerinse, rinse-hold, and heat-dry features of the cycle—none of them get the dishes any cleaner, and they all use extra energy.

Refrigerators

Refrigerators and freezers can be responsible for 25 percent of a home's energy use. Energy Star refrigerators use at least 15 percent less than the minimum federal standards. Choose Energy Star qualified refrigerators,[3] or Super Efficient Home Appliance (SEHA) Tier-2 refrigerators, which save at least 20 percent more than the federal minimum.[4] If you just changed all your lightbulbs after reading the last section, now consider this: replacing a standard 1990 refrigerator with a new Energy Star fridge saves as much energy as four and a

half months of lighting the average household. An Energy Star fridge can reduce the total power bill by more than 10 percent.[5] You can increase these savings by making sure your fridge has a tight seal around the door and is located as far as possible from any heat source, such as an oven or sunny window.

Clothes Washing Machines

Energy Star washing machines use 50 percent less energy and 45 to 60 percent less water, but perform as well as conventional washers. For maximum efficiency, choose models with a water-factor rating of 6.0 or less.[6] Most Energy Star washing machines are front loading. They not only wash and rinse with less water, but most models have a high-speed spin cycle that removes more water than conventional models, thus saving energy on drying.

Whether your washing machine is Energy Star or not, you can use less energy by always washing a full load and by washing in cold water.

Clothes Dryers

Energy Star does not certify clothes dryers because they are all pretty inefficient. In fact, they waste energy twice. While it may seem that a warm and toasty dryer is heating up your house as it tumbles your laundry, in fact it's doing the opposite. Your clothes dryer draws air from inside your house. This is air you've already paid to air-condition or heat. Either way, once inside your dryer, it's heated to dry the clothes and then blown outside of your home. At an average flow rate of around 150 cubic feet per minute, in less than two hours a clothes dryer can move all the heated or air-conditioned air in a 2,000-square-foot house out through the dryer vent.[7] You might as well open all the windows and put fans in them.

As quickly as air is blown out, new air is sucked in through all the cracks and gaps in the house. This new air, then, is newly air-conditioned or heated as your thermostat dictates to keep a steady temperature inside the house. So you're paying to heat or cool new air as quickly as your dryer can spit it back outside.

If possible, the best way to dry your clothes is on a clothesline or a drying rack. If this is not an option, try spinning your clothes on high speed or extended spin before putting them in the dryer to get as much moisture out as possible first. If you must use a dryer, try locating it in a garage, back porch, or some other area that is not regulated by your heating, ventilating, and air-conditioning systems. As long as your garage or porch is not airtight, the changes in airflow there will not affect the rest of the house.

Alternatively, there are a few models that feature a secondary supply vent, which draws air from outside the house. This is a common feature on foreign models, but is not common here, due to lack of demand from American consumers. It's time for us to request this feature from appliance manufacturers and dealers.

Notes

1. Energy Star, www.energystar.gov.
2. "Green Building Guidelines, Appliances," www.co .contra-costa.ca.us/depart/cd/recycle/gbg/Grnbldg -NewConstruction-9Chap4-2.pdf.
3. Energy Star.
4. Consortium for Energy Efficiency, www.cee1.org/.
5. "Green Building Guidelines, Appliances."
6. Ibid.
7. American Solar, "How to Use Your Heater Board," americansolardepot.com/solar_heat_howto_clothes _dryer.htm (accessed November 2006).

Your House as a System

In addition to lights and appliances, the main energy draw in a home is the heating and cooling system. For energy-efficient heating and cooling, a home should be well-insulated and airtight, with controlled airflow.

Much of your home's airflow is determined at the time the house is built by such factors as the type and degree of insulation in the walls and how extensively the cracks and gaps are caulked and sealed. But no matter what your situation is, there's plenty you can do to improve your home's heating and cooling efficiency.

A house's weakest points are doors and windows, which are most often leaky. Fortunately, it's easy to find and fix leaks.

Doors

To check a door for leaky drafts, have a friend stand outside the door at night with a flashlight. Have the friend shine the flashlight slowly along each edge of the door. Any place where you can see light shining between the door and the frame needs sealing.

Alternatively, shut the door and try to thread a dollar bill through the doorjamb on the edge with the knob. If you can get the bill through, such that one end of the bill is on either side of the closed door, the door needs sealing.

A popular weather sealant for doors is a thick, foam-backed adhesive tape that comes on a roll. To install it, simply run it along the frame or the door itself over any leaky spots. Its spongy thickness will block drafts. If the gap below your door is so large that it would require multiple layers of tape, a new door sweep or threshold (the rubber and metal strips across the bottom of many doorways) will create a better seal. Make sure the door shuts smoothly and snugly with the new threshold in place. Hardware and home-supply stores carry a variety of other materials, sold as strips or rolls, that can be installed around doors or windows to block drafts.

Windows

You can use the flashlight method to test windows too. Or, if the light shining through the glass makes it hard to see any leaks, try wetting your hand and moving it slowly around the perimeter of the window close to the surface but not touching it. You should be able to feel a cool draft blowing on your wet hand anywhere there is a gap, even if you can't see it.

Weather sealant tape also works on windows. Another option is a rubber-gasket style of sealant that compresses to fill gaps and cracks.

After checking doors and windows, don't forget your attic door, air vents, and even electric sockets. Hardware and home-supply stores carry a variety of tapes, strips, and caulks that can be installed around windows, doors, or other leaks to stop the flow of air. The more gaps you block, the cheaper and

easier it will be to maintain a pleasant environment inside your home.

Setting the Thermostat

One of the easiest ways to save energy and money is to turn thermostats down in the winter, up in the summer, and off in the spring and fall. Just a few degrees can make a big difference.

The amount of energy required to heat or cool a home is a product of the difference between the inside and outside temperature. For instance, if it's forty-five degrees outside and seventy-two inside, the temperature difference is twenty-seven degrees. Lowering the thermostat inside to sixty-eight degrees makes the difference only twenty-three degrees. This 17 percent reduction in temperature difference also drops your heating bill and energy consumption by 17 percent.

You can adjust the thermostat even more dramatically at night. On a forty-degree night, turning the thermostat down from seventy-two degrees to fifty-five degrees reduces the temperature difference from thirty-two degrees to fifteen degrees, a 47 percent reduction in heating costs. And it won't bother you because you're tucked up cozily in your bed!

The cozy bed can also be a problem, though, because it's so unpleasant to climb out of the covers and into a fifty-five-degree house in the morning. The problem is easily solved, however, by a programmable thermostat. These useful devices automatically turn the heat down at night and back up just before you awaken—to a comfortable house.

In contrast to heating, air-conditioning is

a luxury. After all, a hundred years ago, no one even had electric fans, let alone air-conditioning. You'll read later on in this chapter how home design and the placement of trees can cool your home without air-conditioning. (See pages 67–68.)

But if you do use air-conditioning, a dehumidifier can help you adjust your thermostat to save money and energy. Humid air feels hotter than dry air of the same temperature. When excess moisture is removed from summer air, you can be comfortable with less air-conditioning.

Your Heating, Ventilating, and Air-Conditioning Systems

We've talked about transforming your house into a vessel worthy of heating and cooling. Now it's time to take a look at the system that delivers that air. After all, if you have leaky ducts, you could be losing as much as 20 percent of your heat and air-conditioning before it even makes it into the house.[1]

The easiest step is to change your air filter. A dirty or clogged air filter forces your air system to work harder just to get the air through the filter. By changing your air filter every three months, you enable your air conditioner or furnace to expend less energy on distributing the same amount of air. Plus, the air you breathe inside your home is of better quality.

Most families change the air filter inside their furnace often. However, they may not be in the habit of changing air filters elsewhere in the house. You can easily unscrew the vent covers and remove the dirty filters, if there are any. Cut an extra filter into rectangles the size of your floor or ceiling vents and place

them over the opening of the air duct before replacing the vent covers.

Second, check the ducts themselves. Before plunging into your crawl space, attic, basement, or garage, arm yourself with a tube of mastic sealant, which is available at any hardware store. It's a kind of goo, somewhere between putty and glue, that you can squeeze into cracks to fill them up. Also, grab a roll of metal-backed tape, which is shiny like foil. Ironically, duct tape isn't tough enough for this job.

Now examine your ducts. Check everywhere the ducts connect to an air vent or to each other. Wrap tape around the connection, or squeeze some mastic into the corners.

Once you're done, take an appraising look around. Are the ducts wrapped in insulation? Are there any exposed places? If you can afford it, insulating your ducts keeps heat from dissipating into unheated space. Bring a sample of whatever insulation is present to the hardware store and ask them to help you match it.

Now check the attic. Is there insulation between the attic's floor joists? Or can you see right down to the sheetrock that forms the ceiling of the room below? Adding insulation is a worthwhile investment. Remember, heat rises. All that heat you're pumping into your house rises to the ceiling, and if you don't have enough insulation, it goes right through into the chilly attic. But adding insulation is relatively easy.

Green Insulation

Any kind of insulation is green in a way, because it reduces the energy needed for heating and cooling. But beyond that, there are two ways to assess just how eco-friendly a particular kind of insulation is.

First of all, does it outgas and thus reduce air quality inside the home? Many insulation products emit formaldehyde and other volatile organic compounds for long periods of time after they've been installed. To avoid these insulation materials, look for products that have been tested for low emissions by a third-party organization or by the government.[2]

Most fiberglass insulations release toxic gases and irritating particles into the home. Some, however, are better than others. A few manufacturers are incorporating recycled materials into their products, and some brands, including Certain Teed and Owens Corning, have lower emissions than most.[3]

A far better solution, however, is to avoid fiberglass insulation entirely. Insulation made from shredded newspaper or cotton can be made from up to 80 percent postconsumer recycled products,[4] which uses less raw materials and industrial energy and reduces the flow of waste into landfills.

Cellulose insulation, made from finely shredded newspaper, can be blown into your attic or walls through a giant hose. Because this technique provides a tighter fit around pipes and wires than batt fiberglass insulation, it saves as much as 20 percent on heating and air-conditioning costs.[5] This is more than enough to offset the slightly higher cost of installation.

Cotton-fiber insulation works similarly. It's made primarily from trimmings from denim manufacturing that would otherwise wind up in the landfill. It's also nontoxic and doesn't offgass. A leading provider of cotton insulation made of denim is Bonded Logic.[6]

A slightly more expensive option is spray polyurethane foam (SPF). It sounds toxic, but it actually doesn't offgas and can cut home energy costs up to 35 percent. *Green Builder* magazine endorses Icynene SPF in particular.[7] A soy-based version is also available from BioBased Systems.[8] Homeowner Jeff Martin paid about $2,500 per 1,000 square feet to insulate his home with SPF. "If you put your hand over a light socket in a traditional house, you will almost always feel a breeze," he told us. "In our house, there is no movement of air around the sockets because of the expanding foam. It also provides the secondary benefit of wonderful soundproofing."

If you are considering new construction, a final option is to choose a wall material that doesn't require additional insulation. Rammed earth, straw bales, and autoclaved aerated concrete (AAC) blocks are all examples that are discussed later on.

Saving Energy Is Surprisingly Easy

So far we've covered changing lightbulbs, checking appliances and insulation, sealing cracks, and adjusting thermostats. When it comes time to replace your air conditioner or furnace, choosing Energy Star models is another way to save money on power bills, *and* to reduce your personal reliance on coal, nuclear, and other conventional energy sources. In the next section, we'll consider how to harness energy from better sources.

Notes

1. DIY Network, Weather Sealing, www.diynetwork
   .com/diy/he_weather_sealing/article/0,2037,DIY
   _13897_2277540,00.html.
2. California Integrated Waste Management Board,
   "Standard Practice for the Testing of Volatile Organic
   Emissions from Various Sources Using Small Scale
   Environmental Chambers," www.ciwmb.ca.gov/
   GreenBuilding/Specs/Section01350.
3. "Green Insulation: Some Insulations Out-Green Others,"
   Builder News, www.buildernewsmag.com/viewnews
   .pl?id=157.
4. "Green Building Guidelines, Insulation," www.co
   .contra-costa.ca.us/depart/cd/recycle/gbg/Grnbldg
   -NewConstruction-9Chap4-2.pdf.
5. "Green Insulation," *Builder News*.
6. Bonded Logic, www.bondedlogic.com/.
7. "Icynene Shows its True Color: Green," www.icynene
   .com.
8. BioBased Insulation, www.biobased.net/.

Photovoltaic Living

Going off the grid has such a nice ring to it. It means achieving independence from the electrical companies who are wreaking havoc with our wilderness and our atmosphere.

We've interviewed a number of homeowners who have achieved some degree of independence from utility companies, but most have not severed ties completely, even if they have enough power to do so. For one thing, they may sell their extra power back to the electrical company, and for that, they need to maintain the connection and have an electrical meter. Second, they may keep an account as a backup source of electricity.

There are various avenues to electrical independence, but all of the homeowners we know who generate their own electricity do so with photovoltaic, or PV, panels that trap solar energy. While a PV system requires a significant financial investment, it eventually pays for itself, although the payback may take decades. Photovoltaic panels are most often installed on a slanted roof that faces south, or a homeowner may use PV shingles that have the PV technology built into them. When a roof is not suitable, PV panels can be mounted just as effectively on a small tilted platform in the yard. Most effective of all, yard panels are sometimes mounted on trackers, which rotate

The Solar House at North Carolina State University uses both PV panels and solar-thermal panels to heat water.

This garage/workshop at the Solar House has PV technology built into the roofing material, making maximum use of the roof's area.

during the day to track the arc of the sun through the southern sky.

Homes with PV systems often have a completely separate solar-thermal system that heats water for domestic use and can heat the home's air as well. More homeowners have solar-thermal systems than have PV systems because solar thermal is significantly cheaper.

Solar-thermal panels on this house absorb solar energy and heat water for domestic use.

But What About Clouds?

Using a PV system doesn't mean you don't have electricity when it's cloudy. Most PV owners have batteries for storing surplus electricity generated on sunny days. On cloudy days and at night, the home draws power from the batteries. Other PV homeowners may send surplus power to their utility company, building up credit on their account. They then draw electricity from the power company during periods of low solar production.

Cost

The main drawback to a PV system is cost. Many experts recommend reducing home energy use to around 400 kilowats per month before considering a PV system in order to decrease the number of costly panels needed. A couple of green builders we interviewed told us that the energy-bill savings from a PV system can take as long as thirty to fifty years to outweigh the cost of the system. For that reason, many designers of eco-friendly and energy-efficient homes don't include PV systems in their plans.

Still, homeowners we've met who do have PV panels find the investment worthwhile; some are very enthusiastic. To evaluate the relative merit of PV systems, we profiled three PV-using households to see how their finances work.

Homeowners One: The Elpels

Thomas Elpel, an environmental homesteader and author in Montana, posted on his website a detailed account of his family's transition to a PV system.[1] The Elpels got a system that cost about $20,000 and included sixteen solar panels mounted on two solar-powered trackers in the yard. They applied for and received a grant from their local power company for more than $11,000, and a Montana tax credit of $500, that together reduced the family's cost to just $8,000. The Elpels' two trackers were expensive—more than $3,000 together—but the family saved money by not buying batteries to store excess power. Instead, they signed a net-metering agreement with their power company. Any excess electricity the Elpels produce during summer months is fed back to the power company, for which they get credit on their account to be used during any future month when they draw more power than they produce.

At least thirty-nine or forty states now have net-metering options. When you purchase blocks of green power through your utility company (see pages 48–49), you are, in part, buying power from families like the Elpels and the Martins, described below.

Homeowners Two: The Martins

The Martins power their expansive 4,200-square-foot home with an arsenal of thirty-three PV panels. In addition to the panels mounted on the south-facing roof, the system includes batteries to store power for nighttime use, an inverter to convert the direct current (DC) power harnessed by the panels into alternating current (AC) power for home use and other assorted hardware. All in all, the home's PV system cost more than $60,000.

The south-facing roof of Jeff Martin's home is covered with PV panels to generate electricity and, above those, solar-thermal panels to heat water.

That's a hefty price tag. But the family is earning it back penny by penny by selling excess power they produce to NC Green-Power,[2] a nonprofit organization, who pays them 18¢ per kilowatt hour. They collect an additional 3.5 to 4¢ per kilowatt hour from Duke Energy, the local power company.

The Martins could bypass NC Green-Power and participate in the power company's net-metering system, as the Elpels do, but would be paid less for the electricity they generate (8.5¢ per kilowatt).

In North Carolina, two factors dissuade families like the Martins from participating in net metering with their power company. One is that families or other providers who sell power directly to the utility must pay more than other customers when they buy electricity from the utility. The second discouraging factor is that the net-metering program forbids participants from using batteries to store their own power. The North Carolina Sustainable Energy Association is working to have that stipulation removed.[3] Information on net metering in other states is available at the U.S. Department of Energy's Green Power Network website, www.eere.energy.gov/green power/markets/netmetering.shtml.

During months when their home power use is high, the Martins draw some electricity from the local power company. Their maximum monthly power bill thus far has been about $150, when they cranked up the air-conditioning for visiting out-of-state friends. In contrast, during construction of their current home, they rented a house next door that was one-fourth the size of their current home. In that house, they paid $400 per month for power.

Homeowners Three: The Overholts

Trip Overholt lives in a 1,500-square-foot house he built himself using recycled and salvaged materials and walls of straw-bale infill (straw bales between the wall studs). His eight solar panels are in the yard. They don't track the sun, but have a fixed position that maximizes exposure at his particular latitude.

Trip Overholt's PV panels are mounted on brackets in the yard rather than on his roof.

Overholt's house is completely off the grid. In addition to the yard panels, he has an inverter to change the power from DC to home-usable AC, and a battery to store the power for nighttime use.

"I live way out in the country," he explained. "When I found I would have to cut a swath through the woods for power lines to my house, I decided to use a supplemental generator instead. I am completely off the grid, and I like it that way. I use the electrical things in my house freely, and from April to December, I can do whatever I want. From December to April, when days are shorter and the sun is lower in the sky, I sometimes have to use a backup generator."

His cost calculations are more in line with the Elpels than the Martins. "For a 1,200- to 1,800-square-feet house in a good solar area—more than 300 sunny days a year—a PV system to supply all of the more modest electrical needs would cost probably $25,000. If you need to cut costs more than that, and you're willing to limit or monitor your use of all your electrical appliances, then you might be able to spend less."

Solar Thermal for Hot Water and Warm Air

"The solar-thermal system is really the star of our house," said green homeowner Jeff Martin. "While the PV system gets all the press, it's the low-tech solar-thermal system that should make the headlines."

The south-facing roof of this home sports both PV panels and solar-thermal panels. The smaller roof on the left has only PV panels.

Solar-thermal panels, often mistaken for PV panels, are simpler, cheaper, and lower tech than their flashy cousins. Solar-thermal systems use water to capture solar energy. The warm water can either be used for washing and bathing, or in conjuction with a radiant-floor system to heat the home. Given that heating and cooling air, and heating water, are the biggest energy guzzlers in American homes, the $2,000 to $3,000 spent on solar-thermal panels is well worth it.

Solar-thermal panels are generally black, to increase the absorption of heat, with tiny channels for water inside. A typical solar-thermal system has two to four solar collectors or panels on the roof, each measuring about four by eight feet.

Said Martin, "We have a 1,000-gallon hot-water tank in the basement that's fed by the solar-thermal absorber panels on the roof. Any time the temperature of the roof is 10 degrees higher than the water in the tank, up to 150 degrees, small pumps automatically move water from the tank to the roof to harvest that thermal energy."

The water in the tank stays between 140 and 150 degrees during spring, summer, and autumn. "The really amazing thing about the solar-thermal system is that even when it is below freezing outside, if the sun is shining, you can get 150-degree water. That is one thing people really marvel at when they see the system in operation." In winter, if a cloudy spell causes the tank temperature to drop below 100 degrees, a backup gas boiler comes on to heat it. But that's rare, Martin said.

Martin emphatically recommended a solar-thermal system to other households. "In my view, virtually every home should have solar-thermal assist, because hot water is a high-energy-use application and because solar thermal is well understood and cost-effective today. I say solar assisted because you do not have to design it for 100 percent load, as we did, but rather large enough to dramatically reduce your reliance on traditional fuels."

Jeff Martin keeps a solar-thermal panel mounted on his garage wall for curious visitors to see up close during the annual local tour of green homes.

Jeff Martin says his heavily insulated 1,000-gallon hot-water tank is the "living, breathing heart of my house."

Professional solar-thermal installer Mike Beaver recommends to his customers that they plan on getting 50 to 70 percent of their home's hot water from solar panels. One hundred percent is impractical, he explained, because the number of panels needed to meet peak demand would be underutilized most of the time. A number of variables are involved, but he estimates that a system will typically range from $5,000 to $8,000 dollars, for either retrofitting or new construction.[4] State and federal tax credits can knock more than $3,000 off that cost.[5]

During our tour of the Martins' solar home, Jeff seemed much more enamored of his solar-thermal system than his photovoltaics. "PV gets all the attention," he said. "It's sexy, high-tech, Silicon Valley. But heating is the star in this home. Solar thermal is low-tech. I've been to lots of developing countries, and every one of them have it—because it makes sense. This," he said, hugging his heavily insulated 1,000-gallon hot-water tank, "is the living, breathing heart of my house."

Radiant-Floor Heat

Solar hot water also heats the air in Martin's home by way of radiant-floor tubing. After a thermostat triggers the system into action, whatever hot water is not diverted to showers, sinks, and appliances travels through tubing embedded in the floor. Heat from the hot water in the tubes radiates up through the floors, warming the room.

For a new home, the cost of the radiant tubing and the flooring can be an additional $8,000 to $10,000, said Beaver.

Radiant tubing embedded in the Gyp-Crete floor carries hot water that warms the floor and thus also warms the air of the Martins' home.

"You can choose from several floor systems, but concrete is the best emitter of heat." Alternatively, the Martins' radiant tubing is embedded in a layer of Gyp-Crete, which is covered with bamboo wood flooring.

The future seems brighter when eco-friendly choices are reasonably priced, comfortable, *and* aesthetically pleasing. Solar thermal is all of the above. Photovoltaic technology is a great move, too, for those who can afford it. Both PV panels and solar-thermal panels make a highly visible statement to your community; this can educate others and encourage them to follow suit. Hopefully, as our fossil fuels continue to diminish and our climate continues to change, PV technology will become more affordable and accessible to those with limited incomes.

Notes

1. Thomas J. Elpel, "We've Gone Solar! Installing our 2528-Watt Tracking Photovoltaic Array," www.hollowtop.com/cls_html/solar_power.htm (accessed May 6, 2006).
2. NC GreenPower, www.ncgreenpower.org.

3. North Carolina Sustainable Energy Association, www
   .ncsustainableenergy.org/.
4. Mike Beaver, personal communication.
5. The Database of State Incentives for Renewable Energy,
   http://dsireusa.org. (Click on your state for a listing
   of state tax credits and other financial incentives for
   going solar.)

Additional Resources

The American Solar Energy Society (publishers of *Solar Today*
    magazine), www.ases.org.

Beaver Brothers, Inc. (installers of solar-thermal systems and
    radiant-floor heating systems), www.beaverbrosinc.com.

Co-op America (find thousands of green, environmentally
    responsible, and socially responsible products and ser-
    vices), www.coopamerica.org/pubs/greenpages/.

Find Solar (connections to prescreened solar professionals who
    can estimate costs, benefits, and savings of solar-energy
    power systems for homeowners), http://findsolar.com.

Home Power magazine, www.homepower.com.

Main Solar House (house built by Solar Design architects),
    www.solarhouse.com.

National Renewable Energy Laboratory (provides a broad
    overview of everything you might need to know about
    solar), www.nrel.gov/index.html.

Real Goods (books to help solar consumers get started),
    www.realgoods.com.

Rocky Mountain Institute (a nonprofit that promotes renew-
    able energy), www.rmi.org.

Solar Design (architectural firm), www.solardesign.com.

Solar Today magazine, www.solartoday.org.

U.S. Department of Energy, www.eere.energy.gov/ and www
    .eere.energy.gov/state_energy_program/grants_by_state
    .cfm. (Select a state for summaries of State Energy Pro-
    gram projects, links to state energy office websites, and
    links to state publications on renewable energy and energy
    efficiency. You can probably locate state grants and tax
    credits for solar construction via contacts from this site.)

U.S. Department of Energy, Energy Information Administra-
    tion (official energy statistics from the U.S. government),
    www.eia.doe.gov/basics/energybasics101.html.

The resources below are state organizations,
but they often have information relevant to
any consumer and can make referrals or provide leads to professionals and organizations
in other states, including to power companies
that offer grants and state governments that
offer tax credits for PV construction.

Green Building Guidelines, Contra Costa County, California,
    www.co.contra-costa.ca.us/depart/cd/recycle/gbg.

North Carolina Solar Center, www.ncsc.ncsu.edu.

North Carolina Sustainable Energy Association, www.nc
    sustainableenergy.org.

Solar Power the Bootleg Way

Solar technology is indeed expensive—but
it doesn't have to be. After all, if you've ever
climbed into a hot car parked in the sun, or
walked on scorching pavement on a summer
day, you know that solar heating is inadvertently all too easy.

Avid do-it-yourselfers have found many
ways to harness this energy. Using mostly
salvaged materials, you can build a variety of
very simple solar collectors that could make
your house the talk of the neighborhood (for
better or for worse).

A Solar Air Heater

The most enticing design we discovered is
for a solar-heat grabber, or furnace, of sorts.
This plan was first outlined in *Mother Earth
News* in the mid-1970s, but has since become
commonplace for grassroots activists who
like to tackle projects of their own.

This very simple panel will generate free
warm air for your house. Better yet, it takes
about two hours to build and costs about
$5. Folks who have made this device report a
steady flow of 120-degree air on sunny days.[1]

The panel has a glass top, just like a traditional solar panel. When you look through
the glass, you see a black, heat-trapping surface, just as in a purchased solar panel. However, beneath that black rubber surface lies a
second, insulated chamber. Air flows between

the two through a gap in the rubber divider.

The panel functions by allowing sunlight to shine through the glass and heat the black rubber. If you stand the panel on one short end facing the sun, with the other short end opening into your house through a window, the air warmed by the sun will rise through the open end of the panel and flow into your house. Meanwhile, chilly air from the house is drawn into the insulated lower layer of the panel. It flows through the gap at the lower end of the rubber layer and replaces the recently warmed air.

For construction details and more explanation of the unit's operation, see the *Mother Earth News* web page below.

Note
1. "Mother's Solar Heat Grabber," *Mother Earth News*, September/October 1977 www.motherearthnews.com/ Green-Home-Building/1977-09-01/Mothers-Heat -Grabber.aspx .

A Solar Water Heater

A water-heating panel is more complicated because the materials are harder to come by, particularly if you scavenge them. But after you have the supplies, building takes about three hours and can be close to free.

This device works by pumping water through metal tubes inside a warm solar box. By the time the water has passed through all the tubing, it has absorbed much of the solar heat captured by the box around it. You can collect this water in buckets and pour it into your tub for a hot bath or into your sink for dishes or delicate laundry. By the time it empties into the bucket, it will be warm. If

the water flows continuously on a reasonably sunny day, it will heat from 70 degrees to 110 degrees by the time it has passed through the system. If you stop the flow and allow the water to sit in the panel for a few minutes, it can get as hot as 170 degrees.[1]

For construction details, see the website below.

Note
1. The Sietch, "Build Your Own Solar Thermal Panel," www.thesietch.org/projects/solarthermalpanel2/index .htm.

Building Techniques
Passive-Solar Design

Altering your existing home is one thing, but building a new home opens a world of opportunity for going green. If you're considering building an energy-efficient home, the most important concept to understand is passive-solar construction.

The south side of Kathleen Jardine and Jim Cameron's passive-solar home features solar-thermal panels and a broad expanse of windows.

Passive-solar design doesn't involve technology, hence the word *passive*. Rather, it prescribes the layout of the home and how the building is situated on the lot. A passive-solar design captures the sun's heat and light in winter and deflects it in summer. We visited Kathleen Jardine and Jim Cameron's passive-solar home to see what this means in action.

Approaching Cameron and Jardine's cottage on foot, we walked through the lush flower and vegetable gardens that surround the south and southeast sides of the house. Although it was autumn, sprightly orange blossoms stood tall, profusions of pink and purple blooms nodded gently in the breeze, and a fat green bullfrog burped a greeting from the handsome stonework around a burbling fishpond.

Buck Naked Outdoors

As it turns out, the outdoor charms are a big piece of the puzzle in the passive-solar strategy for energy efficiency. By incorporating pleasant outdoor areas into their living space, homeowners can be comfortable with a smaller house without feeling crowded. A smaller home is cheaper and more efficient to build as well as maintain.

In addition to the verdant gardens and ponds, Jardine and Cameron have maximized their outdoor space with shady, covered porches. The east porch offers inviting benches, while the west porch features a gas stove—and a shower stall!

As if the pleasure of cooking and showering in the sweet, fresh summer air weren't enough, the heat and humidity associated with cooking and showering also disperse into the great outdoors. Of course, there is an indoor kitchen and bathroom as well for chilly times—and for modest visitors.

The outdoors is also made accessible by the home's low floor, with just one step down to the ground. In addition to making the outdoors feel more available, the easy transition also helps older people to stay in their home longer as their knees and hips grow weaker.

What Is *Passive-Solar*, Exactly?

Unlike photovoltaic homes, passive-solar design does not use panels to harness energy. Instead, the house itself captures and stores the sun's energy. The design and orientation of the house trap the sun's heat inside the house in winter and block the sun's rays in summer in order to reduce the amount of fuel or electricity required for heating and cooling.

A passive-solar house should be rectangular in shape, with its longest walls on the north and south sides. In the northern hemisphere, the south side of such a house will

Kathleen Jardine and Jim Cameron's south-facing windows overlook a beautiful garden and pond. The midday winter sun floods the home with heat.

get the most exposure to the sun, so it should have many large windows to admit the rays of the sun in winter. To get the maximum warming benefit of the sun in winter, the long southern wall should face within fifteen degrees of true south.

Interestingly, virtually all caves that once housed humans open to the south, as do all the pueblos and cliff dwellings in the southwestern United States. People who lived in these places learned long ago the principles of heating homes with the warmth of the sun.

A Wide Overhang Blocks Summer Sun

Every day, the sun rises in the east and sets in the west, regardless of the season. But during summer, the arc that the sun travels every day is higher in the sky than it is during winter. So during summer, the sun shines on the house from a relatively high point in the sky.

This is crucial to solar design. At a latitude of 35° north (around the middle of the United States), the roof on the southern side of a passive-solar house needs a two-foot

overhang about seven-and-a-half feet from the floor. The overhang blocks the rays of the high midday summer sun and keeps them from hitting the windows directly. But during winter, the sun is low enough in the sky, even at midday, to peek under the overhang and send its warming rays inside the house. As you move farther north, the summer sun is less high in the sky, so you need a bigger overhang. (There are formulas for calculating just how wide this overhang must be. Sustainable By Design has a number of useful calculators online at http://susdesign.com/tools.php.)

Climbing Vines Galore

Jardine and Cameron's passive-solar house is adorned with lush climbing vines above the windows on all sides of the house. The east side, with its main entry, features jasmine, climbing aster, and old rose; on the south side are grapevines. During summer, when the vines are full and leafy, they help the overhang block sunlight from entering the windows. During the winter, when the vines lose their leaves, they allow solar heat in through the windows.

The wide overhang on the south side of Kathleen Jardine and Jim Cameron's home blocks the higher rays of the midday summer sun.

When leafed out during summertime, vines help shield these east-facing windows from the morning sun.

Deciduous trees, which lose their leaves in winter, perform the same function. But evergreen trees, which keep their leaves or needles all year, have to be dealt with differently. Cameron and Jardine explained that an object ten feet tall casts a shadow seventeen feet long; the shadow is 1.7 times as long as the object's height. So if you have a ten-foot-tall evergreen tree on the south side, as Jardine and Cameron do, then it must be seventeen feet from the south wall or else it will block your solar gain in winter. One way to get around this and to keep more trees is by positioning the house on the northern edge of a downward slope so that the trees on the south side are shorter in height relative to the south-facing windows.

An outbuilding or neighbor's house on the south side requires similar considerations. If the ridge of the building's roof is twenty feet tall, then it will need to be thirty-four feet from the south side of your passive-solar home.

Cameron and Jardine have resolved the sunlight issue by locating their gardens on the south side of their home. On the north side of the house, close shrubs and trees help block cold winter winds and don't interfere with light.

A Gorgeous Thermal Mass

If your bare feet have ever felt the warmth of a paved road after the sun has gone down, you've experienced a thermal mass. A substantial thermal mass—something that absorbs solar heat during the day and releases the heat slowly after the sun is gone—is an essential part of a passive-solar home—it

helps heat the home in the evenings after the sun is gone. Early solar homes in the 1970s sometimes had barrels of water standing around to serve as thermal masses. Cameron and Jardine have a prettier solution.

One of the first things we noticed when entering their home for the first time was the lovely red stonelike floor throughout. Like the charming red roof and the golden stucco exterior, the red floor lends the inside rooms a warm and cozy feel. But we learned soon after our arrival that their floor is neither stone nor ceramic tile, as we had assumed. It's actually scored and tinted concrete. *Scored* means that the surface has narrow grooves that appear to be seams between large squares. Adding pigment to the concrete before it comes out of the mixer results in a varied tint with slightly different hues and irregular patterns, such as one might expect in natural stone or marbled tile. The effect is beautiful. As solar designers, Cameron and Jardine know that concrete is an excellent thermal mass, and the least expensive option for flooring that can serve that purpose. As an additional bonus, the floor is maintenance free forever.

Does the Passive-Solar Design Take Care of All Their Heating Needs?

Cameron and Jardine's home has other sources of heat in addition to the solar gain from their southern windows in winter. Their radiant-floor tubing that circulates solar-heated water just under the surface of their concrete floor also heats the indoor air in winter.

Cameron and Jardine also have a woodstove in their living room, which they use on some cold evenings, often for atmosphere more than for heat. Their Jack Russell terrier, Sleety, spends evenings on her back near the stove, sprawled on their handmade rug, her feet twitching as she dreams of squirrels.

We probably learned more from Jardine and Cameron than from any other single source we interviewed or visited. Over the course of several visits to their home, we found that passive-solar is only one part of their approach to sustainable and energy-efficient building. They are equally passionate about using non-toxic and durable materials. Their ardor on the subject really raised our consciousness about the environmental merits of durability.

Durable Green Building Materials

In addition to passive-solar design, durable green building materials are key to designing an energy-efficient and nonpolluting home. Two main problems with conventional building materials are toxicity and disposability.

Many conventional building materials are made with chemicals that can be hazardous to health or to the environment, though contractors tend to ignore toxicity. For example, popular oriented strand board (OSB), a type of chipboard used for indoor walls, is made of formaldehyde, polystyrene, and wood chips. Not only does OSB give off toxic fumes in the home, but it's also toxic to factory workers, and the production of the wood chips is decimating southeastern forests.[1]

Another potentially toxic building material to look out for is insulation. According to Cornell University, "the manufacture and installation of foam insulations commonly

involves the use of CFCs [chlorofluorocarbon] or HCFCs [hydrochlorofluorocarbon], both of which should be avoided. Some other types of foam insulation offgas formaldehyde or contain harmful chemicals. Fiberglass contains small particles that can cause respiratory irritation when released into the air."[2]

That said, *Builder News* magazine reports that some brands of fiberglass are better than others. A few manufacturers are incorporating recycled materials, and some products have lower emissions of formaldehyde and other pollutants than others. The magazine mentions CertainTeed's and Owens Corning's insulations as those that have lower emissions.[3]

In addition to OSB and some insulations, other potentially harmful materials include treated wood, carpets, vinyl siding, and some paints. Offgassing is only part of the problem. These products also harm the factory workers who produce them and the environments in which they are manufactured and where they are eventually thrown away. According to Jardine, carpets and shingles are the two largest single fillers of landfills. If you've ever lived with wall-to-wall carpeting, you know how quickly it becomes trodden and stained. And shingles, which need to be replaced every fifteen to twenty years, are essentially disposable roofs.

For nontoxic and sustainable walls and roofs, Jardine and Cameron use auto-claved aerated concrete (AAC) blocks and steel roofing.

Autoclaved aerated concrete blocks, erroneously called Hebel blocks (the Hebel company is defunct), are white and smooth, similar in size to cinder blocks. They lack the recessed surfaces and holes of a standard concrete block. They are made by adding foaming aluminum powder to concrete, which makes it fluffier and lighter than plain concrete. Said Jardine, "It's mostly sand. There are no pollutants in the manufacturing of it, no offgassing in the home. And it's hypoallergenic to live in—it doesn't mold."

When Jardine and Cameron found out about AAC blocks from a friend in Israel, no one had heard of them in the United States. Now, more customers are demanding them than manufacturers can keep up with.

Green builders often prefer AAC blocks because they are are energy-efficient, durable, and work well with passive-solar design. They also function as a thermal mass to some degree and are inherently airtight, conserving indoor heat in winter and cool air in summer.[4]

A house made of AAC blocks can last for hundreds of years, keeping truckloads of waste from our landfills. The concrete is also

All the homes in this progressive community have durable, colorful steel roofs.

termite proof and very sturdy in hurricanes, earthquakes, and fires. It also requires no maintenance. Blocks are covered with mineral plaster on the inside and stucco on the outside. Once applied, the stucco needs no repainting or retouching—unless you feel like changing the color.

Steel roofs last 100 years, about six times longer than a shingled roof. They come in cheerful shades of red, blue, green, purple, and traditional silver. A steel roof gives a house old-fashioned charm, but some cities have covenants against them, claiming they look like barns. "Rules like that account for what our environment looks like," said Cameron. "People don't think about the long-term effects. ... They just don't think about the consequences."

Double-Hung Windows Save Birds

Some green builders choose casement windows, which open by cranking outward, over traditional double-hung windows, which open by sliding up and down. While casement windows are more airtight, they have a hidden flaw: their indoor screens make them invisible to birds. According to the Wild Bird Center[1] and David Sibley,[2] collisions with windows kill 100 million to 1 billion birds every year in the United States. The external window screens on double-hung windows not only reduce the number of collisions, but also cushion the blow for birds that still strike the window. If you choose casement windows, try to protect birds by relocating bird feeders to within three feet of a window, or decorating a window with decals or stained glass. However, these efforts are much less effective than exterior screens.

Notes
1. Wild Bird Center, "Project Prevent Collision," www.wildbird center.com/content/project_prevent_collision.
2. Sibley Guides, Bird Conservation—Mortality, www.sibley guides.com/mortality.htm.

Cost and Maintenence

A passive-solar home like Jardine and Cameron's, built with AAC blocks, a concrete floor, and a steel roof, requires about $25 of electricity a month. Hot water is free, thanks to the solar-thermal panels on the roof. Gas is needed only for cooking. No furnace is needed, and an air conditioner is optional. Cameron and Jardine cut a cord of wood per year for the woodstove. With stucco on the home's exterior, there are no repainting needs. The steel roof means no shingles to replace. Inside, the concrete floor means no waxing or replacing of flooring materials. In short, maintenance and operating costs are almost nil.

Notes

1. Denny Haldeman, "The Environmental and Health Impacts of Chipboard," *New Life Journal: Bringing Roots to Modern Culture*, www.newlifejournal.com/junjul02/haldeman.shtml (accessed February 14, 2006).
2. Cornell University, Department of Design and Environmental Analysis, Ecotecture, "Insulation/Energy Efficiency," http://ergo.human.cornell.edu/ecotecture/insulation.htm.
3. "Green Insulation: Some Insulations Out-Green Others," www.buildernewsmag.com/viewnews.pl?id=157.
4. "Concrete Building Systems, Aerated Concrete Blocks," www.scrapbookscrapbook.com/DAC-ART/concrete-building-systems.html (accessed February 16, 2006).

Additional Resources

Kathleen Jardine, "5 Ways to Build a Better House," *Smart HomeOwner* magazine, September/October 2005, www.smart-homeowner.com/ME2/dirmod.asp?sid=&nm=&type=Publishing&mod=Publications%3A%3AArticle&mid=8F3A7027421841978F18BE895F87F791&tier=4&id=0B62169DEC424961B42C05FD5865CFBD (accessed July 1, 2006).

Kathleen Jardine and Jim Cameron, "Building for Affordability and Energy Efficiency: Walls of Aerated Concrete Block, a Passive-Solar Design, and a Truss Roof All Make it Possible," *Fine Homebuilding* magazine, www.taunton.com/finehomebuilding/pages/h00002.asp (accessed February 14, 2006).

Sun Garden Homes, www.sungardenhouses.com.

Straw-Bale Homes

Thinking Outside the Box

Straw and mud as building materials are also compatible with passive-solar design. Both are currently gaining popularity in sustainable building.

Straw-bale houses have a number of environmental merits, great aesthetic appeal, and can be very economical to build. By itself, straw-bale construction does not have the potential to drastically cut our nation's energy consumption in the same way that passive-solar design can. But when paired with passive-solar design, straw-bale construction is a very environmentally friendly choice.

There is no standard way to build a straw-bale house, but in general, straw-bale homes have walls made of bales of straw or hay that are stacked like giant building

Trip Overholt's passive-solar straw-bale house. The solar-thermal panels above the roof and PV panels in the yard contribute to the home's energy efficiency.

blocks. The straw bales can be load bearing; that is, they can hold up the roof without needing additional structural support. Or the bales can be used for in-fill in combination with some type of structural support, such as post-and-beam construction.[1] In either case, after they're stacked, the bales are generally smoothed on the inside and out with a chain saw or a weed trimmer. Then, most often, the inner walls are covered with plaster and the outer walls with stucco. Edges and corners of the building are often somewhat rounded, giving the home a soft, cozy feel. One straw-bale enthusiast told us that he chose that kind of home because his childhood home was emotionally cold. "I wanted a house that was an emotional sanctuary for me, a house that would provide a soft, nurturing, organic feeling, with these deep window wells that would muffle the sound. I wanted a cross between a church and my grandmother's house on the lake." For him, his straw-bale home provides just that.

Sadie admires the fresh stucco over an inside wall in a straw-bale home under construction. Many straw-bale builders use plaster instead of stucco on inside walls.

How Is a Straw-Bale House Visually Different?

A single bale of straw is big. The shortest dimension of one bale is often fourteen or sixteen inches, so the outer walls of a straw-bale house will be that thick if the bales are laid on edge. The outer walls may be as thick as twenty-three inches if the bales are laid flat. Either way, straw provides excellent insulation, with an R-value of thirty-two to fifty-four, depending on the width of the bales and how they're stacked. (*R-value* is a measure of the insulative power of building materials; the better the insulator, the higher the R-value.) This is two to three times as good as new homes with R-11 fiberglass insulation, and often five to ten times as good as older homes, which may have no insulation at all.[2] The U.S. Department of Energy recommends an R-value of thirteen for wall cavities and five for wall sheathing in new homes.[3] The thickness of the straw-bale walls also muffles sounds from the outdoors.

Straw-bale homes with exterior stucco in earth tones often look like adobe structures, which are common in parts of the Southwest, especially New Mexico. Both interior and exterior surfaces may be somewhat irregular if the home was built by novice homeowners. But folks who live in these houses feel that such irregularities add to the charm.

If the straw is in-fill for a house whose structural support is wood, the final result may look like a conventionally built home. It may be indistinguishable except for the thickness of the walls. After the plaster and stucco are added, there's no way to tell that straw hides inside.

Because the walls are thick, window wells are deep. This can be an asset in passive-solar design—the top of a window well on a south-facing wall functions like an overhang.

The Environmental Merits of Straw-Bale Construction

The high insulation value of straw means that a straw-bale home can be very energy efficient. However, to capitalize on the benefit of the insulated walls, the home's attic or roof will need to be well insulated too, and doors and windows need to be well sealed to minimize leaks and drafts.

In addition to offering superior insulation value, building with straw also makes good use of a product that might otherwise be considered waste. Straw is the stem of a grass that produces grains, such as wheat, and is left after the grain has been harvested. This is different from hay, which includes the grain and is therefore rich in nutrients.[4] For that reason, hay is used as livestock feed and is much more expensive than straw. Straw is not useful as feed, and the stems are too long and tough to be thoroughly tilled back into the soil.[5] So straw truly is waste and is often burned. In 1991, the state of California created more carbon monoxide and particulates from burning straw than from all the power plants in the state combined.

This is partly a regional issue, however. Most grain is grown in the West, so most of the 200 million tons of waste straw created in the United States each year are out west as well. In the eastern states, straw is not burned as frequently as it is in the West, although some farmers sell it for less than a dollar a bale

to get rid of it. In gardening and farm-supply stores, straw may be sold for landscaping and livestock bedding for $3.00 or more per bale.

Building with straw is less polluting than building with standard construction; it reduces the need for the paints and solvents used on conventional homes that often contain noxious ingredients. Straw walls are typically covered with a nontoxic plaster or stucco. Straw-bale construction also bypasses OSB, the commonly used chipboard that offgases formaldehyde and contributes to deforestation.[6] If more homes were built with straw bales, particularly homes without wood framing, we would need much less timber for home construction. According to Matts Myhrman of Out on Bale, "If all the straw left in the U.S. after the harvest of major grains was baled instead of burned, 5 million 2,000-square-foot houses could be built every year."[7] Unlike wood, straw can be grown and sustainably harvested in less than a year, every year.

Building with straw has an advantage over the use of adobe or earth blocks as well. Harvesting straw does not disturb or damage the topsoil, while cutting earth blocks does disrupt the fertile layer of soil. This is not a sustainable practice, although it is widespread in some countries, such as Egypt.[8]

According to *Green Building Guidelines* from the U.S. Department of Energy, "Up to 70 percent of the total energy invested in a building's construction is embodied in the materials themselves."[9] Researchers from the University of Washington report the same thing—that most of the energy in home construction is consumed not by the power tools, machines, and trucking during construction, but during the manufacture of the building materials.[10] In this matter, straw-bale construction truly shines. It bypasses much of the energy and waste involved in producing industrial building materials. The production of one ton of straw requires 112,500 British thermal units, in comparison to 5,800,000 British thermal units needed to produce concrete. According to Richard Hoffmeister of the Frank Lloyd Wright School of Architecture in Scottsdale, Arizona, straw-bale walls are at least thiry times less energy intensive than a wood-frame wall with equivalent fiberglass insulation.[11]

Is Building with Straw Cost Effective?

Straw-bale homes have counterculture appeal. Building with straw is attractive to get-back-to-the-land types and independent do-it-yourselfers. This is partly because a straw-bale house can be really cheap. Jennifer and Joe Gonsalves built a 1,000-square-foot straw-bale house for themselves and their three children for $20,000.[12] That doesn't include the $6,000 they spent for their three-acre lot in rural Maine. They didn't build a wood frame for the house; rather, all the weight of the house and roof rests on the straw. They built the walls by impaling the bales on threaded rods that were embedded in the concrete slab and extended upward to the roof. The couple had no prior construction experience, but built the entire house by themselves with no assistance other than a copy of the book *The Straw-Bale House* by Athena Swentzell Steen, Bill Steen, and David Bainbridge, which details a variety of construction methods. Straw-bale homes can be easier to build and require less precision than conventional homes, so in general they are more approachable for the novice.

Is There a Downside to Straw-Bale Construction?

Physically, no. The straw has to stay dry so that it won't mold, but that's not hard to achieve. The straw must be properly dried and compacted when it's baled, before the house is built. Then certain precautions must be taken to keep it dry. The site must be graded so that rainwater flows away from the foundation—which is true of any house. The coverage of the stucco on the outside and plaster on the inside of the house must be thorough to seal against moisture. And the roof must be leakproof.

At times, homeowners may have trouble with local building codes that do not permit unconventional construction. Urban or suburban codes are often more restrictive than rural communities in allowing deviations from usual methods. Certain strategies can help you get a permit. Making personal contact with local building officials, citing historical precedents, and offering results of fire and structural testing on straw-bale houses can help.[13]

Prospective straw-bale builders may also have trouble getting a loan to build a house or have trouble getting insurance. One owner of a straw-bale house told me that home builders may need to use euphemisms in describing straw-bale and other "outlaw" wall systems in order to gain approval from agencies and institutions. Said Bruce Glenn of the Northwest EcoBuilding Guild, "When talking to the building department or insurance company, the way one communicates the type of home is important. If you say, 'I live in a straw home,' most people think the straw is exposed and you're living on a dirt floor. If you describe the home as a post-and-beam frame on a continuous concrete foundation, [with] cellulose insulation, exterior stucco, and interior plastered walls, you are telling the truth."[14]

We interviewed Barry Ford, owner of a straw-bale home, about his straw-bale construction experience. His home was so inexpensive that he didn't need to consider a bank loan. See the following sidebar to learn how Barry, his pregnant wife, and eight-year-old son built a 2,200-square-foot straw-bale home entirely by themselves, while Barry and his wife were working other full-time jobs.

Notes

1. Athena Swentzell Steen, Bill Steen, and David Bainbridge, *The Straw-Bale House* (White River Junction, Vermont: Chelsea Green Publishing Company, 1994), 49.
2. Ibid.
3. U.S. Department of Energy, "R-Value Recommendations for New Buildings," www.ornl.gov/cgi-bin/cgiwrap?user =roofs&script=ZipTable/ins_fact.pl.
4. Steen, Steen, and Bainbridge, *The Straw-Bale House*.
5. Ibid.
6. Denny Haldeman, "The Environmental and Health Impacts of Chipboard," *New Life Journal*, www.new lifejournal.com/junjul02/haldeman.shtml (accessed February, 14, 2006).
7. Steen, Steen, and Bainbridge, *The Straw-Bale House*.
8. Ibid.
9. *Green Building Guidelines: Meeting the Demand for Low-Energy, Resource-Efficient Homes, Fifth Edition* (Washington, DC: Sustainable Buildings Industry Council, 2007).
10. Sandra Hines, "Environmental Costs of Home Construction Lower with Wise Choice, Reuse of Building Materials," University of Washington Office of News and Information, August 24, 2004, www.uwnews.org/article .asp?articleID=5360.
11. Steen, Steen, and Bainbridge, *The Straw-Bale House*.
12. Joyce White, "Living within Their Harvest," *BackHome* magazine, no. 76, (May/June 2005): 39–41.
13. Steen, Steen, and Bainbridge, *The Straw-Bale House*.
14. "Straw Bale and Ecological Home Questions and Answers," Terrasol Designing and Building, www.straw balehomes.com/Strawbale%20FAQ.html (accessed February 22, 2006).

Barry Ford and His Truth Window

Barry Ford's straw-bale home is located outside of Lancaster, South Carolina, in a suburban neighborhood with large lots. Although Barry's property is home to horses, hogs, and emus, in addition to his family, it measures just 100 feet wide at the road, and neighbors' houses are visible through a thicket of trees. Barry was proud to tell me that they didn't cut down a single tree during construction of their house.

Legs Sticking Out

The Fords' straw-bale house is a two-story box with an arched silver roof. The house is covered by dark brown stucco with red trim. From the back of one side of the house juts a two-story addition with a flat roof.

The Fords' straw-bale home. Barry and his family chose to build with straw because material costs were low and labor costs were nonexistent.

As we approached the house on the day of our visit, Barry scrambled out from beneath a pickup truck to greet us. We chatted for a few minutes about the truck, the house, and the emus wandering around the backyard, then went indoors to look around. We noticed right away that the window wells and doorjambs were very deep, more than a foot deep, due to the straw bales in the walls. But that was really the only thing about the house that suggested anything unusual about its construction—that is, except for the truth window. Barry took us right away to a glass window set in an interior wall that reveals the straw behind it. All straw-bale homes should have a truth window, he said—it's the only way to know for sure if a house is constructed of straw, since the straw is concealed everywhere else.

The Ford family chose to build a straw-bale house because material costs were low, and labor costs were nonexistent—the simplicity of the construction allowed the family to build the whole thing themselves.

Some straw-bale homes have a truth window to show off the straw behind the plaster.

Because straw bales are thick, the window wells in the Fords' home are deep, making them the perfect spots for houseplants.

What Do They Know?

Barry used university engineering departments, particularly at Cornell and nearby Clemson University, as free informational resources during the building process. However, he said, much of the university advice was overkill or too late. "Engineers overbuild everything. I would send them a problem, which they used as grad-student projects. But they took so long to work it out, I would get tired of waiting and figure it out myself. Typical engineers, they even came down from Cornell because they wouldn't believe what I was doing would work as good as what they were planning. It was fun showing them that the way they were overbuilding wasn't practical."

Besides the advice from the two universities, the Fords did not use any other outside information. They didn't look online or at any books—well, eventually they looked at one book. Midway through, they checked out a book from the public library on straw-bale construction. "It was so different from what we were doing, we just decided it was better not to look," said Barry.

"It's Not Allowed"

The Fords hit the first bump in their process before they'd even begun, when the zoning department told them their project wasn't possible. Their neighborhood is zoned residential, with the stipulation that the homes must all be either modular or stick-built (with standard walls of drywall nailed to two-by-fours). The Fords were not pleased with that roadblock. "The boss man down here told me that I just could not—he would not *allow* one built in Lancaster County. He said, 'It'll never happen.' And that's not their job. Their job is to oversee compliance, to make sure it's structurally safe, that type of thing. It's not their job to say no, you can't do it."

So Barry called the legal department at Cornell and asked the secretary there to help him find a student in the law school who would help him for free. She shuffled him to a professor who hooked him up with a sharp student. The student told him to just build the house, with no permit, then he and Barry would petition Congress for "the right to build a house within his means." So that's what the Fords did. After the house was built and the petition filed, the county replied that if Barry could find an engineer who would sign off on the house, they'd give him a permit. He got the engineer, and the county did issue the permit. The Cornell law student said the county had to give in in order to avoid the exorbitant legal expense of pursuing the matter in court.

Aside from the legal logistics, the most formidable task was collecting all the necessary straw bales before construction began. "If you have all the materials sitting there," Barry said, "you do it ten times faster than if you have to go get things all the time."

It took a few months to collect enough straw. "We would drive out in the back country until we saw a farmer who was baling, and we'd stop and talk, and end up buying 50 or 100 bales." They paid between $0.75 and $3 a bale, and picked up the bales themselves.

Back at the lot, they stacked more than 1,000 bales under a tarp. Condensation and mold were not a problem, said Barry, but compressing the bales was. "If you find a farmer that will square bale, or will use an old baler to compact the bales at the time in the field to the right specs, then you've saved yourself tons of work." Otherwise, the bales have to be compressed by hand. The university engineers tried to help the Fords by designing a complex gizmo to condense the bales for them, but Barry preferred a more direct method. "The engineers designed this big, monstrous thing that takes you two weeks to build … or you can do what I did: just set a couple strings down on the ground, set the bale on the strings, then put my chest and my weight on the bale, pull the string tight, put a loop in it, and pull it tight. Turns out that works better."

Meanwhile, the Fords poured and insulated a concrete-slab foundation for the house. When the concrete was ready, it was time to begin building.

Pregnant Mother Builds Home

The Fords chose to build their home without post-and-beam structural support; rather, the straw itself bears all the weight of the roof. They chose this design because it's more economical and simpler, allowing them to do all the labor themselves. "My pregnant wife and eight-year-old stepson could readily do this with no problem. It wasn't driving nails; it was helping put bales up and running string," Barry said. He pointed out that hiring a contractor to build post-and-beam support would've made the cost prohibitive because a straw-bale house takes longer to build than a conventional house. So Barry, his wife, Carrie, and their young son built the house entirely by themselves. The construction took them ten months, with only one day off. They worked every night until 10:00 and every weekend, while both maintained full-time jobs.

Technique

The Fords kept their building technique simple. "We would stack three rows, then we would put the first layer of stucco on the three rows. Three more rows, then stucco those rows. The reason was, once you put the stucco on, you could put ladders against it,

and you didn't have to build lots of scaffolding."

Straw-bale homes with no wooden posts in the walls often have vertical metal rods embedded in the concrete footer at regular intervals. The straw bales are impaled upon these rods to stabilize the walls. The Fords, however, decided against using rods at the advice of their engineering helpers. As the engineers told Barry, if you drive bamboo or steel rods into the bales to hold them in place, it separates the straw and makes a space for condensation. Every impaled bale that the engineers have pulled apart has had the straw rotted away from the steel because of the condensation.

Instead, the Fords anchored their house to the foundation with straps that go up around the first bale and back down into the foundation. "We have no bamboo, no steel rods, no nothing in the bales," said Barry. "It's all held together with 18,000 feet of baler twine. It goes around and around each bale. You compound that with up to twelve layers of bales, and it becomes very, very strong."

As for the roof, some straw-bale builders bolt the roof onto the vertical rods to anchor it, but clearly the Fords couldn't do that since they didn't have any vertical rods. Instead, they cabled the roof right down into the foundation.

To finish the walls, many straw-bale builders use weed trimmers, electric carving knives, or chain saws to smooth the surface of the straw before applying the stucco and plaster to the walls. The Fords just used extra baling twine. By running a piece of twine from top to bottom and left to right on each wall, they could eyeball any irregularities in the distance between the wall and the string. This same technique is used to straighten stick-built walls in conventional construction. The Fords, however, left the string in place, snug against the wall at six-inch intervals, to reinforce the walls. Each strand supports about 120 pounds.

A visit from the Underwriters Laboratories, a non-profit product-safety testing and certification organization, proved the strength of this technique. "They came out here and built a wall using our technique, brought in a jet engine on a trailer, and tried to burn the wall down," said Barry. "Then they tried to blow it down. They brought another machine in and shook the wall. They did it for twice the time they would have for any other structure, and the stucco cracked, but the wall stood. It never collapsed. After the earthquake and fire and compression tests, they gave us a rating of three, which is the best rating they could possibly give." The family had no problem getting new homeowner's insurance.

Five Dollars a Square Foot!

With no labor costs, the Ford's entire 2,300-square-foot house cost them only $13,000 to build, an amount so low they didn't even need a bank loan. The numbers work out to $5.65 per square foot, a figure so far below customary home-construction costs that we had to recalculate the numbers several times before we believed it.

So, what's the catch? "What about resale value?" we asked Barry. He replied that he had the house appraised recently and its value is 20 percent higher than his neighbors' homes.

Resale value in a straw-bale home depends a lot on the character of the home. The Fords' living room floor is made of warehouse pallets that they scavenged and refinished. The floor looks beautiful; it never occurred to us that the wood was less than top of the line. "The wood is soft," he said. "Every time you drop something, it leaves a dent. But that just adds to the charm." We couldn't argue with him. The circular staircase to the second floor, which Barry built himself, has a rail that appears to be made of a polished and finished tree branch. The effect is charming.

Renovating Made Easy

An additional benefit to straw-bale construction is the ease of renovation. The Fords decided to add a small room onto their home to accommodate a heated pool. Since all of their water pipes and electrical wires run under the floor, and the walls have no studs, Barry simply knocked a hole in the outer wall with a sledgehammer to open up a door to the new pool room. He just shoved the bales to the outside and tied the horses up outside the hole. Even though straw isn't edible, the horses entertained themselves by yanking out the ragged straw remnants and tidying up the new doorway. Much cheaper than contracting a labor crew, Barry observed.

Barry Ford made his living-room floor using wood from warehouse pallets. The circular staircase incorporates free or previously used materials as well.

While working on a farm in Spain, Sadie whitewashed a rammed-earth house. Rammed-earth buildings are commonplace in the Mediterranean. Courtesy of Sadie Kneidel

Rammed Earth—An Ancient Tradtition

Working on a rammed-earth construction crew was fascinating, but it was living in rammed-earth buildings that taught me the greatest respect for this simple form of housing. With their thick walls and smooth whitewash, these earthen buildings stay cool even in the blazing sun. Both of the farms I worked on in southern Spain, as well as virtually every building I entered in Morocco, were built from mud and rocks in the centuries-old style of rammed-earth construction. (See the sidebar on page 79.)

Many Moroccan towns are hundreds if not thousands of years old and often still consist of the original buildings. A typical town is centered around a *medina*, or old city, surrounded by the *ville nouvelle*, or expanded new city. The medina is enclosed by a massive rammed-earth wall, sometimes as thick as fifteen or twenty feet. Once a barricade, this wall is perforated by only a few keyhole-shaped gateways, often one facing each cardinal direction. Pedestrians, bikes, donkeys, and carts bustle through—but not cars. The screeching tires and chugging tailpipes of the modern world don't fit inside the compact labyrinth of the medina.

The structures are old, but life is fresh and vibrant. The narrow roads are still cobblestone; the earthen buildings are still solid and smoothed, gleaming with centuries of polished whitewash in shades of pink and brown. Breezes enter through open windows, but the sturdy walls keep out the dust and clatter of the streets. Each building shares a wall with its neighbor, creating a long row along the street. Stepping inside any door along the cobblestone road, a visitor enters a square central courtyard, open to the sky above and rimmed with balconies whose walls are covered with small and colorful tiles. The complex tile patterns were long ago pressed into the mud walls as they dried—a built-in wallpaper that will never be painted over. Gazing into the twisting shapes and colors, you can imagine the generations of lives that have come and gone while these sturdy tiles and walls have persisted. This world was built to last.

—Sadie

On a Rammed-Earth Work Crew in Spain

Rammed earth is a phrase that encompasses a range of techniques. In southern Spain, where I first encountered rammed earth, most rural homes—indeed, entire towns—are built of rammed earth, some of them very old. Historically, they were built by simply piling and shaping moist or wet earth to create a thick wall, then trimming away the bulges to make the inner and outer surfaces more or less smooth and vertical. Old homes built in this way have uneven walls that are charming; they feel like

A rammed-earth farmhouse in the mountains of southern Spain shows its age. Courtesy of Sadie Kneidel

country farmhouses—they *are* country farmhouses. Virtually all of them are painted with whitewash, a waterproof mixture of water and limestone.

While in Spain, I got a job helping to build a two-room rammed-earth house. My two friends Nicci and Catherine and I worked with a crew of four men to build the walls, which had to be completed within two weeks. As is customary now in rammed-earth construction, the walls were made by packing damp soil between two boards that were bolted together to form a mold. When the mud had dried enough to hold its shape, the boards could be unbolted and moved to another section of the wall.

The men stood on a simple scaffolding to tamp

79

Sadie's rammed-earth crew puts the finishing touches on the walls. Courtesy of Sadie Kneidel

buckets of mud and rocks into the wooden form. They packed it down by stomping on it and pounding it with their hands and big stones. Because we were in a hurry, trying to get a building permit by a certain deadline, we removed the form within hours, long before the wall was dry, in order to mold the next section of wall.

Our part of the job was to whitewash the completed sections. The soil was still damp enough that it bled into the whitewash, turning it pink. The walls needed several coats to override the pink tint. Whitewash goes on watery and translucent, but it dries thick and opaque, smoothing over imperfections and irregularities. It's the only protection needed against rain or drainage over the surface of the ground. In that arid climate, this system has been in use for centuries.

—Sadie

A Rammed-Earth Cottage Today—
Gary Phillips's Modern Approach

Rammed earth has been popular for hundreds of years, particularly in the arid regions of northern Africa, southern Europe, and the Mediterranean. But rammed-earth homes aren't just for arid climates. Realtor and rammed-earth homeowner Gary Phillips has seen rammed earth in wet climates ranging from riverfronts in southern France to the coastal town of Charleston, South Carolina,

a humid area regularly slammed by hurricanes.

Although it's an old technique, rammed earth is currently experiencing a resurgence in popularity as interest in green building picks up. The thick walls of rammed-earth homes are energy efficient, nontoxic, and they buffer sound. They're also resistant to termites, fires, and, with rebar reinforcement, to earthquakes. Rammed-earth walls are extremely durable as well. Parts of the Great Wall of China are made of rammed earth.

To see a more modern approach to rammed-earth construction than the buildings Sadie saw on her travels, I tracked down Gary Phillips for an interview and a tour of his new rammed-earth cottage.

At first glance, Phillips's home almost looks like a gingerbread house in a fairy tale, with its warm brown walls and royal blue front door. The colors, he said, were inspired by beautiful 500- and 600-year-old rammed-earth buildings he'd seen in Morocco and Mexico. Phillips decided to build with rammed earth "to avoid poisons and build in a sustainable manner."

Gary Phillips's modern rammed-earth house.

Rammed earth is indeed a good choice for sustainable building. The thick walls are excellent insulators and lend themselves to passive-solar design. Not only do the walls serve as an effective thermal mass, but they also fulfill the function of a southern overhang—because the walls are so thick, little sunshine comes through the windows when the summer sun is high in the sky. When the sun is lower in the sky in the winter, it shines more directly through the windows, warming the house.

In addition to thick walls, Phillips's house has other features that save energy. He intentionally built a small house, around 1,100 square feet, and has expanded his living space into an inviting outdoor courtyard and covered back porch. Like Jim Cameron and Kathleen Jardine, Phillips has made these areas more accessible by avoiding or minimizing steps at the home's outside doors.

Construction Methods Have Evolved

As interest in rammed-earth construction has grown in the United States, certain building methods and tools have evolved that are not always available in rural communities worldwide. For example, Phillips had his soil delivered from a company that specializes in fill, rather than using soil from the excavation and leveling of the building site. Phillips said his on-site soil had too much clay and too many rocks to be useful for the walls. By purchasing soil, he was able to get an optimum blend of sifted organic matter, sand, and clay.

Dump trucks delivered seventeen-ton loads of his prescribed soil blend for $300 to $400 per load. His work crew then added

cement to the blend, 5 percent of the total volume. Phillips rented eight-feet-by-eight-feet wooden forms that are designed for making concrete walls and are held together with big metal screws. The space between the forms, and consequently the wall itself, should be at least eighteen to twenty-four inches wide, Phillips said, because the workers need to be able to stand inside the form to compact the soil. Phillips's walls are twenty-four inches thick.

Phillips used a forklift to dump soil into the forms—obviously, this was much faster than carrying buckets up a scaffold. About eight inches of soil were added at a time, then tamped down, reducing the layer to about five inches.[1] Phillips's crew used a handheld hydraulic tamping machine to compress the soil instead of the hand-stomping-and-stone-method that Sadie saw in rural Spain. A tamping machine is similar to a jackhammer, but it has a small flat circle of metal at the end rather than a cutting wedge. It took three men one day to do each wall.

Typically, the soil is about 8 percent water when it's added to the form.[2] It takes up to a year for the soil to dry completely, but within twenty-four hours, it is cured enough to remove the forms. The finished walls look and feel as solid as a poured concrete wall—but the warm earthen tones make them much more attractive.

Artistic Touches

Traditional rammed-earth houses are coated with whitewash inside and out, but Phillips chose to cover his interior walls with clayote for a smoother finish. (Clayote is a plaster made from water, sand, and a dash of tint.)

The interior of Phillips's home also features several appealing traits unique to earthen homes. One is the niche holes, small recessed areas in the walls that were created by volume displacement. Said Phillips, "Since you have two-feet-thick earth walls, any shape you put in the earth wall as it's being formed, and have a means to pull out, will then leave a permanent opening or space in the wall." Phillips used his niche holes to maximum advantage. He installed a small recessed light in the top of each hole to illuminate the small sculpture or other object now displayed in the finished space. This method of highlighting his art has a stunning effect.

Gary Phillips uses the niches in the walls of his rammed-earth home to display works of art.

Phillips also pointed out that, because the walls of a rammed-earth house are so thick, the builder has to choose whether to locate the doors and windows closer to the outside or inside of the wall. If you put your windows at the outside, then you have huge, wide windowsills that also serve as niche holes. If you place the doors to the inside, then you have the wide sill in front of them to protect the door from the weather. Gary has used his windowsills for family photographs, books, and artwork—another personal touch that adds to the warm atmosphere of his home.

Good Shoes and a Good Hat

All rammed-earth houses need a solidly waterproof top and bottom—or "good shoes and a good hat," as Phillips calls them. The good shoes are the foundation, or stem wall, a low wall of poured concrete that starts below ground level and protrudes above. The rammed-earth wall rests on the stem wall in order to elevate the earthen portion of the wall above the possible eroding effects of surface rainwater. Of course, as with any home, this problem can also be averted or minimized by grading the site so that rainwater flows away from the house.

Vertical steel bars called rebar are often anchored in the stem wall and extend up into the earthen wall to strengthen the structure, a stabilizing technique Phillips used in his home.

The good hat for a rammed-earth home consists of wide overhangs to keep rain away from the wall, and, in modern construction, a concrete cap around the top of the wall, just below the roof. This cap, called a bond beam, is created by pouring concrete into the top six inches of the form, on top of the rammed earth. This ensures stability against any possible pressures from the sides, such as earthquakes or strong winds. The roof is attached to the bond beam.

Expense

As with straw-bale construction, the earth-based materials for rammed-earth homes are not very expensive. Phillips estimates that the materials for his house were 25 to 30 percent cheaper than for a conventional stick-built home. However, because rammed-earth requires more skilled labor and specialized equipment, the labor costs are much more than for straw-bale building. It would be difficult for a family to do all the labor themselves, as Barry Ford's family did with their straw-bale home, but *The Rammed Earth House* by David Easton is a helpful guide for anyone who may be interested.[3]

The steel roof adds to the durability of Gary Phillips's home. The thick earthen walls provide excellent insulation.

Construction costs are also mitigated by the extremely low maintenance costs of a rammed-earth home. With tinted concrete flooring and a steel roof, a rammed-earth home like Phillips's will need little maintenance for 100 years.

Zoning Restrictions, Building Permits, and Insurance

Phillips prevented logistical difficulties from the beginning of his project by using pre-drawn plans for a rammed-earth cottage in New Mexico, which he then had altered by a professional architect to meet his needs. The only hitch in his plan turned out to be a false alarm. "After we built the stem wall, the county sent out an inspector to look at it. He didn't say a word, but got in his car and left. I thought, 'Oh, Lord, now we're in trouble.' He came back with the entire department. He had rounded them up [from] all over the county and he told them, 'I want you to look at this stem wall. As far as I'm concerned, they can build a fourteen-story building here if they want to.' He recognized that we weren't taking any shortcuts, and he never gave us any more grief about it.

Phillips had no problem getting insurance through a national insurer. "I said to the insurer, if the people you're dealing with don't understand rammed earth, ask them to contact their New Mexico or Californian or British Columbian or Canadian branches and talk about it. They did, and they came back and reduced my insurance premium by about $300 a year because it's considered a construction that's not likely to be harmed either by an earthquake or severe flooding or fire."

Notes
1. Rammed-Earth Development, Inc., "What Is Rammed Earth?," www.rammedearth.com.
2. Ibid.
3. David Easton, *The Rammed Earth House, Revised Edition* (White River Junction, Vermont: Chelsea Green Publishing Company, 2007).

Earthships

Earthships are passive-solar homes that incorporate a wide spectrum of green features. Constructed from natural and recycled materials, they are usually independent from the grid. Most earthships are built from recycled car tires packed with soil to form a "rammed-earth brick encased in steel-belted rubber."[1] According to Earthship Biotecture, a firm based in Taos, New Mexico, the walls built from these bricks are "virtually indestructible."[2]

Earthship homeowners pride themselves on their completely self-sustaining homes. The home's water needs are met by rainwater, which is collected on the roof and funneled through a system of cisterns, pumps, and filters. Water is used and recycled many times throughout the home before being treated on-site in a "jungle," a nonpolluting sewage-treatment process. Hot water is heated by the sun and by an on-demand natural gas heater that is activated only in the event of insufficient sunlight.[3]

Earthship electricity is harvested through PV panels, with the assistance of generators and the grid, if necessary. As with other passive-solar homes, very little energy is required for heating and cooling the home. As a result, it's easy to capture enough energy for other household needs.[4]

In the absence of recycled tires, earthships can be made from other materials, such as concrete, adobe, or even bales of paper trash.

To find out more about earthships, and for practical information about design and construction, check out www.earthship biotecture.com. You can even rent an earthship for a week to try it out for yourself.

Notes
1. Earthship Biotecture, "Learn: What Is an Earthship?", 2005, www.earthshipbiotecture.com
2. Ibid.
3. Ibid.
4. Ibid.

Paper-Bale Homes

A paper-bale home is one in which the walls are made of baled paper and trash. Homeowners Ann Douden and Rich Messer astonished their neighbors by constructing their cozy Colorado home from bales of postconsumer paperboard and polyvinyl chloride trash.[1] These materials—glossy, coated cardboard (such as laundry soap boxes), and waste plastic (broken toys, laundry baskets, and shampoo bottles)—are hard to recycle and usually end up in landfills. But for Douden and Messer, they provide inexpensive yet sturdy walls. With an insulation value of R-30, this recycled home exceeds many times the energy-efficiency standards of conventional housing.[2]

As with any first-time venture, building a green and energy-efficient house of any kind can be a major undertaking. But satisfied do-it-yourselfers are convinced the final product is worth the effort. Energy-efficient homes made of recycled or waste materials are the ultimate in earth-friendly building, and that's bound to be a feel-good choice for any environmental consumer.

To learn more about paper-bale homes, contact Rich Messer at rmesser@rkymtnhi .com, or search for Maureen Drummey's "Paper Bale House" online.

Notes

1. Robin Griggs Lawrence, "Classy Trash," *Natural Home* magazine, July/August 2002.
2. Ibid.

Recycled Homes

Recycling a home means buying an older house that would otherwise be torn down to make room for a new mall or subdivision and moving the house to a new location.

Moveable houses are most likely to be available in communities experiencing rapid growth. After a tract of land is purchased, the developer must make monthly payments on the new purchase and wants to get any obstacles off the property as soon as possible so cash flow can be generated from the sale of the new construction. It's much cheaper for a developer to sell an old house that stands in his way than to pay for it to be torn down.

Relocating an older home is perhaps the greenest of all housing choices, at least in terms of the environmental costs of construction. It not only saves the physical materials that go into a new home—the wood, concrete, drywall, wiring, shingles, ducts, fixtures, glass, and so on, but also saves all the energy needed to extract, process, manufacture, package, and transport all these materials. Just how much energy does this save? Building 1.7 million houses consumes as much energy as heating and cooling 10 million or more homes a year.[1] Reusing a home also saves the energy that would otherwise be used in recycling or disposing of materials if the house were demolished.

Moving a recycled home is also much more cost effective than building a new home. The average cost of relocation is $10,000 to $20,000. Even with the added costs of buying a site, building a new foundation, and repairing any damages incurred in the move, the expenses still come out lower than the construction costs of an equivalent custom-built new home. Excluding the cost of the land, recycled homes generally range in price from 50 to 90 percent of the cost of a comparable new custom house. The final cost depends in large part on the amount of renovation and the value of the new features.

Moved houses tend to be quality homes that appreciate well. Most are thirty to fifty years old—old enough to have plaster walls and crown molding, and often hardwood floors. They're solid and well-constructed; many have timbers in the ceiling and heftier joists under the floors than are normally used in new construction. These older homes often have charm or character that adds to the appreciation of the home.

Please Take This House

To better understand the process of recycling houses, we got together with professional house mover Trip Overholt. He and a friend founded a home recycling business, Sustainable Living, to save family farmhouses in their area that were being destroyed to make room for new development. In the years since they started the business, Overholt has cultivated lucrative relationships with local developers. "I got a call this week from a company that bought land just south of here with a thirty- or forty-year-old house on it," he told us. "They said if we don't take it, it's going to cost them $7,000 to demolish it. So they gave it to us. That's not always the case, but it was this time."

A free house seems like a great deal, but it's not that simple. The market for relocated houses is not very strong. Overholt and his business partner are actually marketing to people who don't have much discretionary income, a market few businesses pursue. Their potential buyers tend to be people who have a patch of land, but little cash. Overholt said finding a buyer for a newly acquired

Trip Overholt relocates and sells houses that are displaced by commercial developments.

home may take as long as a year. Meanwhile, storage costs for the home are high, and the stored house is uninsured—a situation Overholt feels is not a good business risk.

Plus, moving the house is a big ordeal, and the move itself can be expensive.

Birthing a Whale

An ideal house for moving is narrow, with a low profile, such as a rectangular ranch no wider than thirty-four feet, no longer than sixty feet, and no more than fifteen feet from the sill plate to the peak of the rooftop. Such a house can be maneuvered down the street on a set of beams without the use of dollies.

Any larger than that, Overholt said, and they have to move mailboxes to get the house down the road. "We can pull fifty, sixty, seventy mailboxes out of the ground on a move," he said. "We usually start at 7:00 in the morning and get to the lot at 3:00 or 4:00 in the afternoon, but sometimes we have to park the house and finish the next day. It's pretty stressful. I'm at the front, helping the troopers deal with traffic. I might have 3,000 interactions in a day with motorists; some of them are angry, some are late, some are intrigued."

Who wouldn't be intrigued? Overholt's latest move sounds like it was quite a spectacle. The house was 120 feet long, twice his ideal maximum, and cost $85,000 to move—five times the usual cost. "It was an amazing event!" said Overholt. "We took it *over* the mailboxes, instead of pulling them up. There were people out there at 5:00 in the morning with their digital cameras. I don't know if they were out there to see if we messed up their expensive mailboxes or whether they were really excited about it, but this was like birthing a whale out of a Chihuahua. It was absolutely brutal."

One of the houses Trip Overholt has moved, which would otherwise be in the landfill.

We wished we could have witnessed that adventure. Instead, we had to content ourselves with seeing the house itself, now gracefully settled on its new lot. Although the house had been sawed in half for the move, there was no obvious evidence of recent trauma. The elegant interior, with its hardwood floors and crown molding, granite countertops, and stainless steel appliances, was immaculate. The only clue to the move was a narrow floor seam filled with a mosaic of ceramic tiles—like a scar left from surgery. Of course, Overholt reminded us, the house didn't arrive in such pristine condition, but required months of repairs and upgrades to get it so. As we spoke, a lone workman with a tool belt around his waist moved from room to room, still at work on a few finishing

touches to ready the house for listing.

Overholt stopped to talk to the workman for a moment and we wandered outside into the shade of the tall pines behind the house. As we looked for a good photo angle, we reflected on the fact that almost the entire house was salvaged. Were it not for Overholt and his business partner, this whole house would be at the landfill. In its place, instead,

Buying a relocated home such as this one saves materials, energy, and money.

would eventually be a new home constructed from scratch—much more costly all around.

With a little ingenuity, a fresh approach, an old home gets a new start. More important, the most basic green principles—reduce, reuse, recycle—are applied to a community on a grand scale. Buying vintage clothes and using waste vegetable oil as fuel are great, but this is grassroots green activism at its best. We hope the neighbors are paying attention. And we hope they notice not just the economic and aesthetic success of the move, but the sentiment of sustainability behind it.

Note

1. Sandra Hines, "Environmental Costs of Home Construction Lower with Wise Choice, Reuse of Building Materials," University of Washington Office of News and Information, August 24, 2004, www.uwnews.org/article .asp?articleID=5360.

Doing It Right

Trip Overholt, professional house mover, is doing it right. Overholt is a one-man embodiment of just about everything we know about sustainable choices. He lives in a straw-bale house he built himself, 80 to 90 percent of it from salvaged materials. His home is off the grid—he gets all of his electrical power from photovoltaic panels in his yard. The panels collect and store solar energy in batteries for later use. He has a composting toilet. He also built a small refinery to produce his own biodiesel fuel from waste vegetable oil, which he uses instead of petroleum diesel in both of his diesel vehicles—a pickup truck for the company and an old Mercedes wagon to drive his two young daughters around. For seven years, Overholt was the owner and proprietor of Earthwares, an environmental-products store he closed a couple of years ago to seek more income for his family.

Need we say more? We were encouraged to see that it's possible for one person to do so many things right.

Trip Overholt fills the tank of his Mercedes with biodiesel that he made in his own small refinery.

Chapter Three
Land Use—Green Choices for Yards, Streams, and Habitats

Lawn Is a Dirty Word

Did you know that lawns are the fifth biggest crop in the United States? That's right—after corn, wheat, soybeans, and hay, we devote more land area to lawn than to any other cultivated plant.[1] Additionally, the per-acre application of pesticides to lawns is typically twenty times greater than pesticide application to farm crops.[2] This seems absurd when you consider that lawns don't fulfill any purpose other than to match our arbitrary idea of what looks good in front of a house. Lawns are an American phenomenon, an obsession that the rest of the world doesn't share. The British refer to the yard as a garden—because it usually *is* a garden. In other countries, yards are tiny and usually covered with leaves, bare soil, or native plants.

Yet lawns are serious business in the United States. We spend more than $30 billion per year on lawn installation, lawn-care products, equipment, and the lawn-service industry in pursuit of our ideal lawn: one composed of grass species only, free of weeds, always green, and regularly mowed to a low and even height.[3]

Our green urban spaces—lawns, roadsides, and parks—add up to a staggering amount of space that we are not taking advantage of. With a little attention, however, the 30 million acres of lawn in this country could become 30 million acres of native plants, creating habitat for crowded and endangered animal species. Habitat destruction is the number one threat to wild species. Converting lawn to native habitat could also provide a natural air filter and temperature regulator against pollution and heat-trapping materials from cities. In addition, this conversion would reduce or eliminate the chemicals, intensive watering, and power machinery required to maintain lawns and other nonnative landscaping.

In this section, we'll explore what you can do with your lawn, as well as what conservationists are doing on a larger scale to ease the impact of development.

The Lawn-Service Offer

To begin investigating landscaping choices, I started with the enemy: I called a professional lawn service and asked them to give me a free estimate. That's how I met Bob.

Bob was a friendly guy. He looked like a college student doing summer work. He took out his wheel on a stick and measured off the yard, then pulled out his clipboard to write up a contract for his company's lawn program. He recommended the economical Custom Care Program, which includes five visits a year from their lawn technician at $37.80 per visit. During each visit, Bob assured me, the lawn tech would apply a slow-release chemical fertilizer, herbicides to kill everything except

the few blades of grass in the yard at present, an insecticide for turf-eating insects, and, if needed, a grub-killing chemical to get rid of moles (which depend on grubs for food). The chemicals, he said, are only toxic as long as they're wet; after they dry, we could romp on the lawn at will. When I asked Bob what chemicals in particular would be applied to my lawn, he replied that he had no idea what the chemicals were, but he'd be glad to ask and call me back.

Bob did call me back the next day. The slow-release fertilizer, he said, is 16-0-8, meaning 16 parts nitrogen, 0 parts phosphorus, and 8 parts potassium. A 50-pound bag is applied for every 4,000 square feet of turf. The herbicides, he continued, are Ortho Weed B Gon Pro and Scotts Halts. The grub-killing chemical is Scotts GrubEx. The insecticide used to kill turf-damaging insects is Ortho Max Pro. He still didn't know what was in these products, but, according to his boss Nate, "Runoff is not a problem."

Bob asked if I was interested in the Custom Care Program he had described or in their more deluxe Complete Care Program, which would offer me seven services per year, at $59.79 per service, to include seeding, aeration, and the application of yet another chemical, a fungicide. He offered me a $20 discount off my first treatment.

I told him I'd have to get back to him about that. I had a different kind of landscaping in mind.

—Sally

What's Wrong with Lawns?

The displacement of native habitats by lawns and manicured arrangements of ornamental plants uses resources and generates pollution unnecessarily. Think of all the noisy mechanical equipment, fossil fuels, and limited water resources needed to maintain a typical suburban property. Gasoline-powered mowers, blowers, trimmers, and so on, account for more than 5 percent of urban air pollution.[4] Nonnative plants typically need much more water than do native plants, and they squander the water they get. Lawns absorb only 10 percent of the water that a woodland would absorb; the rest runs off into streams. Because of this, lawns contribute significantly to suburban flooding and to stream degradation.

Also, as noted above, lawns are dosed with a daunting array of pesticides. Of course, most of these chemicals don't stay on your lawn; they wash into the street, sewers, and then streams, where they kill wildlife and comtaminate human drinking water.

And chemicals aren't the only things creeping out of a landscaped yard. According to our county's conservation office, 28 percent of the plants in our local nature preserve are nonnative species that got their start in someone's yard. Next time you go to a state park or nature preserve, ask the naturalist on staff how many of the plant species are introduced. You may find that the dominant plants there are nonnative, like the signature golden grasses in Mount Tamalpais State Park along the California coast.

Lawns and ornamentals also overload our landfills. In spite of the efforts of some communities to recycle yard waste as mulch, grass clippings and shrub trimmings—materials that could easily be composted—comprise a fifth of all municipal waste.[5] Or if the nonnative plants from which this bulk was clipped and trimmed were instead native plants, most of the clipping and trimming would have been unnecessary.

In short, the planting and maintenance of lawns and ornamentals displaces native species, pollutes our air and water, contributes to flooding, generates noise and landfill waste, and uses fossil fuels unnecessarily. And why are we doing all this? The lawn-service brochure tells me that an emerald green lawn will improve my property value. But that's not true. Some of the most desirable neighborhoods in our city have completely wooded lots with no lawn at all, and last we checked, these lots were selling briskly for much more than we can afford. And we did check, because we wanted one.

Many folks would probably opt for a wooded lot if we could get it overnight. After all, mowing grass is a headache. The problem is, it's sort of like letting your hair grow out—the yard has to go through an awkward stage where it doesn't look its best. One of our neighbors is letting his yard undergo succession with almost no interference or management. He stopped cutting the grass a couple of years ago. The plants are about six feet tall now, and the house is dwarfed behind exploding bushes. Although his approach is interesting and somewhat refreshing, most of the plants that are flourishing in his yard are not native species, and are not nearly as helpful to wildlife as a native plant community would be.

There are better options than just abandoning all yard care. You can replace your lawn with something useful, such as a money-saving vegetable garden. Or you can convert your yard to a beneficial natural area by replacing one invasive species at a time. Native plants are part of the local ecosystem and play particular roles in the life cycles of the local wildlife. Native plants also add character and give an area its sense of place, such as the longleaf pines in the Southeast coastal plain, or aspens in the mountains of Wyoming and Colorado.

Thinking Outside the Box

While I enjoy my current job building houses with Habitat for Humanity, there are a few parts of our development process that make me bite my tongue. I have a hard time landscaping, for instance, when I know what else could be done with those precious green areas.

The frustration begins when I am sent to pick up our order of plants from the shrub nursery—all nonnative species, like Beale's Oregon Grape and Chinese Privet. As I plant them around the house, I can't help but imagine the urban forests, wild spaces, and gardens that could instead occupy this area. Without saying anything, I dutifully mulch with pine needles and spread grass seed, fertilizer, and straw across the rest of the yard. Within a few weeks, the new lawn looks like any other house on the block.

But when the families move in, my hope is restored. Many of our families are immigrants or refugees from around the world, and often you can pick out their houses without even meeting the inhabitants. One of my favorite houses belongs to a Somalian family. Not a trace remains of the carefully installed bushes and lawn; rather, their yard is a shoulder-to-shoulder sea of okra, pepper, and tomato plants. Basil bursts out of the flower beds; green bean vines climb the side of the house. Although it's a tiny lot, they're growing more food than one family could possibly eat.

Another favorite of mine is a house belonging to a family from Kosovo. They've augmented the one modest Japanese maple offered by Habitat with a veritable forest of baby sycamores, sweet gums, and oaks. The front stoop is shielded by a lush green curtain of grapevines that is more inviting than any vinyl porch railing we could have installed.

As I reluctantly spread each handful of fertilizer, I hope that the future inhabitants of that house will soon be undoing my work. I hope that our American clients take a lesson from their less traditional neighbors. However small the yard, those few square feet of land are bursting with potential!

—Sadie

Create Backyard Habitat

In addition to making your yard safer and easier to maintain, a primary goal in native landscaping is to create a healthy environment for wild species. The National Wildlife Federation has developed a certification program to assist you in creating backyard wildlife habitats, although you can include front yards, too, of course.[6] To be certified, a yard must provide food in the form of native plants, water for drinking and bathing, cover as protection from weather and predators, and nest

Beth Henry checks a monarch chrysalis in her backyard. She established the native meadow after killing and removing the lawn without using herbicides.

sites. Also, an applicant must commit to the use of sustainable practices in maintaining the habitat, such as avoiding toxic chemicals.

Providing food means planting native shrubs, trees, and flowers that provide berries, seeds, acorns, and other edible plant parts for birds, butterflies, and other animals.[7] Healthy soil with lots of organic matter will support soil organisms to feed birds and other animals, and rotting logs will harbor invertebrates to feed larger animals.

A source of water could be a birdbath, pond, or shallow dish that can be used for drinking and bathing. Unless it is a pond, the water container should be flushed and cleaned daily to avoid the spread of disease.

Cover can include brush piles, rock piles, deep water, hollow logs, tall grasses, dense shrubs, and stone walls with nooks and crannies.

Breeding sites may include mature trees and tall shrubs for birds and squirrels. In our yard, an old and stable brush pile has been home to many mammal species. And amphibians will take advantage of a pond, even a small one. We've had mature bullfrogs in a pond that's only five feet across. Host plants for caterpillars will help birds feed their young.

Sustainable gardening practices include using native plants, reducing the use of power tools and chemicals to manage them, building healthy soils, maintaining creek buffers, and reducing runoff by landscaping your yard to retain water.

Refer to the National Wildlife Federation for more information on appropriate plants

for your area (www.nwf.org/backyardwild
lifehabitat/whatisrequired.cfm).

Native Landscaping Step-by-Step

For a crash course in native landscaping, we
turned to landscape restoration experts Beth
Henry and Mollie Brugh. These innovative
women were the masterminds behind the conversion of a bedraggled hillside on a nearby
school campus into a lush native meadow of
flowering plants. They did the same on two
open acres of property at Henry's home. In
addition, the two women have planted hundreds of native shade-tolerant plants, such as
ferns and native lilies, in the understory of a
forest at the same school and at another site.

When we visited the restored sites, we
were astonished at how beautiful and healthy
the native meadows and the forest understo-
ries were with no watering at all. Normally,
August in our area is very hot and dry, a
time when ornamentals and nonnatives grow
parched and die if not tended to regularly.
But we found that the native plants were
flourishing, entirely untended.

From Lawn to Meadow

According to Henry and Brugh, the first step
in converting a lawn to a meadow is to kill
the grass. This can be achieved by spreading a thick layer of newspapers or flattened
cardboard boxes all over the lawn and cover-
ing that heavily with mulch. Henry ordered
two dump trucks of mulch to kill her own
two-acre lawn. She left the mulch in place all
summer, and by the end of August, the grass
was dead. Henry told us not to till the grass

under. No tilling is needed for native plants,
and a single tilling reduces the earthworm
population by a third.

After Henry removed the cardboard and
dead grass from her yard, she was ready to
plant her native meadow. She placed plugs of
very young, already-sprouted seedlings about
a foot apart from each other. She planted
each seedling by plunging a narrow shovel
into the soil and pushing it forward, creating a slit just wide enough to put in the plug.
Then she tamped the soil around it with her
foot. She watered them for only a week or
two until they were established.

Henry started her home meadow with six
species of native grasses and seventeen species
of native wildflowers, planting just three or
so plants of one type together, but not all the
plants of one type in the same spot—a small
group of coneflowers here, and another small
group of coneflowers over there, with several
other types of plants in between.

Gardeners Mollie Brugh and Beth Henry in the native meadow at
Henry's home. Purple coneflowers can be seen in the left foreground.

Henry stressed the importance of finding native seedlings that have been propagated by growers rather than dug from the wild. Removing wild species from nature, plant or animal, depletes the natural populations. Many nurseries and greeneries, as well as local native plants societies, supply native seedlings. You should be able to find sources in your area by doing a quick search on the Internet. Or, try asking around at local nurseries or gardening clubs; you may find a seed-exchange group that meets periodically in your area to trade seeds, or your state's native plant society may have a Listserv to help find such a group.

When adding plants, choose regionally native plants that are appropriate for particular sites on the lot. Consider shading, slope, drainage, and soil condition. Your county cooperative extension agent can help. Native plants have evolved to local conditions over millions of years and, if placed in the right habitat, won't need any special attention. A friend gave us three native plants recently for our yard: passionflower, milkweed (for monarch butterfly caterpillars), and morning glories. We dug three shallow holes in the compact clay soil of the side yard, stuck the three plants in the holes, tamped the soil gently, watered them once, and forgot about them. A month later, we were amazed to see that they were all blooming and thriving.

Skip the pesticides and chemical fertilizers. Native plants generally don't need chemical assistance. Composted vegetable and yard waste makes an efficient fertilizer. Autumn leaves can be a useful ground cover and mulch rather than a troublesome burden that must be raked. Mulching reduces the need for watering.

If you do have pests, choose natural alternatives to pesticides. County cooperative extension agents can help you choose a treatment suitable for your plants and climate.

If you must choose some exotic (nonnative) plants, avoid invasive species—those that spread aggressively and dominate native species, resulting in a loss of biodiversity for both plant life and the animals that depend upon them. Invasive exotics that can pose a serious threat include English ivy, Chinese and Japanese privet, Japanese honeysuckle, Bradford pear, sacred bamboo, mimosa, johnsongrass, and many others. Choose drought-resistant species to reduce watering needs, and arrange them informally to minimize or eliminate the need for power trimmers.

A ground cover of pine needles or leaves between plantings is suitable for a children's play area.

From Lawn to Woodland

Replacing lawn with woodland is more difficult than starting a meadow or adding native understory to an existing woodland, though it certainly can be done. If you're willing to be patient, the trees will self-establish, or volunteer, from acorns buried by squirrels or maple seeds blown in on the wind. If time is of the essence, you can buy wildlife-friendly native trees from a local nursery.

If you're starting from scratch, first protect the existing natural areas as much as possible, including at least 100 feet on each side of streams to reduce flooding and to provide a wildlife corridor between bigger tracts of undisturbed land.

Unlike an existing forest, your baby woodland may not have a ground cover of dead leaves to suppress weed growth. If not, expect an abundance of weeds, by which we mean invasive and nonnative species that self-colonize. You can use the grass-smothering technique detailed above, or just pull up the weeds as they sprout.

Start by buying shade-loving native wildflowers and shrubs and planting them, a few at a time, under the canopy of trees. The few humble shrubs that started Henry's woodland now form a substantial multilevel understory of native plants with seeds that are edible for wildlife.

Visual Aid

If you need help identifying invasive plants, you may find the website www.invasive.org helpful. A joint project of the University of Georgia and the United States Department of Agriculture, the site features excellent identifying photos of hundreds of nonnative plants. You can look up any exotic species to see photos of its foliage, fruit, flowers, and bark.

Plant to Reduce Air-Conditioning Needs

In the Passive-Solar Design section, we described how a carefully planted yard can save energy for home heating and cooling needs by shading the south side of the home in summer and blocking the north side from winter winds. For those who cool their homes with air-conditioning, here's another tip: deciduous trees planted along the south side of the house can reduce air-conditioning costs by up to 20 percent by shielding the house from the summer sun.

Imagine ...

What if every yard were converted to native meadows and native woodlands instead of pointless, chemically sustained green lawns? Imagine the benefits to our native wildlife. Imagine the return of croaking toads and climbing tree frogs, lumbering box turtles and timid lizards, and birds of prey darting from the sky. Even the weasels and foxes would come back, with small mammal populations to sustain them.

It could happen. Imagine your children growing up in a place so rich with wildlife. As humans grow more and more numerous on the planet, beneficial landscaping is a crucial step toward preserving the wildlife we have left. Loss of habitat, as we've said, is the number one threat to wildlife worldwide.

Notes

1. Environmental Protection Agency, Green Communities, Beneficial Landscaping, "Environmentally Friendly Landscaping," www.epa.gov/greenkit/landscap.htm.
2. Ibid.
3. Ibid.
4. Center for Watershed Protection, "Feeling Smart? Take Our Watershed Quiz!" www.cwp.org/watershed_quiz .htm.
5. National Wildlife Federation, Create a Certified Wildlife Habitat, www.nwf.org/backyardwildlifehabitat/whatis required.cfm.
6. Ibid.
7. Ibid.

Additional Resources

Cornell Lab of Ornithology, www.birds.cornell.edu/school yard/all_about_birds/feeding_birds/plant_types.htm.

Dan L. Perlman and Jeffrey C. Milder, *Practical Ecology for Planners, Developers, and Citizens* (Washington, DC: Island Press, 2005).

eNature, www.enature.com/native_invasive/.

Invasive and Exotic Species (source for information and images), www.invasive.org/.

Martin F. Quigley, "The American Lawn: An Unrequited Love," Ohio State University, Extension Research Bulletin, 2000, http://ohioline.osu.edu/sc177/sc177_14.html.

Sara B. Stein, *Noah's Garden: Restoring the Ecology of our Own Backyards* (New York: Houghton Mifflin, 1995).

Sara B. Stein, *Planting Noah's Garden: Further Adventures in Backyard Ecology* (New York: Houghton Mifflin, 1997).

A Billion Birds per Year

We are in the process of killing invasives in half of our front yard right now using Beth Henry's cardboard-and-mulch method as outlined on page 93. The other half of the yard remains a scraggly assortment of grasses and low-lying plants, mostly nonnatives that we'll eventually get rid of, that colonized the area on their own. In that untended half of the yard, we have twenty-seven chipmunk holes. Close observation has revealed that all twenty-seven holes apparently lead to the same burrow, occupied by a mother with a notched ear and her three youngsters.

The chipmunk family provides daily entertainment, as our computer and desk are stationed in the bay window overlooking the yard. Unfortunately, the entertainment often turns to rage over the neighbors' Siamese cats. These cats constantly invade and patrol our yard, looking for songbirds, chipmunks, and other small mammals. Despite repeated conversations and confrontations with the neighbors, the cats keep coming back. Just two hours after our last discussion with the neighbors, we spied one of the kitties trotting down the driveway with a wriggling cotton rat in its mouth. (Cotton rats are native woodland rodents that bear little resemblance to the introduced Norway rats that invade houses and carry diseases.)

Have you ever thought about how your domestic pets interact with the wild animals in your neighborhood?

While predation is natural, cats are not. Cats are an introduced species, just like kudzu or starlings. Because they are sustained artificially by their owners, house cats operate totally outside of the limiting factors that control wild populations, such as parasites, food scarcity, predators, and disease. Thanks to their human care, cats are unusually fit and capable predators of native animal species. In fact, house cats are the third largest threat to songbird survival after habitat loss and crashing into windows. A recent Wisconsin study cited by the U.S. Fish and Wildlife Service estimated that domestic cats kill more than 39 million birds annually in Wisconsin alone.[1] If it's that many in just one state, then cats kill approximately 1 billion birds annually, nationwide.

Despite these numbers, just 53 percent of cat owners are concerned about cat predation, and 64 percent believe that putting bells on cats keeps them from killing—which is not true.[2] The only way to keep a cat from killing is to keep it indoors. Two-thirds of vets recommend keeping cats indoors at all times.[3] Many shelters now require adopters to agree to keep cats indoors; more and more communities are passing leash laws for cats as well as for dogs.

In our yard, the cat war rages on. Nationally, the cat war has barely begun. We're not sure we've ever met a single person, other than a biologist or serious birdwatcher, who is aware of the menace that domesticated cats pose to native wildlife. Here's what you can do to spread the word: write a letter to the editorial page of your local newspaper. Print out a couple of the online articles listed below and give them to the cat owners you know—with a smile. Start with the cat-safety angle; maybe they'll listen. And if you have a cat, please keep it inside.

Notes

1. U.S. Fish and Wildlife Service, "Migratory Bird Mortality: Many Human-Caused Threats Afflict Our Bird Populations," www.fws.gov/birds/mortality-fact-sheet.pdf (accessed September 4, 2006).

2. The American Bird Conservancy, "Human Attitudes and Behavior Regarding Cats," www.abcbirds.org/cats/fact sheets/attitude.pdf (accessed September 4, 2006).

3. "Keep Your Cat Safe at Home: Humane Society of the United State's Safe Cats Campaign," www.hsus.org/pets/pet_care/cat_care/keep_your_cat_safe_at_home_hsuss_safe_cats_campaign/index.html (accessed September 4, 2006).

Additional Resources

American Bird Conservancy, Birds and Cats—The Cats Indoors! Campaign, www.abcbirds.org/cats/.

C. A. Lepczyk, et al., "The Effects of Free-Ranging Cats on Birds in Wisconsin: Wisconsin Bird Conservation Initiative Issues and Guidelines," www.wisconsinbirds.org/CatsBirds.htm.

Joe Schaefer, "Impacts of Free-Ranging Pets on Wildlife," University of Florida, IFAS, http://edis.ifas.ufl.edu/UW090.

Project Bay Cat (a cooperative effort to manage feral cats in California). A tool kit for others who wish to take similar action can be obtained free from info@homelesscatnetwork.org or by calling 650-286-9013. www.cimeron.com/html/project_bay_cat.html.

Minnesota Department of Natural Resources, Minnesota's Killer Kitties, www.dnr.state.mn.us/fwt/back_issues/december98/cats.html.

What Conservationists Are Doing on a Larger Scale
Easing the Impacts of Development

Growing up in a city, I didn't notice as our population burgeoned from half a million to nearly 2 million in just twenty years. People were already everywhere; a few more didn't seem to make much difference—other than the condominiums popping up on street corners where small islands of trees had once stood.

In contrast, I spent my first year out of college living in Madison County, one of the most rural counties in North Carolina. Hot Springs, one of the county's three main towns, boasts just 639 inhabitants. Well, 640 once I got there. Madison has been this way for quite some time. Much of the farmland has been in family hands for generations. At the first community meeting I attended, I listened in fascination as locals recited their family history in the area before offering their opinion; implicitly, the legacy suggests a legitimacy of their perspective. I, the newcomer, kept quiet.

However, the county is undergoing a sudden and disastrous change as wealthy homebuyers seek pristine and quaint vacation land. A new residential and vacation development, Scenic Wolf Mountain Resort, will include the construction of 910 homes, a restaurant, a hotel, and lodge, just five miles from tiny Hot Springs—instantly quintupling the population of the area and dumping 33,000 gallons of sewage per day into the currently unsullied Laurel River. While this development will raise property values in the area, it will also raise property taxes to potentially unpayable levels, forcing some families to mortgage or sell their farms. The existing mountain roads, the local water and sewage systems, the power supply, not to mention the rural Appalachian culture, will be severely impacted by such an instant population boom.

And yet, that boom is happening. Hundreds of thousands of people are born every day. As we keep creating more and more humans, where will we put them all? This is a question that conservationists and wildlife advocates around the United States are struggling to answer. As development gathers speed, it's crucial that we preserve the few wild places and green spaces we have left. But how?

—Sadie

A Man with Answers

Just a few counties in the entire country have employees dedicated solely to answering this question. One of these is Mecklenburg County, North Carolina—home to Charlotte, one of the fastest growing cities in the nation. The scientists who work in this densely populated county's division of natural resources wage an uphill battle against explosive growth and the ravages of suburban sprawl. In our investigation of how humans and wildlife can coexist, we turned to these dedicated professionals for answers.

As manager of the department, conservation scientist Don Seriff's job is threefold: to wage war on invasive species, to document threatened native species and advocate their protection, and to encourage builders to use conservation development practices. All three of these agendas urgently require the support and cooperation of the public. We asked him to explain the particulars of his job and to tell us how citizens can support local governments' efforts to protect land—a task Seriff takes very seriously.

Kill Invasives

One of Seriff's most difficult challenges in managing nature preserves is getting rid of exotic and invasive species. An exotic is a species not native to the area, one that has been introduced from somewhere else. An invasive is an exotic species that is spreading aggressively. Exotics and invasives are catastrophic to wild areas because they displace native species and send the entire food chain topsy-turvy. If you've ever seen Japanese kudzu vines draped like a blanket over entire forests, you know what introduced species are capable of.

Seriff battles invasive species that escape from manicured lawns and city plantings. A glance at his list of public enemy number one—also known as Level I invasive species—reveals many popular yard plants, such as English Ivy, Japanese honeysuckle, autumn olive, mimosa, Chinese privet, and tree of heaven. In one city woodland, 35 of the 124 plant species are nonnative exotics—spread from yards by bird droppings, wind, and the dumping of seed-laden plant waste. Perversely, many of the most reputable birding websites recommend that birders plant berry-laden bushes, such as Beale's Oregon grape, although they are invasive exotics.

Even more ironically, many invasive species, such as Chinese lespedeza and Bradford pears, spread rampantly from plantings by state departments of transportation or city landscaping departments. They escape in woodlands by vegetative reproduction and by way of birds and other animals that eat the fruits and drop the seeds.

Seriff's crew tackles invasives by hand. In some areas, they dig and pull up targeted plants. In others, they transform the entire ecosystem back to its natural state. The division is currently restoring a native Carolina prairie—an ecosystem so destroyed that most human residents aren't aware it ever existed.

As noted above, citizens can support professionals' attack on invasives by managing their own yards carefully by removing exotic species and choosing native plant replacements.

Natively landscaped yards create corridors between habitat islands, such as city parks and urban forests. Connected habitat fragments are much more useful to wildlife than isolated fragments because animal populations in the connected fragments can

An orange sulfur butterfly on a black-eyed Susan. Don Seriff and his coworkers manage this native Carolina prairie, an ecosystem undergoing restoration. Courtesy of Alan Kneidel

interbreed, thus perhaps doubling the effective population size. (All animal species have a fixed minimum number of individuals that must be able to interbreed in order to sustain a healthy population.) A string of backyard habitats along a couple of streets might connect two patches of forest—imagine a wildlife underground railroad scurrying through your yard. These corridors are vital not only for breeding and foraging purposes, but also for the dispersal of young from their parents.

Citizens can also support large-scale efforts like the Carolina prairie by visiting, appreciating, and voicing their support for these projects. On our last visit to the piedmont prairie, in just half an hour we saw several grassland birds that are rarely seen here, including a field sparrow and a loggerhead-shrike. In a bog between the prairie and the adjacent woodland, we heard five frog species calling, an indication that these amphibians are breeding. Under old boards placed by Seriff's staff, we found snakes and salamanders seeking refuge.

Keep Records

Seriff's second task is to keep careful and thorough records of wildlife species on all undeveloped county properties. These meticulous wildlife records are the tools Seriff uses to argue for conservation when county planners envision a new soccer field or a new elementary school. When a school is needed, it *will* be built somewhere, but Seriff can tell county planners which potential site is the most expendable in terms of wildlife needs. Quite simply, he's the voice of the county's wildlife.

But Seriff's efforts at wildlife and habitat protection are more effective when the public pitches in to help. He encourages local wildlife enthusiasts and birders to report species seen on walks through county properties, from prairies to woodlands to wetlands. Seriff particularly seeks numbers and species of breeding birds—the most visible and audible vertebrate species. I worked for a summer entering these sightings reported by citizens into the county's database. Many sounded as simple as, "I saw a vesper sparrow today," but this is a seasonal sighting that tells biologists migration has begun.

Every year, Seriff's division publishes a spiral-bound volume listing the species records for all undeveloped county properties, with the dates and the names of the people who reported the sightings. These public records are one of the most effective tools Seriff uses to influence development.

Conservation Development

But even when development on a particular site is inevitable, it's not an all-or-nothing proposition; it doesn't have to mean destruction. Far from it. Seriff's job includes consulting with state and federal officials, developers, and county planners on using low-impact designs and techniques—principles that he calls conservation development. Said Seriff, "It's not really an oxymoron."

The goal of conservation development is to maintain a viable, intact, and functioning natural community that is not disturbed or impacted by human development for the long term. A human development that has true conservation value leaves at least 50 percent of the existing natural ecosystems on the land parcel unaltered and undeveloped.

Communities that are planned along these guidelines have multiple advantages for people and for animals. Such developments provide habitat for wildlife, maintain wildlife corridors between adjacent unaltered properties, protect farmland, and retain the rural character of a region. They also offer natural and wild areas that many people desire, complete with hiking trails. In addition, the green spaces improve water quality by filtering rainwater through the soil rather than sending it into storm-water drains.

Due to shorter roads and shorter utility distances, conservation development can also reduce the cost of site development, a benefit to developers.[1]

People who live in conservation development with clustered housing report social benefits too. Shared green space and walkways create social meeting places and opportunities for a cohesive neighborhood spirit.[2]

The concept of conservation development is gaining momentum among planners and developers. This approach to community design includes clustering homes to maximize the common space that's left undeveloped. The most common designs that preserve large amounts of green space include at least some multifamily housing, often condominiums. Shared walls not only minimize land use, they also reduce the amount of materials needed per home, and reduce the energy required for heating and cooling.

Conservation development also includes sensibly planning roads and lots for newly acquired land parcels, with narrower roads and the retention of native topography and native vegetation, as opposed to wide, straight roads, and unnecessary reshaping of hills and slopes, which destroys large amounts of native habitat.

Walkways between clustered homes facilitate socializing and a sense of community.

Communities with clustered homes like these often share green space and have more recreational options, such as hiking trails. Clustering conserves wildlife habitat too.

Homeowners can augment these design techniques with smaller changes on their own property. Low-impact management techniques can be as simple as using water-permeable paving for parking lots and driveways. Permeable pavement can include porous asphalt and concrete, lattice paving stones filled with turf, and chamfered paving stones with spaces between stones. These options, best suited for low-traffic areas, allow storm water to infiltrate the soil underneath rather than shoot over the surface into storm drains that feed streams with heated and dirty water. Households can also add rain gardens or bioretention areas to yards and lawns—again to encourage the slow seepage of rain into soil, and from the soil into our groundwater that replenishes streams with cool and filtered water.

Residents can also support conservationists' efforts by seeking out conservation developments when they move. Beware, however, said Seriff, that some new subdivisions that are marketed as conservation developments really aren't. One development in our area that was promoted as a conservation development, for instance, really retained only 20 percent of the natural habitat, even though the site includes a population of an endangered flowering plant. Another development nearby, also self-advertised as a conservation community, features huge single-family homes widely dispersed on large lots—the antithesis of clustering, which is optimal for conservation. If you're thinking about moving, check out *Practical Ecology for Planners, Developers, and Citizens* by Dan L. Perlman and Jeffrey C. Milder for more information on

how to recognize good conservation development when you see it.

Speak Up

If you don't have a yard to tackle, or if moving is beyond your means, there's still plenty you can do. "Tell them to bug the government," Seriff told us earnestly. "Speaking out is the most important thing." Just a handful of calls—three or four calls about a certain issue—can seem like an avalanche of interest to some governmental offices, he said.

Voting is also important. In local elections, voter turnout is often as low as 10 percent, and just a few votes can decide issues such as crucial funding for natural resource and land-use plans.

Keep an Eye Out

Be vigilant. Departments and agencies assigned to protect our natural resources—air, water, habitat, and wildlife—don't have enough staff to monitor everything. A watchful public can help tremendously in forcing businesses to adhere to regulations. The appropriate governmental departments do respond to complaints, Seriff said, and they appreciate the information. What's more, calling communicates to local governments that citizens care and are concerned. This makes a difference when shaping the direction a community wants to take.

Call Water Quality

Call the water quality department, Seriff said, if you see something unusual in a stream. If a normally clear stream turns red or brown,

it's probably carrying sediment from development upstream. It isn't unusual for a subcontractor to illegally channel waste into a stream to save money, and if no one reports it, the problem can remain undetected for years. If a stream smells funny, or bubbles, or has a strange color, someone may be clandestinely dumping. Seriff told us about a local shopping center that was pumping all of its waste—from sinks, toilets, and floor drains—into a nearby stream and went undetected for years.

If you see a neighbor pouring motor oil, antifreeze, or paint into a storm drain on the side of a street, tell him that it feeds directly into a stream—most people don't know that, nor do they know that pouring such substances into storm drains or onto the ground is illegal. If it continues, report it to the water quality department. According to Seriff, mobile car wash businesses are major offenders. They travel to their customers and generate quite a volume of liquid waste that runs into storm drains and hence streams, and eventually into the source for our drinking water. If you see one in operation in the street or a driveway flushing wastewater into a storm drain, call water quality. Some of the major commercial car washes with their own sites have systems for recycling their water and treating their waste. He mentioned Auto Bell, in particular, in a positive light.

Call Erosion Control

Seriff recommended calling your erosion control department if a stream bank is eroding into a stream, or if any yard or property is eroding into a stream. All developments must meet a governmental code for erosion control. Sediment is the single biggest pollutant of surface waters that provide municipal drinking water.

Call Natural Resources

Hopefully, conservation and natural resources departments will welcome information about wildlife sightings of any kind. They also field calls from citizens concerned about wildlife safety, such as when wild turkeys, coyotes, or bears wander into neighborhoods. They appreciate calls about illegal activities, such as hunting on nature preserves or park properties and the collecting of plants from protected properties. These calls help the natural resources staff protect our remaining undeveloped land and wildlife.

Take Note of Positive Trends

In a world of dismaying environmental news, sometimes progress seems too good to be true. But Seriff has quite a few success stories to encourage his department and other conservationists in their quest to protect wildlife and habitat. "Wild turkeys have moved back into the county since reintroductions in surrounding counties fifteen years ago. They're breeding in many nature preserves," Seriff told us. And in 2004, after stream-restoration projects in the city, a variety of wildlife species returned to suburban creeks on their own, including spiny soft-shell turtles, redbreast sunfish, belted kingfishers, and even river otters. "It's great that our citizens have a chance to see these beautiful creatures swimming and playing in our creeks again. The return of otters [in particular] is an important sign of our increasing sensitivity to water quality and our success in cleaning up our local rivers and streams,"[3] Seriff said. But we shouldn't get complacent. Streams are still threatened by too much sediment, excessive runoff from pavement, pollutants from lawn treatments, and so on. "It's a tough world for wildlife," said Seriff, "especially [for] those dependent on clean water."[4]

After talking with Seriff, we have a better understanding of the challenges facing wildlife in a world of expanding human development. No matter how motivated and industrious, no matter how well funded, government officials can't protect wildlife and their habitat alone. The public has to help, and now we know better how to do just that.

Notes

1. University of Illinois Extension, Local Community Resources, "Cluster/Conservation Development," www.urbanext.uiuc.edu/lcr/LGIEN2000-0010.html.
2. Goodhue Land Design, "Alternative Models," www.goodhuelanddesign.com/4alternatives.html#conservation.
3. Wendy Waite, "River Otters Return to Briar Creek: Mecklenburg Lures Wildlife Back to Cleaner Stream," *The Charlotte Observer*, September 7, 2004.
4. Ibid.

Additional Resources

Environmental Protection Agency, Green Communities, Beneficial Landscaping, www.epa.gov/greenkit/landscap.htm.
The Nature Conservancy, The Global Invasive Species Team, http://tncweeds.ucdavis.edu/worst.html.
U.S. Department of Agriculture Forest Service, Invasive Species Program, www.fs.fed.us/invasivespecies/index.shtml.
U.S. Department of Agriculture National Agricultural Library, National Invasive Species Information Center, www.invasivespeciesinfo.gov/plants/main.shtml.

Saving Streams

Suds and Slicks

Growing up, I lived in a house on a hill as the youngest kid in a household that was often in chaos. My refuge from the bedlam was the meandering rocky stream in the lower part of the yard. I waded in the riffles, peeking under rocks and finding crayfish and dusky salamanders in the cool, clear water.

During heavy rains, the creek flooded—the lower yard was a naturally occurring floodplain. I loved the drama of the floods, but my dad didn't. He had the stream dredged and straightened so it didn't flood anymore. There were no more salamanders, either. I still poked around in the stream, but it wasn't the same species-rich, complex ecosystem. It was just a channel, a straight shot to the much wider and deeper Sugar Creek at the end of the street, which had also been dredged and straightened. Sugar Creek was so polluted, we were forbidden to play anywhere near it. I remember the suds and slicks and trash carried along in its waters, and the rusty nail I stepped on while walking along its banks. I remember the foul smell too.

That was many years ago. Today, Sugar Creek is unrecognizable as the stinky creek of my youth. The creek is still huge, but it is no longer a straight-shot flood-control channel. The stream now twists and turns—it even has pools and riffles! The bank slopes gently down to the water now, and is covered with native plantings to stabilize the soil and stop erosion. Best of all, the invertebrates are back, and with them, the fish, ducks, soft-shell turtles, and river otters. This restored stream goes right through the middle of town. It's now part of the city parks' greenway system, and a shaded bike and hiking trail follows the course of the creek. The buildings along portions of the stream have been torn down and converted to green space, allowing groundwater to recharge during rains. You'd never guess what a wasteland it was years ago.

This is no coincidence, of course. Rather, the changes in Sugar Creek have been the work of a dedicated stream-restoration team, headed by environmental engineer Shawn Wilkerson. We sat down with Wilkerson to learn about how human development impacts streams and what citizens can do to mitigate it.

The two biggest problems Wilkerson sees are stream straightening and pavement. "An undisturbed stream," he told us, "is usually a meandering stream. The meanders create different kinds of habitats—riffles and pools—that play different roles in the stream ecosystem." A riffle is shallow water that gurgles over rocks, picking up oxygen, which

is, of course, vital to stream organisms. Stone fly and mayfly larvae and hundreds of other macro-invertebrates live in riffles, Wilkerson said, while the deeper pools between riffles are good fish habitat. A healthy stream has trees along the bank that drop leaves and woody debris into the water. These are essential sources of food for the macro-invertebrates, which in turn feed the fish, salamanders, frogs, birds, turtles, snakes, small mammals, and other wildlife that depend upon streams. Without a healthy stream, there wouldn't be a woodland community.

When humans first settle a rural area, "they clear out all the trees and usually straighten the stream, and they move it way over to the side of the valley," Wilkerson said, so the stream doesn't interfere with farming. Straightening destroys the riffle and pool habitats, and the entire riparian community collapses. If the trees have been removed, there's no riparian buffer or vegetation in the bank, so the banks erode and you get sediment inputs in the stream. "Most people attribute sediment to construction sites and runoff, where people have cleared the land. But a lot of sediment comes from unstable stream banks that are eroding." As mentioned above, sediment is the single biggest pollutant to our drinking water.

Urban streams have the additional problem of pavement, which keeps rain from infiltrating the ground and recharging groundwater. Instead, dirty rainwater runs along the pavement, picking up oil, gasoline, dirt, and heat before plunging into the creek through a storm drain.

This group of birders enjoys the city's greenway system, which includes green space and trails along streams, boardwalks over wetland areas, and stream-restoration projects. Courtesy of Mecklenburg County Division of Natural Resources

Pavement also inhibits streams from refilling naturally. "If it hasn't rained in a week, where is the water in a stream coming from? Have you ever thought about that?" Wilkerson asked us. Without waiting for us to respond, he answered his own question. "It's coming from groundwater. Groundwater is water from the storm ten days ago that has soaked into the ground, slowly moved through the ground, where it's filtered by soil and rocks, and is slowly seeping out to streams. That's nice clean freshwater. If you pave over a big portion of your watershed, there's no way for water to soak into the ground. Even if you have a nice meandering stream with a riparian buffer," said Wilkerson, "if it's surrounded by pavement, it's in trouble."

Powerful Grassroots

In North Carolina, where Wilkerson works, a troubled stream has more chance of recovery than in most places. The reason for this, according to Wilkerson, is grassroots organizing.

"Ten years ago, when I was getting my masters degree," he recollected, "ten of us who were interested in stream quality got together in somebody's basement and started this thing called the Hydrology Task Force. We started doing research on how to get funding, getting agencies that fund stream work to look at our ideas, and pretty soon the task force turned into the Stream Restoration Institute, which is now at North Carolina State University. The last SRI conference we had, in Winston Salem, had over 200 attendees from all over the country. This year, instead of the NCSRI conference, it's going to be the Southeastern SRI conference.

"We were ten individuals who shared a vision. We didn't always coordinate perfectly, but we all pushed it in our own way. I pushed it through the city of Charlotte and Mecklenburg County while I was working there. Will pushed it through education at the university. Angela pushed it by getting grants and getting federal groups interested in it. And today, North Carolina is one of the best-funded states for watershed protection and restoration work. I had no idea it would get to this point. I think it's a good example of how something that starts at the grassroots level—a few people in somebody's basement—can, with persistence, grow and take hold."

What Can We Do?

This same tactic works in every state. Even if you're not a water-quality professional, you can organize in your community. Join an advocacy group or a land conservancy and help them seek funding for environmental restoration projects. The Waterkeeper Alliance, for example, has affiliates in every state.

Vote for city bonds to support water-protection projects, and vote for local candidates who support them.

Support the preservation of green space in general. Specifically, support low-impact-development legislation, such as a stream-buffer policy. This restricts how much of the buffer around a stream can be removed when creating a subdivision. "Keeping wooded

Land Use—Green Choices for Yards, Streams, and Habitats

buffers intact along streams, the riparian corridor, and leaving the streams alone is key," said Wilkerson. This is not a costly priority—a stream buffer network that extends a distance of 100 feet on each side of every stream takes up only 5 percent of the land in a watershed.[1]

Wilkerson also suggested supporting an ordinance that requires developers to protect groundwater too. Developers or homeowners can protect groundwater by creating infiltration basins (also referred to as rain gardens or bioretention areas) so rainwater can seep back into the ground rather than running into storm drains that feed streams with hot and polluted water. We can also encourage legislation to preserve extensive wetlands, which are disappearing to development, along with their indigenous wildlife.

"What kind of choices might homeowners have on their own property?" we asked Wilkerson. In response, he described his experience with his own new home, which he built as in-fill in an older, established neighborhood close to downtown. "All the runoff from our lot and 90 percent of the runoff from our driveway, instead of draining to the storm drain in the street and right into a stream, runs to a grassy low point in the back of the lot, and then into a natural area, then runs through somebody else's backyard and through their natural area, so it can infiltrate. It was our way of creating our own bioretention area."

Finally, to echo Don Seriff, keep an eye on streams in your area and report abuses to your city or county's water quality department.

Note

1. Center for Watershed Protection, "Clean Water Project," www.cwp.org/watershed_quiz.htm.

Community Voice

Alan Kneidel: Vipers and Tanagers—A Chance to Heal Scarred Land

Most streams have been altered in some manner by humans, whether straightened by farming, poisoned by fertilizers and invasives, or removed entirely. I'm a full-time student at the University of North Carolina, but during the last two summers, I've worked for a stream-restoration firm. Our job is to help undo these alterations and return these waterways to their natural state. By doing this, we reduce the erosion and scouring of the land while improving habitat for native flora and fauna.

Our firm designs new stream channels, and by studying the topography of the land, we can determine which style to implement. To begin such a project, we must first assess the existing conditions of the stream that we are potentially restoring. This often involves walking the length of the stream—in the water.

One of my most vivid memories of such an outing is from rural Rockingham County, North Carolina. It was mid-June, with steaming heat in the low nineties. The tannin-filled water was up to my waist as I slogged and crawled through laurel thickets, machete in hand to clear a route. Eastern cottonmouth vipers as thick as my forearms lined the banks, at times sitting at eye level, only inches away. Choruses of warblers and tanagers sang above us, occasionally offering a dashing glimpse of gold or scarlet. At the end of each day, I passed over my scratches, more focused on the poison ivy rashes and itching bites of fire ants, chiggers, and mosquitoes. This particular water system was completely pristine, and we were happy to recommend to the county that it be preserved rather than altered or restored in any way.

On some trips, while doing this grueling kind of field work, I have questioned whether I can handle day after day of such exertion. But inevitably, I've come to the conclusion that it's worth the effort. At times, I've been able to work at stream sites that our company has already restored. One site was

106

adjacent to some farmland in the mountains of North Carolina near Morganton. Farmers had long ago degraded the stream channel by straightening it and pushing it to the side of the fields, as is typical on farmland, destroying the riffles and pools essential to a healthy stream. The stream banks were choked with invasive bamboo and Chinese privet. But the subsequent stream-restoration project had removed the bamboo and privet and restored the natural meanders with a new channel, full of riffles and root wads (bundle of roots introduced to a stream during restoration). The root wads and riffles create habitat for the fish, invertebrates, and salamanders that will return to a restored stream. An assortment of native plants and trees had been planted along the new banks and nearby wetland. The stream and the surrounding land would now be protected. Here I realized that a bit of grueling work was little sacrifice when the reward was the restoration of stream habitats that all wildlife depend on, and the preservation of the riparian corridor, hopefully forever.

Land Conservancies

In the interviews with Don Seriff and Shawn Wilkerson, we identified lots of actions citizens can take to protect wildlife habitats and water quality, from choosing native plants to keeping cats indoors to using pervious paving stones for driveways.

Another way to participate in conservation efforts is to become a member of an environmental advocacy group or land trust. Advocacy groups such as the Sierra Club get involved in political matters, endorse candidates, and pressure corporations and government officials.

Land trusts such as The Nature Conservancy are the behind-the-scenes partners to the highly visible advocacy groups. While advocacy groups are very vocal in seeking public support for their agendas, a land trust quietly works with families and businesses to permanently protect land from development.

To learn more about how these organizations work, we tracked down Sonia Perillo,

assistant director of the very successful Catawba Lands Conservancy. During our conversation, she explained the inner landscape of the land trust world—their goals, their challenges, and their strategies for saving land, and, most importantly, why it's so crucial that citizens support their work.

Communities Are Making Their Own Decisions

Perillo sees land conservancies as a keystone of grassroots activism. During the seven years she has worked in the conservancy world, the number of trusts nationwide has increased by more than 50 percent. "The reason for this increase," she told us, "is that more and more people are starting to see changes in their own communities. So local groups have formed all over the country to protect the most important natural areas and open spaces right in their own communities. It's a powerful thing for communities to make their own decisions about what land they want saved."

A land conservancy can acquire land through purchase or through conservation easements. With an easement, the owner maintains ownership of the property, but signs a contract waiving some development rights. The owner of a forest, for example, might sign an easement agreeing that the forest could never be logged. This contract is permanent; it accompanies the land when it is sold.

According to Perillo, easements are harder to come by as property values rise. "It used to be somebody telling their children, 'You're going to get the land. You'll be able to build a house on that hill over there, but you won't be able to develop it.' You weren't taking that much value out of their pockets. But now, it's just obscene. There was a property in Union County that just sold for $110,000 an acre—not a lot, just a property for development, twenty-five or thirty acres. It's crazy!"

For this reason, building relationships with landowners is the most important and the most difficult aspect of what a land conservancy does. "These are really huge decisions these families are making about permanent land conservation," Perillo reflected. "If they've owned the land for six generations, and they're the one that's going to decide how their kids will manage it and how their children's children will manage it, that's a huge decision. It's very challenging to work with multiple generations and the elders' concerns about tying their children's hands. But it's so satisfying … to be able to take part in their process of doing that."

Like Seriff and the Division of Natural Resources, land conservancies also work with developers to promote conservation-development practices. According to Perillo, "Our actions are sometimes different from national-scale wilderness protection. We're saving small family farms, and in urban communities it may be only a tenth of an acre lot for community gardens—but it's communities deciding what's important for them to protect." And even these small spaces are crucial in rapidly developing areas. The fourteen-county region where Perillo works loses forty-one acres per day to development.

The faster this development happens, the more crucial the work of a land conservancy. Conservancies often have an advantage over advocacy groups because they are regarded as less threatening by the nonconservationist public. Cooperation is often the result of working for years to build a relationship with developers "to bring them to understand that we're not going to protest their developments in the area. That's not what we do. So we are available and familiar to them when they have a project that has conservation value. If we fought their past developments, those agreements wouldn't happen, and the land they have available wouldn't get protected. So we can't really cross that advocacy line."

Cooperation from developers and the public is vital for land conservancy work. But equally important is the participation of folks who don't have land to contribute or a subdivision to build—folks like you. For the average citizen, Perillo has a checklist of steps to take to support local land conservation.

Location Is Key

First of all, choose wisely where to live. Perillo faced a struggle with this herself. "When my husband and I were looking for our first house to buy," she recollected, "I said some things that everyone around us thought were strange, like, 'I can't live in the Mountain Island Lake watershed, where the city's drinking water comes from. I just can't do it.'" She is all too aware that development leads to fuel leaks, dirty storm water runoff into streams, and the pollution of streams, rivers, and lakes from construction sediment.

What do you know about the water system in your area? Where does your drinking water come from? How might your neighborhood impact that system? These are questions that most homeowners never ponder.

Suburban sprawl also greatly affects land conservation. Perillo continued, "In the seven years we've been here, I've seen plenty of cow pastures converted to subdivisions. ... We spent about $138,000 on a 1,300-square-foot house close in to the city. For that much in a new development farther out, we might have gotten 2,000 square feet with a nice yard and neighbors with two-and-half kids and a dog, but I know what the impact is." As nice as big suburban yards and wide streets are, compact city living is a much greener use of space and is more likely to leave undeveloped areas alone.

Demand Green Space

Be vocal. Perillo implores citizens to ask for what they want in regard to land use. She offered an example: "Even within developments, residents could demand open space instead of swimming pools and tennis courts. Everything is consumer driven. If people moved to areas where developers save more than the fifty-foot required buffer around a lake or stream and have trails and those sorts of things, eventually that message gets through to the people who make decisions about land-development patterns."

It's the same message we've heard about food and clothes and fuel and timber products and everything else: we all vote for sustainable or unsustainable practices with our consumer dollars. Perillo confirms that.

Get Political

Voting with ballots is crucial. One person's vote has a huge impact on questions of land use because all zoning and land-use regulations are local, not state and federal, decisions. Many people don't bother to vote in these small elections, so your opinion is all the more powerful. The Sierra Club (www.sierraclub.org), The League of Women Voters (www.lwv.org), and the League of Conservation Voters (www.lcv.org) all offer online information about local political candidates who support conservation legislation.

Tax Write-Offs

Finally, financial support of land conservancies is always helpful, and contributions are tax deductible. The donation of land and conservation easements are also tax deductible. These big deductions can be a major incentive for some landowners. The Land Trust Alliance has established an independent accreditation program that gives landowners and donors a way to ensure that any local land trust that they are interested in partnering with is really solid. For more information, see the Land Trust Accreditation Commission website (www.lta.org/accreditation/).

Where Will She Find Tadpoles?

As a mom and as a person who enjoys a walk in the woods, what does land conservation mean to Perillo?

"The area is developing so fast," Perillo said with a sigh. "I want my daughter to have places to look for tadpoles, and I don't know where that might be. I want her to be able

to enjoy natural places, to have clean air and water and green spaces to play in. And trails to hike on. I want her to value the environment and to be able to experience it."

Perillo made a good point that we sometimes forget: preserving clean water, air, and land is important for the sake of wildlife and healthy ecosystems, but humans, too, need and benefit from thriving green space. Fortunately for us, professional conservationists will be there to remind us.

said that he wrote his famous field guides to birds because he felt strongly that "out of awareness comes concern."

Do the people playing golf near this small woodland or the people speeding along the beltway even know that something as glorious as this little bird exists? And if they did, would it make a difference in how we might plan the conversion of the woodland into a recreation area? I don't know. But I do know that for me, hooded warblers are special. That's why I made a point to submit this sighting to the county conservation science office. They play a role in determining how county property will be developed. It's comforting to know that this warbler's voice has been heard.

Community Voice
Ken Kneidel: Woodland Voices

On more than one occasion, I've recognized that I'm happiest when I'm walking alone in the woods. Not that I'm antisocial; I just get such pleasure from being outdoors with wildlife.

Last summer, my best day came while walking in a small woodland surrounding an abandoned farm near my home. Our county is experiencing some of the fastest population growth in the country. As I walked along in this particular woodland, I suddenly heard the "weeta-wee-teo" of a hooded warbler. I stopped abruptly, astonished and thrilled to the

core. I knew from regular birding in the county that this was a rare find. Although hooded warblers are relatively common in extensive undeveloped areas, I was sure that I was hearing one of the very few breeding pairs left in my urban county.

Within a mile, a golf course had just been built and the city's new outer beltway had been constructed. I believe there are plans to turn the woods where I was walking into soccer fields as well. Soccer crowds and hooded warblers certainly won't mix. This made the moment all the more special. If only the developers who trade woodlands for malls and highways would take the time to look at a hooded warbler. The bird's brilliant yellow plumage sets off a black mask that covers the head and throat—such a handsome contrast. The great birder Roger Tory Peterson

Chapter Four

Food 101—Your Diet Matters More Than You Think

Contemplate, for the moment, all the environmental problems you read about in the newspaper: deforestation, climate change, pollution of our rivers and drinking water, erosion, mass extinctions—let your imagination wander. Now think about the underlying causes that connect all these serious problems.

Would you believe us if we said our *food* is one of the biggest causes?

It's true, as you'll see in the pages ahead. From the heavy emphasis on meat to the negligent use of our land, the American food industry is launching a serious assault on our planet and our future.

Efficient for Consumers and for Corporations

Our food system is remarkably convenient from a customer's point of view. We can pop by the grocery store on our way home from work and find meals available in every degree of readiness. From microwaving a frozen dinner to dumping the contents of a can into a saucepan, food preparation could hardly be more efficient for the consumer. The system is also extremely efficient for agribusiness companies, which are making record profits, allowing them to expand overseas.

Chemical Management

To make their record profits and to deliver food so cheaply and conveniently to consumers, the giant food corporations have changed the face of farming and of food production.

They have not changed it for the better.

Nationwide, small family farms are rapidly being engulfed by corporate monoliths. In 1900, the United States had 10 million farms; today, we have 2 million.[1] While these large factory farms are more efficient than their smaller predecessors, their high output is possible only with the intensive aid of chemical pesticides, herbicides, fertilizers, antibiotics, and genetically modified crops. These methods are efficient in the short term, but disregard the true costs to American society and to the planet, as reflected in the degradation and depletion of our natural resources.

In general, corporations are not interested in sustainability. The chief executive officer of today will not be held accountable for the state of the world's ecosystems or soil health of our farms twenty-five years from now. Instead, CEOs are motivated by the annual report on profits for their shareholders.

Wandering Genes

Food corporations are toying with our future in more sinister and covert ways as well. In order to grow plants more resistant to insects and crops that withstand long transport, corporations are genetically modifying our seeds. Modified genes disperse to all sorts of unintended targets, polluting other seed stocks, as well as natural ecosystems, with genes whose effects are little understood. Nor do we understand the health effects of eating genetically modified foods. And yet, we are all eating genetically modified foods and funding their development without even knowing it. Like farming with chemicals, these methods may increase profits in the short term, but the future costs to worldwide ecosystems and to future seed banks far outweigh any short-term gains.

Too Much Truckin'

The transporting of corporate foods is among the most detrimental of current food practices. The average food item in the supermarket has traveled hundreds or even thousands of miles to reach us. The plastic packaging, the refrigeration, and the trucks and planes needed for carrying food long distances take a heavy toll on our remaining fossil fuels and generate the smokestack and tailpipe emissions that are warming our planet. In this section, we'll consider the merits of shopping for locally produced food.

Manure on the Move

Land use is another hot potato we'll consider in the following pages. Raising livestock and their feed crops uses much more land and water than is needed for raising plant-based foods. In addition, the demand for animal products and the corporate competition to provide them cheaply lead to farming practices that damage our agricultural land and water, often irreversibly. Confined animal operations create waste-management problems with no good solutions. Waste inevitably washes into rivers and groundwater, with ill effects for wildlife and well users.

Just Ahead …

In this chapter, we'll examine all of these issues. They all have solutions that we can easily contribute to. Not only can we make different choices for ourselves, we can shape the future of the food industry through selective buying. We can choose to fund producers that are using sustainable methods and whose products are safe and nutritious. Or we can choose to fund corporations that are out for profit alone by whatever means—corporations that disregard the damaging effects of their methods and their products on our bodies, our planet, and our future.

Note
1. Michael Pollen and Ira Flato, "Science Friday," National Public Radio, November 24, 2006.

Seafood—Here's the Catch

It's early morning. You step outside to get the newspaper, and when you come back inside, you find that your toddler is not where you left him at the breakfast table. Running through the house, your heart pounding, you find him on the back porch playing with a bottle of fabric dye. With a lurching heart, you realize he has eaten some of it. Frantically, you grab the bottle. The label reads "*POISON*: Decreases food intake, growth, and fertility rates; causes damage to liver, spleen, kidney, and heart; inflicts lesions on skin, eyes, lungs, and bones; causes genetic mutations and developmental abnormalities; carcinogenic to the liver and thyroid; and causes tumors in the lungs, breasts, and ovaries."[1]

Gasping in horror, you drop the bottle,

grab your child, and run to call Poison Control. As you grab the phone, you wake up in a cold sweat. What a terrible nightmare!

Relieved that it was only a dream, that evening you take little Jimmy out for a celebratory dinner. For a treat, you order a special hors d'oeuvre: a platter of thinly sliced smoked salmon. How delicious it looks. You urge your little one to eat up, reminding him that the fish is full of healthy oils, protein, vitamins, and minerals. What you don't know is that it's also laden with the very same poison from your dream—only this time, the nightmare is real.

The unfortunate reality is that malachite green, the chemical described above, is only one of scores of toxic substances contaminating our seafood and waterways. If this is news to you, as it was to us, you better listen up. There are a few things you should know.

Our fish and seafood are produced in two ways. One way is by harvesting wild fish from their natural environment using trawlers or other mass-collection techniques. The second is through aquaculture in which fish are farmed in crowded indoor tanks or offshore sea cages. The aquaculture industry is skyrocketing; by 2007, more than half of food fish will be farmed rather than wild, an increase from just 3.9 percent in 1970.[2]

In this changing market it's important for consumers to know the difference between the two types of seafood as they have drastically different impacts on both the environment and your health.

Scraping the Oceans Clean

I remember catching sunfish with a bamboo fishing pole at my granddad's lakehouse as a little kid. There's nothing wrong with lassoing your own fish from time to time, at least in terms of environmental impact. However, rustling up 30 billion pounds of seafood per year is a whole different ballgame.[3]

In order to meet burgeoning demand, wild fishing consists not of lines and poles, but of trawling, blast fishing, and poison fishing. Bottom trawlers drag weighted nets across the ocean floor, scraping up everything in their path and destroying entire ecosystems. Blast fishing and poison fishing target entire areas, killing indiscriminately, while only a small fraction of the kill is actually used. In the Indo-Pacific, blast fishing has destroyed precious coral reefs that were once highly productive and diverse ecosystems as well as a sustainable livelihood for local peoples.[4]

These mass-fishing techniques have sacrificed caution in the name of efficiency. Decades of overfishing have depleted wild fish populations to the point that, currently, most stocks of wild fish are classified as "fully exploited," with more and more categorized as "overexploited" or "in decline."[5] Many of these populations are not even the targeted food species; they are merely the unfortunate bycatch. In fact, nearly one-fourth of the world's fish catch—20 million tons a year—is bycatch, or unwanted fish that are the wrong species, the wrong size, or otherwise undesirable.[6] These fish are captured, killed, and tossed back into the waves. This bycatch needlessly destroys fish populations and creates vast expanses of decomposing waste in the water. The magnitude of this is hard to imagine. For every shrimp caught, for instance, 1,000 other organisms are caught and thrown away.[7] Think about that while you eat your next shrimp cocktail.

On a recent visit to the fishing village of Sekiu on Washington's Pacific coast, we met a salmon fisherman who told us about throwing back 700 dead dogfish, bycatch from a single haul with a gill net. (See the following sidebar for more information on gill nets.)

The harvesting of wild fish has ripple effects far beyond the obvious, damaging entire ecosystems, including seabirds and marine mammals. Marine communities worldwide are vanishing as a result of these practices.

Gill Nets and Longlines

The albatross, a magnificent bird with a wingspan of up to seven feet, is one of many oceanic birds in serious trouble from the mass-fishing techniques of today. If you've been to the Pacific Northwest, you've probably spotted dozens of oceanic birds from coastal ferries and cliffs. These birds spend most of their lives floating on the ocean and swimming underwater for fish. Many species, such as puffins, guillemots, auklets, murres, and murrelets, stay relatively close to shore. But pelagic birds, such as albatrosses, shearwaters, and petrels, stay miles offshore and are seldom seen closer to land.

All seabirds of the Pacific Northwest, both coastal and pelagic species, are feeling the impact of the fishing industry—some more than others. As we learned while staying in the remote salmon-fishing village of Sekiu, Washington, the marbled murrelet is endangered by the gill nets that snag fish by the gill covers.

Nets can be tied together to stretch for 3,000 meters. In the coastal straits of Sekiu and Neah Bay, gill nets are submerged to catch salmon as they fish toward their spawning rivers. One Sekiu fisherman confirmed that gill nets trap much more than their targeted species; the bycatch includes other fish species, seals, sea otters, and diving seabirds such as the marbled murrelet. All the air-breathing species drown; most of the fish bycatch are killed by the hauling-in process, and are thrown back dead. Gill nets are also commonly set in open waters where they catch and drown porpoises and whales.

Longlines are another fishing technique that endangers offshore pelagic seabirds such as albatrosses, as well as whales, dolphins, and porpoises. A longline is a fishing line up to *60 miles long* with up to 30,000 shorter lines with baited hooks trailing from it. Seabirds often take the bait and are then dragged underwater and drowned.

For more about the dangers of gill nets, longline fishing, and other mass-fishing techniques, see the Cetacean Bycatch Resource Center (CBRC)[1,2] and the American Bird Conservancy.[3] This CBRC report on longlines concludes with a list of measures you can take as a citizen to protect wildlife from mass-fishing techniques.

Notes
1. Cetacean Bycatch Resource Center, Gillnets, www.cetacean bycatch.org/gear_gillnet.cfm.
2. Cetacean Bycatch Resource Center, Longline, www.ceta ceanbycatch.org/gear_longline.cfm.
3. American Bird Conservancy, "Sudden Death on the High Seas. Longline Fishing: A Global Catastrophe for Seabirds," www.abcbirds.org/policy/seabird_report.pdf.

The Global Fish Market

Human communities are also heavily impacted by the indiscriminate harvesting of wild fish. When fish populations are depleted, families that fished using modest and sustainable methods are forced to change jobs and relocate. Traditional ways of life along the world's coasts are disappearing.

Developing nations, mostly China and southeast Asia, are responsible for two-thirds of wild fish harvesting.[8] Most of their catch is shipped for long distances, often to other countries, wasting huge amounts of energy, fossil fuels, and packaging. While these countries earn money from exporting seafood, the profits benefit large companies rather than the traditional fishermen. The cost of certification in accord with international safety standards costs hundreds of thousands of dollars a year and can be afforded only by large corporations in developing economies. Economists predict that as current demand for seafood increases, "large-scale, capital-intensive operations are likely to emerge in developing countries at the expense of traditional and small-scale commercial fishers."[9] This is what you are supporting when you buy imported fish.

Poison in Pens

Well, you might think, *wild fishing is destructive, but at least farmed fish are contained in pens. You don't have to scrape up the entire ocean searching for them, and we can grow them right here in the United States. Right?*

Wrong. While the fish may be physically contained in pens and cages, their diet and waste heavily impact the wildlife around them. Nearly one-third of wild-caught fish are ground into feed for captive fish. This greatly increases the amount of wild fish that must be caught in order to maintain the seafood industry, and therefore also increases the destructive wild-fishing practices described above.

And sadly, much of this fish food goes to waste. Laced with antibiotics, pesticides, growth hormones, dyes, and other chemicals, the uneaten food rots in the water. In both indoor tanks and offshore pens, fish are packed very tightly. The regulation of sixty kilograms of fish per cubic meter of water for trout, for instance, comes out to twenty-seven one-foot-long fish in a tank the size of a bathtub.[10] You can imagine how concentrated

the feces and uneaten food must be with so little extra space.

In sea cages, as the ocean water laps through the bars of the pen, it carries away the excess feed, feces, and fertilizer. The antibiotics, pesticides, and other drugs in this waste are released into the ocean environment, poisoning wild species. In fact, 80 percent of antibiotics used on farmed fish wind up in the aquatic environment. A recent study of antibacterial residues, as reported in the scientific journal *Aquaculture,* found that wild crabs contain thirty-eight times the acceptable limit of oxytetracycline, a potent antibiotic.[11] And those are the *wild* crabs. Can you imagine how high the concentration must be in the animals that were intentionally exposed to it?

Occasionally, the farmed fish escape into the wild, introducing nonnative genes into local fish populations—genes that are unlikely to benefit a finely tuned ecological balance. Genetically modified fish have been developed but are not yet on the market. If this changes in the near future, crossbreeding could become an even bigger concern than it is now.

Aquaculture damages marine habitats as well. Thailand, for instance, has lost 17 percent of its mangrove forests to shrimp farms in just six years.[12] If you've ever seen a mangrove forest you know what a magical and unique ecosystem it is. Spidery, finger-like roots grow right down into the smooth black water, creating a dense, gnarled forest seemingly floating on the water's surface. One spring break, two friends and I rented

a canoe and paddled through the mangroves of the Everglades in south Florida. As we navigated these secret canals, I felt that I had slipped into another universe—a savage, wild universe, untouched by human hands.

Unfortunately, that could hardly be farther from the truth. Fish farms have degraded hundreds of thousands of hectares of this unique habitat, though we depend on these fragile forests to filter water, protect water quality, harbor newly hatched fish, and maintain healthy aquatic systems. They also shelter many unique species, from magnificent frigate birds to the highly endangered royal Bengal tiger. As mangroves are destroyed to make way for fish farms, such species are vanishing and water quality is declining.

Regretting All Those Fish Sticks ...

Fish-farming veteran Dr. Gloria Brady* opened my eyes to the world of aquaculture. Over a pancake breakfast, she spoke to me candidly about her experience as a microbiologist in the pathology lab at a fish-processing plant in the Pacific Northwest.

The factory made surimi, she explained, which is basically "the Spam of the fish world." Fish are ground up and compressed into fish sticks, imitation crab, and other processed fish products. "The fish come in on boats, where they're held in tanks in the hull." She gestured in the air, marking the dimensions of an imaginary ship. "They suck them out of these tanks through tubes and spew them onto a conveyor belt, which dumps them into a holding tank in a silo at the plant. Some fish are alive at this point, but some are already dead."

"One day," Brady continued, "the spinning device in the finishing vat got stuck. The foreman stuck his foot in the vat and gave it a kick to get it going again, and his boot came off! We watched as it got ground up into the surimi. I kept looking for

* This person's name has been changed to protect her identity.

pieces of rubber in that batch, but we never saw that boot again. I guess it ended up in somebody's fish sticks somewhere."

Just where that boot did end up is hard to say. After processing, the surimi is shipped to Japan, where it is formed into fish sticks. "But why?" Brady wondered and shrugged. "The Japanese don't eat fish sticks. And neither do I." She shook her head. "I will not eat imitation crab. I will not eat fish sticks."

I raised my eyebrows. What compelled her to make this decision? "Well," she explained, "if you'd seen what I saw ... You see, I was required to check for salmonella, but out of my own interest I liked to test for other things as well. I kept a notebook of my own where I would keep track of what I found. They were very paranoid about that notebook. They were afraid it would get out."

And no wonder too. To her surprise, Brady's investigations uncovered strains of hepatitis in the surimi. When she investigated the source, she discovered a leak from the men's bathroom running straight into the finishing vat. She also observed that captains, from time to time, pee into the fish holding tanks. "I don't know why," she said with a half-smile. "It's a fish captain thing."

Brady later also discovered that the surimi were tainted with cholera. "This came from water from the bay," she told me. "They pull water out of the bay to fill the tanks, [but] if you don't draw it from far enough out, it's contaminated with all kinds of nasty things."

When she confronted officials about her findings, she said "they just shrugged and said, 'It doesn't matter. They're going to fry 'em anyway!' And that was that."

Brady left the plant when it closed after a few years. This closing was not unusual, she said. "Those plants operate for a couple years, and then they close the plant down and move it so no one can track them too closely or sue them for what's going on. The government doesn't regulate seafood at all, you know. It's easy to get away with anything."

—Sadie

Health

In addition to these environmental concerns, there are also a number of serious health issues concerning seafood. Ironically, in recent years seafood has become very popular as a "health food." After all, fish is an easily digestible lean protein and offers many vitamins and minerals in addition to omega-3 oils. Understandably, many nutritionists recommend fish as part of a healthy diet.

However, nutritionists rarely make the crucial distinction between farmed and wild fish. Farmed fish have only about one-third the amount of healthy omega-3 oils that wild fish do, yet their overall fat content is two to three times as high.[13] In crowded pens, they cannot get enough exercise and are fed an unhealthy, unnatural diet. Farmed salmon, for instance, are fed oily meal derived from wild fish, which results in gray, fatty flesh rather than the lean pink meat they develop in the wild. The unnatural conditions in the pen also foster the growth of fungi, parasites, and disease, and require a slew of antibiotics, fungicides, and pesticides that accumulate in their bodies. Thus, farmed fish have a higher concentration of toxins in their bodies than wild fish do. An advisory on salmon consumption published in the scientific journal *Environmental Health Perspective* explains that "farm-raised fish contain much higher levels of environmental contaminants than do wild fish because they are fed a diet [of] small pelagic fish [from] polluted waters. ... Fewer chemicals accumulate in wild salmon because their diet contains less of the contaminated fats and because they get more exercise, reducing their own fat levels."[14]

Just as the contaminants are passed from the smaller fish to the larger fish, they are then passed from the larger fish to you. This includes chemicals that the fish are intentionally exposed to, such as antibiotics, as well as environmental toxins that pollute their habitat, and thus their bodies. The largest

study ever to compare contamination in wild and farmed salmon found that environmental contaminants are found in much higher concentrations in fatty farmed salmon.[15]

Environmental Toxins

Farmed and wild fish share the problem of incidental toxins, or stray contaminants, that are found in their environment. These are pollutants that exist in the environment independently of the fishing industry, yet end up concentrated in the bodies of fish. After all, we dump our trash in the ocean and then we eat out of it.

Some of the most toxic environmental pollutants are no longer produced, yet continue cycling through the environment for decades. Polychlorinated biphenyl, also called PCB, for example, once used as a coolant and lubricant, has been banned since the 1970s, but is still turning up in the tissues of fish. Dioxin, a key ingredient in the toxic defoliant Agent Orange, persists as well. "Among the most toxic of man-made chemicals," PCB and dioxin are linked to cancer, as well as to developmental and reproductive problems.[16] A recent study conducted in Canada found that these notorious toxins are still showing up in fish in up to six times the concentration permitted by the World Health Organization.[17]

Other chemicals ranging from flame retardants to banned pesticides bioaccumulate in fish as well. Of particular concern is mercury, which settles on water from the gases and particulates released by coal-burning power plants and is also discharged directly into the ocean by offshore oil rigs.

Food 101—Your Diet Matters More Than You Think

117

Intentional Toxins

In addition to these environmental toxins, farmed fish have the added danger of all the chemicals that they are intentionally exposed to as they grow. These range from dangerous antibiotics to dyes that disguise their discolored flesh.

As much as 433,000 pounds of antibiotics are given to farmed fish in the United States every year, mostly as a strictly preventative measure.[18] Several antibiotics that are known to cause cancer and other deadly diseases in humans and have been deemed unsafe for human use are still used illegally on fish farms around the world. Chloramphenicol, for example, is a broad-spectrum antibiotic. It is used only for the most serious infections in human beings, partly due to its extreme potency, and partly because it is known to increase the risk of cancer, leucopenia, anemia, and aplastic anemia in humans. According to the Food and Drug Administration (FDA), "it has not been possible to identify a safe level of human exposure to chloramphenicol."[19] And yet, despite its ban, shipments of shrimp and other seafood from China and southeast Asia have repeatedly been found to be tainted with the drug.

The routine and regular use of antibiotics for any kind of livestock, including fish and shrimp, contributes to the development of drug-resistant bacteria—a serious health concern as human diseases become less responsive to antibiotics. Studies have shown that there is a clear link between the use of antibiotics in aquaculture and the development of resistant bacteria in the guts of fish.[20]

According to the Center for Disease Control, these dangerous antibiotic-resistant bacteria can be transmitted to humans who handle or eat contaminated fish.[21]

In addition to antibiotics, fungicides and pesticides are also routinely administered to farmed seafood. Although many are illegal, such as the toxic malachite green mentioned above, they are used to prevent fungal growth and parasitic infections in fish packed too tightly into small tanks. Unfortunately, they are also suspected carcinogens and increase the risk of genetic mutation. Yum.

Fish are given hormones for a variety of reasons. They're actually quite handy—they can cause sex reversal, induce the fish to become sexually mature earlier or later, or trigger rapid growth. For example, tilapia given the bovine growth hormone rGBH grow to twice their normal size in just four weeks. This hormone has been banned from dairies in Europe, Canada, Japan, Australia, and New Zealand due to health concerns for both humans and cows. Adding it to fish, therefore, does not seem like a wise choice.

Dyes are also used on farmed fish that do not have access to their natural diet. Farmed salmon, for example, have no access to their natural diet of krill, which turns their flesh pink. As a result, farmed salmon are gray. To make them more marketable, they are treated with dyes like astaxanthin and canthaxanthin, even though these chemicals are known to cause retinal damage in humans and hyperactivity in young children. This is a pandemic problem given that 95 percent of Atlantic salmon are farmed, including imports from Chile, Canada, Scotland, Norway, Iceland, Tasmania, and Ireland.

Genetically Modified Fish

Although not currently under cultivation, the thirty-five species of seafood that have been genetically modified will be proliferating on fish farms before long. Among their genetically engineered traits are the ability to produce human insulin and the ability to grow thirty times faster than their natural rate.[22]

The National Academy of Sciences concludes that consuming this genetically modified flesh is dangerous to human health.[23] Once a gene is altered to cause a certain action, such as producing insulin, it cannot be "turned off." This results in unnaturally high, even toxic, amounts of certain proteins that can cause allergic reactions in the people who consume them. In addition, the altered genes may disable or set off other genes, causing results that have not yet been studied. In fact, very few studies have been conducted in this area at all. We know that we don't want our bodies to be the laboratories for those experiments.

How Can This Be Happening?

If you've been blissfully eating fish all your life as many health-conscious consumers do, all of this probably comes as an unhappy shock. How can all these poisons be in our food? According to the Center for Food Safety (CFS), the problem is that aquaculture and fishing are the least regulated animal product industry in our country.

The FDA is responsible for monitoring the safety of the U.S. seafood supply, but the seafood inspection process is seriously insufficient and unsafe. After assessing current inspection and regulation standards, the Government Accountability Office found that federal oversight of seafood does not sufficiently protect consumers. They found that the FDA inadequately enforces the safety requirements outlined in the Hazard Analysis and Critical Control Points system.[24] The FDA does not test for many drugs used illegally abroad, employs an inadequate number of inspectors, and does not enforce equivalency standards with exporting countries. All of these flaws add up to the production, both domestic and abroad, of unsafe food sources.

The largest domestic seafood industry is catfish, followed by salmon, tilapia, yellow perch, sturgeon, crawfish, shrimp, abalone, oysters, clams, walleye, mussels, trout, and hybrid striped bass. Only six drugs are approved by the FDA for use on these products; however, more than thirty other banned drugs are used in aquaculture around the world—and often within our own borders.[25]

This is often due to uncompleted inspections. An investigation in 1999 found that "48 percent of products scheduled for inspection were not inspected because they were not being processed on the day of inspection."[26] Furthermore, when violations were found, no decisive action was taken to correct the problems.

Canada, for instance, permits twenty-five times as much residue left by Slice, a pesticide used on salmon, as does the United States. And yet, although 95 percent of Canada's farmed salmon is consumed in the United States, the FDA does not test Canadian salmon imports for this drug, which is known to block neural transmitters in the brain and cause behavioral and growth changes as well as pathological brain changes.[27]

Legal drugs are also routinely used in unsafe quantities. After discovering that the salmon dye canthaxanthin causes retinal damage in humans, the European Commission lowered the permissible level by nearly three-fourths. The United States, meanwhile, did not change the allowed levels of the substance.[28]

Our seafood imports come from more than sixty-two countries, from South America to southeast Asia, many of which have even less regulation than we do.[29] There is currently no standardized definition of organic seafood, and few labeling requirements. This inconsistency and chaos make it very tough to choose seafood conscientiously.

Alaskan Wild Salmon— A Kinder Choice?

The Center for Food Safety promotes wild-caught fish as a positive alternative to farmed fish.[1] After learning about the environmental impacts of wild fishing and the lack of federal regulation in the entire seafood industry, farmed or wild, we've been hesitant to agree.

Josh Lewis, a veteran of the Alaskan fishing industry, cleared up some uncertainty for us. Lewis worked for several years with Alaskan Fish and Game, the state equivalent of the U.S. Fish and Wildlife Service, helping biologists monitor salmon populations. Fish and Game, Lewis said, is much more exacting than federal-level regulations because the Alaskan economy depends on protecting these salmon populations. "Fishing employs more people than any other industry in Alaska," he said. "Maintaining healthy fish populations is a question of economic sustainability."

Teamed with biologists, Lewis hiked up Alaskan streambeds, counting the number of salmon. "It's just a rough estimate," he conceded, "but it helped

us keep track of the populations. I'd holler back to the biologists, 'There's 10,000 in this stream,' or 1,000, or whatever. And when there's enough, then they let the fishermen in."

And what happens when the fishermen come in? I imagined bottom trawlers ravaging the wild salmon populations. But Lewis explained that Alaskan wild salmon are caught through less destructive methods. "The lowest impact is hand trawling," he told me. "You have baited lines on manual cranks. You don't catch much that way, but you get a permit for a longer season to make up for it. And then there's power trawling, where you have powered wenches to reel the fish in faster. They also use gill nets—particularly on the Sakai salmon in Bristol Bay. They roll out a long net behind the boat in the fish channel and it catches the fish by the gills." (A gill net snags the gill covers when the fish tries to back out.)

The third practice he described is seine netting. "There are two boats, one with a big net behind it. The other boat sweeps the net in a big circle around the first boat, and then a huge wench pulls the seine together, like a purse." He gathered the corners of his napkin together to demonstrate how the net would form a pouch.

"Wouldn't this sweep up an awful lot of bycatch?" I wondered aloud. But Lewis countered, "The bycatch up there is not terrible. Not compared to trawling on the ocean floor, anyway."

So if you feel that you must eat fish, choosing Alaskan wild salmon may be a way of mitigating your environmental impact.

—Sadie

Note

1. The Center for Food Safety, "The Catch with Seafood: Human Health Impacts of Drugs and Chemicals Used by the Aquaculture Industry," 2005, www.centerforfoodsafety .org/thecatchwithseafoodaquaculturereport.cfm (accessed September 23, 2006).

What's a Consumer to Do?

In short, modern-day fish is often unhealthy and unsustainable for your body, wildlife populations, and the environment, no matter where it comes from. The only exception is a few sources of wild fish, but even this is not a perfect solution. Scientists at the Environmental Protection Agency (EPA) estimate that eating less than one serving of wild salmon per month still places you in the moderate range of their cancer risk scale.[30]

After assessing the damage to human health, the environment, and fish populations, we believe that the most responsible choice is to not buy seafood, be it farmed or wild. However, if you do choose to consume seafood, there are online resources to help you buy carefully. You can help yourself, too, by speaking out about the system you want to create.

Buy Carefully

As of April 2005, the U.S. Department of Agriculture's (USDA) new seafood labeling system requires that the country of origin and method of production be indicated on the label of all seafood. Although this isn't much, it gives you a shot at making an informed choice. If there's a seafood product you really love, read about the countries where it's produced and decide what your safest choice is. For example, if you love salmon, and you know that Chilean exports have been rejected by Europe and Japan due to unsafe antibiotics and malachite green, you may wish to avoid Chilean salmon.[31]

However, trusting a label is a tricky business. Arctic Keta, for instance, is actually low-grade salmon remarketed under a different name. Misleading packaging or blatant exclusion of information is very unfair to consumers who are trying to make responsible choices.

Gone Fishin'

Is it safe to catch your own fish? On one hand, fish you catch yourself have eaten a natural diet and gotten plenty of exercise, unlike farmed fish. Nor are they intentionally exposed to the drugs and chemicals that taint aquaculture products. Catching your own fish by plucking one fish out of the water does not impact the ecosystem the way a trawler does, and the food does not have to be packaged and shipped thousands of miles to your plate.

However, fishing fans should still be wary of their catch. We met a woman named Suzanne whose fishing hobby nearly cost her her life. On a family vacation in 2003, she innocently ate a fresh tuna she and her family caught off the coast of Long Island. "It was delicious," she recollected. "But the next day, I literally fell to my knees in pain, clutching my neck." After extensive medical testing, Suzanne learned she is highly sensitive to heavy metals, such as mercury and cadmium, which are frequently found in fish. The tuna incident was a case of acute heavy metal poisoning that almost killed her. Years later, she is still struggling to eliminate these poisons from her body through medication and strict diet modification.

While Suzanne is an extreme example, the rest of us may soon be reacting similarly if current trends continue. Wild fish are becoming increasingly contaminated, particularly with mercury. Most of our power nationwide is generated by coal-burning power plants, the number of which grows with our population. Consequently, the pollution of our waterways with mercury from their smokestacks is also increasing. The number of dangerously contaminated fish species in North Carolina tripled in just one year, leaping from seven in 2005 to twenty-two in 2006. Due to prohibitively dangerous levels of mercury, a new state advisory warns pregnant women, nursing mothers, and children under age fifteen not to consume any of seventeen marine and five freshwater species, including such common fare as Spanish mackerel, marlin, shark, and tuna. Consumers are warned not to consume largemouth bass caught anywhere in the state for fear of danger to our kidneys, nervous systems, and especially unborn babies.[1]

Until we develop alternative cleaner sources of power and demand that all coal plants are equipped with state-of-the-art scrubbers for their emissions, our surface waters will continue to accumulate mercury—a heavy metal that does not biodegrade, but persists in ecosystems and in living flesh indefinitely.

Note

1. "Authorities Issue Mercury Advisory for 22 Fish Types," *Asheville Citizen Times*, April 21, 2006, B4.

Speak Up

If all of this makes you mad, don't keep it to yourself. After lawsuits targeted the three largest supermarket chains in the country for not labeling dyed seafood, Safeway, Albertsons, and Kroger are now complying with federal law, and many smaller chains are following suit.[32] Demand that the supermarkets in your area do likewise.

Also, let the FDA know you're paying attention. You can send a message to the FDA demanding a moratorium on genetically modified fish at www.centerforfoodsafety .org/action2.cfm.

For frequently updated evaluations of various seafoods in terms of both human health and overharvesting, see the online guide at Oceans Alive.[33]

Whatever decisions you make as a food consumer, keep in mind that every purchase sends a message that you approve of the provider's methods and products. A dollar is a vote. Vote conscientiously for your health and the health of our fragile planet.

Notes

1. The Center for Food Safety, "The Catch with Seafood: Human Health Impacts of Drugs and Chemicals Used by the Aquaculture Industry," 2005, www.centerforfood safety.org/thecatchwithseafoodaquaculturereport.cfm (accessed September 23, 2006).
2. Ibid.
3. Ibid.
4. Christopher L. Delgado, Nikolas Wada, Mark W. Rosegrant, Siet Meijer, and Mahfuzuddin Ahmed, "Outlook for Fish to 2020: Meeting Global Demand," International Food Policy Research Institute, Washington, DC, 2003, www.ifpri.org/pubs/fpr/pr15.pdf.
5. Christopher L. Delgado, Nikolas Wada, Mark W. Rosegrant, Siet Meijer, and Mahfuzuddin Ahmed, "The Future of Fish: Issues and Trends to 2020," International Food Policy Research Institute, Washington, DC, 2003, www.ifpri.org/pubs/ib/ib15.pdf.
6. The Center for Food Safety, "The Catch with Seafood."
7. Andrew Purvis, "Farmed Fish," *The Observer*, May 11, 2003, http://observer.guardian.co.uk/foodmonthly/story/0,9950,951686,00.html.
8. Purvis, "Farmed Fish."
9. Delgado, et al., "Outlook for Fish to 2020."
10. Purvis, "Farmed Fish."
11. Douglas G. Capone, Donald P. Weston, Veronica Miller, and Cynthia Shoemaker, "Antibacterial Residues in Marine Sediments and Invertebrates Following Chemotherapy in Aquaculture," *Aquaculture* 145: 55–56.
12. Purvis, "Farmed Fish."
13. The Center for Food Safety, "The Catch with Seafood."
14. Jeffery A. Foran, David O. Carpenter, M. Coreen Hamilton, Barbara A. Knuth, and Steven J. Schwager, "Risk-Based Consumption Advice for Farmed Atlantic and Wild Pacific Salmon Contained with Dioxins and Dioxin-like Compounds," *Environmental Health Perspective* 552 (6), cited in The Center for Food Safety, "The Catch with Seafood."
15. Ronald A. Hites, Jeffery A. Foran, David O. Carpenter, M. Coreen Hamilton, Barbara A. Knuth, and Steven J. Schwager, "Global Assessment of Organic Contaminants in Farmed Salmon," *Science* 300: 226–229, www.pewtrusts .cpm/pdf/salmon_study.pdf.
16. J. K. Huwe, "Dioxins in Food: A Modern Agricultural Perspective," *Journal of Agriculture and Food Chemistry* 50: 1739–1750, cited in Michael L. Weber, "What Price Farmed Fish: A Review of the Environmental & Social Costs of Farming Carnivorous Fish," SeaWeb, www.seaweb.org/resources/reports.php.
17. M. D. Easton, D. Luszniak, and E. Von der Geest, "Preliminary Examination of Contaminant Loadings in Farmed Salmon, Wild Salmon, and Commercial Salmon Feed," *Chemosphere* 46: 1053–1074, cited in Weber, "What Price Farmed Fish."
18. United Nations, Food and Agriculture Organization, "The State of the World Fisheries and Aquaculture," 2002, www.fao.org/docrep/005/y7300e/y7300e00.htm.
19. The Center for Food Safety, "The Catch with Seafood."
20. Ibid.
21. Memorandum from Angulo, Frederick, DVM, PhD, Medical Epidemiologist, National Center for Infectious Diseases, Division of Bacterial and Mycotic Diseases, Foodborne and Diarrheal Diseases Branches, cited in The Center for Food Safety, "The Catch with Seafood."
22. The Center for Food Safety, "The Catch with Seafood."
23. Ibid.
24. U.S. General Accounting Office, Report to the Committee on Agriculture, Nutrition, and Forestry, U.S. Senate,

"Federal Oversight of Seafood Does Not Sufficiently Protect Consumers," GAO-01-204, January 2001, www.gao.gov/new.items/d01204.pdf.

25. The Center for Food Safety, "The Catch with Seafood."
26. Ibid.
27. Ibid.
28. Ibid.
29. Ibid.
30. Ibid.
31. Ibid.
32. The Center for Food Safety, "The Catch with Seafood."
33. Oceans Alive, www.oceansalive.org/home.cfm.

Genetically Modified Foods: Progress or Problem?

Easy to Overlook

I considered myself a conscious eater for years before I paid attention to genetically modified organisms (GMOs). *Genetically modified food.* Sure, it sounds weird, but secretly I was annoyed by the whole issue. I didn't really know what *GMO* meant, and privately I suspected that people who made a fuss about it were just being whiny—those people who always want something to complain about. *Like tap water,* I would mutter to myself. *All these water filters all over the place. What's the matter with plain old tap water? That's what I want to know.*

Boy, was I wrong. I first got wind of the real deal with genetically modified food when we paid a visit to Tony Kleese, the director of the Carolina Farm Stewardship Association (CFSA). As we parted, he handed us a booklet published by the CFS entitled *Monsanto vs. U.S. Farmers*.[1] I dropped it in my backpack and forgot all about it until it turned up among my things at a booksellers conference in Atlantic City later that fall.

As we settled into our hotel room, I flopped on my bed and pulled out the Monsanto booklet. What was all the fuss about, anyway?

An hour later, I was waving my pen in the air and shouting. "I can't believe this!" I shrieked. "It's a farming holocaust! It's … it's … a military takeover of food! Why isn't anybody doing anything?!"

Sally regarded me mildly. "I know," she said. "It's appalling."

—Sadie

What Is a Genetically Modified Organism?

We were appalled to find out not only the true meaning of genetically engineered food, but the pervasive and insidious way it's spreading throughout our agriculture industry in a seemingly unstoppable tide of economic and environmental destruction. But most of all, I'm horrified that so few people know this is happening.

Genetic modification or engineering means changing an organism's permanent genetic code by adding genetic material from a foreign organism. Along with the desired gene, a package of proteins and other molecules, called a cassette, is also added to the host to aid in the gene's assimilation into the host's system—kind of like loading new software onto your computer. The cassette includes antibiotic marker systems, vectors, and bacterial and viral promoters.[2] All these agents affect the function of the host organism's genes.

A wide array of organisms have been modified, from pigs with human growth genes to tomatoes with fish genes.[3] However, thus far in North America, just four crops have borne the brunt of genetic modification: cotton, corn, soy, and canola. The most common genetic alterations made to these crops are insect resistance and herbicide tolerance, though drought and frost resistance are in the works.[4]

Genetically modified (GM) plants acquire insect resistance with the addition of a gene from *Bacillus thuringiensis* bacteria, or Bt, which causes them to produce a toxin that kills munching insects.[5] Herbicide-tolerant plants have been modified to withstand lethal doses of potent herbicides so that entire fields can be heavily doused with chemicals that kill everything but the crop. The first herbicide-tolerant, or "Roundup Ready," soy was planted in 1996. By 2004, just eight years later, 85 percent of the soybeans grown in the United States were Roundup Ready. Now 84 percent of U.S.–grown canola, 76 percent of cotton, and 45 percent of corn are genetically engineered as well.[6]

Monsanto Monopoly

This rapid growth is largely the result of market takeover by one company, Monsanto. In the late 1990s, Monsanto aggressively bought out every major seed company in the United States, except for one, Pioneer Hi-Bred International. By 1998, Monsanto was the largest marketer of genetically engineered seeds in the world and the second largest seed company. Monsanto currently provides the seed technology for more than 90 percent of the world's genetically modified crops and controls most of the American corn and soybean markets.[7]

Monsanto's monopoly on food production is possible thanks to a peculiarity of the U.S. patent law as determined by the Supreme

Court and U.S. Patent and Trademark Office (U.S. PTO). After the Supreme Court ruled in 1980 that living organisms are patentable, Monsanto began meticulously patenting each new process and discovery in the development of genetic engineering. In 1984, they patented a genetic mechanism called the 35S promoter, which is found in a cauliflower virus and has proved to be an essential tool in almost all genetic engineering projects. Owning this patent has given Monsanto the legal right to control other companies' bioengineering process.[8] That step alone ensured Monsanto's monopoly over the biotech industry in the decades to come.

The deal was sealed in 1985 when the U.S. PTO began accepting patents on sexually reproducing plants.[9] Under a plant utility patent, Monsanto could now claim ownership of not only their genetic modifications, but of the modified plants themselves. The corporation could now deny others the right to use this property or define their terms of usage however they wished. As the coming years proved, the granting of this right would prove disastrous for the future of U.S. agriculture.

Changing the Fundamentals of Farming

Twenty years later, Monsanto now controls 30 percent of all biotech research and development and owns the seed technology for 90 percent of the world's genetically engineered crops. Farmers who plant Monsanto seeds must sign a technology contract agreeing to repurchase the company's seeds each year instead of saving the seed from the previous year's harvest, as farmers had done for thousands of years. The contract also assigns farmers the responsibility of preventing any seeds from dispersing off of their land.

Owning Mother Nature

This is, of course, impossible. Seeds and pollen have evolved features that facilitate their dispersal by way of wind, water, and animals, often over dozens or even hundreds of miles. This phenomenon is fundamental to the successful reproduction of plants in nature and to the survival of ecosystems everywhere. So far, the seeds or pollen of genetically modified plants have been documented to disperse by forces of nature for up to sixteen miles.[10] Although Monsanto's Technology Use Guide acknowledges that "pollen movement (some of which can carry genetically improved traits) between neighboring fields is a well-known and normal occurrence in corn seed or grain production,"[11] the corporation still holds the farmer liable for the random dispersal of their seeds and pollen. In other words, the farmer is guilty of sharing patented material. If another farmer's seeds or pollen blow onto his land, he is guilty of stealing. If plants that result from this random dispersal naturally sprout on their own, or "volunteer," he may be sued.

Seed dispersal and volunteer crops are age-old aspects of farming, but they have been turned into crimes. According to Monsanto Canada's vice president, Ray Mowling, the company "acknowledges the awkwardness of prosecuting farmers who may be inadvertently growing Monsanto seed."[12] Yet the corporation devotes seventy-five staff

members and $10 million a year to doing just that.[13] Many of these farmers are completely unaware of the offenses they have committed. Some never signed a contract with Monsanto at all; their fields are merely tainted by a neighbor's windswept pollen. Others bought the genetically modified seed without realizing it or without signing or reading the contract. To others, it simply never occurred to them that they could be prosecuted for saving and trading seed as they have always done.

At the farm I worked on, we routinely ousted wayward GM corn volunteers from our fields. Although we grew only organic corn, those GMOs sprouted from corn seeds that had accidentally strayed into the ground-up soybeans we purchased as fertilizer for our fields. If we had been less vigilant and the volunteers had grown to maturity, they could have tainted our entire corn harvest or bankrupted the farm.

Prosecution of Farmers

None of this matters to Monsanto. They have gathered more than $15 million in scores of lawsuits, intentionally driving many unsuspecting farmers to bankruptcy. Gary Rinehart, a farmer mistakenly investigated by Monsanto, reported hearing investigators "bragging to other farmers about all of the farmers they had put out of business."[14] Many are threatened that Monsanto will "tie them up in court for years" if they do not agree to settle out of court.[15] Farmers report Monsanto agents employing desperate measures to collect evidence, from bullying their families and customers to lying, forging documents, and trespassing in order to get onto their farms to collect evidence. Extreme cases include investigators posing as members of local Alcoholics Anonymous groups, as friendly neighbors needing a loan of seed, or as land surveyors innocently documenting the lay of the land.[16] Mississippi farmer Earl Scruggs reported that Monsanto investigators went so far as to buy an empty lot across the street from his store in order to track his movements. Tailed by planes, helicopters, and hired agents, Scruggs is still currently embroiled in a lawsuit after four years of battling.[17]

Environmental Damage

If it's this hard to stay on Monsanto's good side, why risk it? Why buy their product in the first place? Many farmers would prefer not to, but find little alternative. Eighty-five percent of U.S. soy is now genetically modified, and 70 percent of that contains Monsanto's patented alterations—down from 90 percent due to government regulations.[18] After searching for other seed varieties, Indiana farmer Troy Roush concluded, "You can't even purchase them on this market. They're not available."[19]

Resistance

This lack of variety in the seed gene pool has dire consequences for the future. After just ten years of commercial cultivation of GMOs, we are beginning to see the biological and environmental ramifications of this unnatural system.

One of the most alarming concerns is the issue of resistance. As mentioned above,

plants can be engineered to produce a toxin that kills insects. The gene for the toxin occurs naturally in Bt bacteria and can be transferred into plants. When entire fields of crops are steadily producing the toxin, of course more insects are exposed to higher levels of this insect-killing toxin. As the susceptible pests are killed off by higher and higher doses, the resistant individuals are left behind to reproduce, creating strains of insects that are resistant to the pesticide.

Because the Bt toxin is a relatively benign and naturally occurring pesticide, it is one of the few pesticides widely used by organic farmers. As insect populations develop resistance to it, this could become a huge problem for organic farmers who can't resort to alternative chemical pesticides. In short, Bt resistance is a major threat to the future of organic farming and to the delicate balance between plant and insect populations.

Resistance is also a problem in herbicide-engineered plants. Crops are usually engineered to withstand just one of the major commercial herbicides, such as Monsanto's Roundup, Aventis LP's Liberty, or Cyanamid's Pursuit and Odyssey herbicides.[20] This way, the resistant crop will withstand applications of that particular herbicide, but can be controlled with other herbicides if the crop itself should get out of control. Many crops, including corn and canola, have weedy relatives that are sometimes fertilized by pollen via wind or animals. Since 79 percent of GM crops are herbicide resistant, this accidental pollination of wild species can transmit herbicide-resistant traits to the wild relatives; it can transmit resistance to more than one herbicide to a particular population of weeds. This flow of genes for herbicide resistance is among the most serious agricultural problems on the horizon for it can create "super weeds" that are resistant to multiple herbicides and impossible to control. Even crops themselves can become super weeds if they acquire resistance to multiple herbicides by way of accidental pollination. A super-resistant strain of canola is becoming a persistent problem in wheat and barley fields. Both weeds and out-of-control crops necessitate the use of higher and higher doses of chemical herbicides, and this has devastating effects on the environment.

These changes in the genetic material of plants are sometimes called biological pollution. Unlike chemical pollutants, which slowly break down over time, biological pollution intensifies with each generation. Just as antibiotic-resistant bacteria eventually predominate in a bacteria population continually doused with antibiotics, so herbicide-resistant weeds will come to dominate wild populations of these plants on agricultural lands continuously sprayed with herbicides.

The Biological Pollution of Animals and Humans Too

In 1998, the EPA approved a certain strain of pesticide-resistant corn, called StarLink, for use in livestock feed, although the added genes were known to cause allergic reactions in humans. Although only 1 percent of Iowa cornfields were sown with StarLink, samples from *half* the state's fields showed contamination with the toxic StarLink allergen—after only one year! In addition, residues of the offending protein persisted in the meat of the livestock that had eaten it. The company that had engineered StarLink eventually conceded "it was inevitable that the commercial introduction of StarLink corn for feed would cause the introduction of Cry9C protein into the general grain supply *because of the biology of corn*."[21]

In the manufacturer's own words, the processes that the biotech industry is trying to control are simply a part of the biology of plants. As prosecuting attorney Terry Zakreski put it, "Monsanto has a problem. It's trying to own a piece of Mother Nature."[22] And that, as all these problems demonstrate, is a pipe dream.

Chemical Pollution

In addition to causing biological mayhem, genetic engineering is also chemically damaging the environment. New studies are showing that Roundup, originally considered benign, is actually quite harmful to natural systems. Researchers at the University of Pittsburgh found that Roundup runoff into surface waters caused an 86 percent decline in tadpole populations and a 70 percent decline in amphibian biodiversity.[23] Amphibians are often indicator species, like canaries in a coal mine. With their sensitive skins, frogs and salamanders react early to chemical problems that will affect other wildlife and humans as they increase in intensity.

This trend is confirmed by recent research in France. A study found that the supposedly inactive ingredients in Roundup are far more likely to cause reproductive difficulties in mammals than its active ingredient, glyphosate, alone.[24] Unfortunately, with the proliferation of herbicide-resistant crops and weeds, the use of Roundup has surged in recent years.[25] Crops can now tolerate high doses, and weeds require ever-increasing doses to control them. Indications are that the use of Roundup will continue to escalate in coming years.

Not surprisingly, pesticide usage is also on the rise. Bt technology was developed assuming that plants producing their own pesticide would not require additional applications of chemicals. However, it seems that Bt engineering may, in fact, be increasing the use of chemical pesticides. In Alabama, for instance, where 60 percent of cotton features Bt technology, pesticide usage doubled between 1995 and 2000.[26] Nationwide, pesticide use on cotton, soy, and corn has increased by 122 million pounds since 1996, according to USDA data.[27]

Systemic Effects

Introducing genetically modified material into an ecosystem affects much more than the altered plants themselves. Plants, even crops, are part of an ecosystem, and any change to them affects the world around them. More than 76 million acres of U.S. farmland are currently planted with GM crops, but neither the FDA, the USDA, nor the EPA has sufficiently tested the impact of these crops on biodiversity or natural ecosystems. According to the CFS, "No federal agency has ever completed an Environmental Impact Statement on any GE organism, and much research into the environmental impacts of GE crops

remains to be done. No regulatory structure even exists to ensure that these crops are not causing irreparable environmental harm. The FDA, our leading agency on food safety, requires no mandatory environmental or human safety testing of these crops whatsoever. Nonetheless, officials at the FDA, EPA, and USDA have allowed, and even promoted, GE crop plantings for years."[28]

Feeling disturbed yet?

Health Woes

The federal government has not required environmental testing for GMOs, but what about testing for human health?

The very first genetically engineered food, the Flavr Savr tomato, gave stomach lesions to the rats that ate it. Although FDA scientists who were aware of this recommended long-term testing of GMOs before putting them on the market, to this day, the government does not require any safety testing or labeling of GM foods. "The agency's failure to require testing or labeling of GE foods has made millions of consumers into guinea pigs," asserts the CFS.[29]

There is, in fact, overwhelming evidence that GM foods are hazardous to human health. One of the first GM products, a dietary supplement called L-tryptophan, caused 37 deaths and 1,500 disabling illnesses in the late 1980s. Investigators suspect that the process of genetic modification created a toxic by-product that poisoned its consumers.[30]

This very same thing could be happening in our corn, soy, and canola, not to mention other GM foods that are not yet on the market. When a gene is inserted into an organism's DNA, it renders the existing system unstable. Genetic engineers do not know where it is safe to place the added gene, nor what side effects a certain location may have. In addition to unknown toxicity hazards, studies performed by the FDA have found that this instability also decreases the nutrient levels in GM foods.[31]

Other FDA scientists acknowledge that the addition of foreign genes into random locations may cause an increase in natural toxins, the production of new toxins, or the concentration of environmental toxins, like pesticides and heavy metals.[32] Despite this information, these foods have still not been tested for safety. "The [FDA's] actions can only be seen as a shameful acquiescence to industry pressure and a complete abandonment of its responsibility to ensure food safety," conclude analysts at the CFS.

Toxins aside, GM foods may also induce unexpected allergic reactions. If you've ever known anyone with a peanut allergy, you know food allergies can be very serious, even life threatening. These risks greatly increase in GM foods with haphazardly placed genes creating unknown substances. As the FDA acknowledges, any one of the genes, viruses, vectors, marker systems, promoters, and bacteria added to a food during genetic modification could cause an unexpected allergic reaction in a consumer who has never been exposed to the substance before. And without labeling, consumers have no way to protect themselves from such a risk. People with nut allergies, for instance, got a nasty surprise

when they consumed soybeans engineered with a Brazil nut gene; they reacted just as if they were eating the Brazil nut itself. This Pioneer Hi-Bred soybean had to be hastily recalled due to the serious reactions in unsuspecting consumers.[33]

One of the potential allergens included in the genetic cassette that accompanies a transferred gene is called an antibiotic marker. These tags are used in genetic modification to indicate whether the foreign genetic material has actually been assimilated into the host. However, these antibiotic-resistance genes also drastically weaken the effectiveness of the antibiotics we use to treat infections in humans and animals, according to the Consumer Policy Institute.[34] The British Medical Association, less blind than our FDA, recommends that antibiotic-resistance marker genes be banned, due to their contribution to antibiotic resistance and the resulting risk to human health.[35]

Watch Out for These

Genetic ID, an independent testing firm, tested a multitude of processed foods for the presence of unlabeled GM ingredients. It's worth reading through this list just to realize the prevalence of soy, canola, and corn ingredients in seemingly innocuous foods. Cornflakes may not be too surprising, but pancake mix? Granola bars? The list is long, but here are just a few examples:

- Alpo dry pet food
- Aunt Jemima pancake mix
- Ball Park franks
- Betty Crocker Bac-Os bacon flavor bits

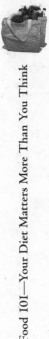

- Boca Burger Chef Max's Favorite
- Bravos tortilla chips
- Duncan Hines cake mix
- Enfamil ProSobee soy formula
- Gardenburger
- General Mills Total Cornflakes
- Heinz 2 baby cereal
- Jiffy corn muffin mix
- Kellogg's cornflakes
- Lightlife Gimme Lean
- McDonald's McVeggie burgers
- Morningstar Farms Better 'n Burgers
- Morningstar Farms Harvest Burgers
- Nestle Carnation Alsoy infant formula
- Old El Paso taco shells
- Ovaltine malt powdered beverage mix
- Post Blueberry Morning cereal
- Quaker Chewy Granola Bars
- Quaker yellow corn meal
- Quick Loaf bread mix
- Similac Isomil soy formula
- Ultra Slim-Fast[36]

Economic Viability

Even though 94 percent of Americans believe that genetically modified ingredients should be identified on food packaging, the United States is one of the few countries in the world that does not require such labeling.[37] This is not too surprising, given that 59 percent of the world's GM food is produced in the United States, and our government often protects corporate interests at the expense of consumers and the environment. But other countries are not so oblivious to the problem.

In fact, there's an interesting correlation between the countries that produce GM crops and those that have lax labeling policies. Argentina, the second largest producer, at 20 percent, also does not require labeling of GM ingredients. Neither does Canada, at 6 percent. None of the large producers have ratified the Biosafety Protocol, the first legally binding international agreement concerning international trade of genetically modified foods. Meanwhile, nearly every other country in the world, from Australia to Ecuador, requires GM labeling, has signed the Protocol, or both. Many countries have actively banned all GM food, either regionally or nationally. And perhaps most tellingly of all, seven of the neediest countries in Africa—Sudan, Nigeria, Angola, Malawi, Mozambique, Zimbabwe, and Namibia—will not accept GM grain as food aid, despite their desperate need.[38]

The trend is abundantly clear. A few countries—particularly the United States—are producing nearly all the world's genetically modified food, and their governments—particularly that of the United States—do not protect their own citizens or environment from the biotech industry. Other countries, those not involved in GM production, refuse to consume GMOs and are doing all they can to protect themselves from this hazardous industry. The U.S. State Department estimates that the United States is losing as much as $4 billion per year in exports to European markets that refuse genetically engineered crops. This loss in revenue falls close to home for farmers who find themselves tethered to Monsanto's production methods, then left on their own to find a market for their GM goods.

Even farmers who have managed to steer clear of Monsanto's contracts are not safe. A study of canola seed found that thirty-two of thirty-three certified non–GMO seed samples were actually contaminated with genetically modified content.[39] The Union of Concerned Scientists suspects that this is also the case with more than half of supposedly non–GM corn and soy crops.[40] David Gould, an expert in organic certification, confirms that "virtually all the seed corn in the United States is contaminated with at least a trace of genetically modified material, and often more."[41] This contamination can persist in the organic varieties for as long as sixteen years, according to a British study.[42] The vice president of Pioneer Hi-Bred concedes that "100 percent purity, either in genetic make-up or in the absence of foreign material content, is currently not achievable for *any agricultural product*."[43]

Them's scary words.

Solutions

So that's what happens when a corporation tries to own and control nature. It seems that this whole mess went awry with the first patent on a living organism. How can a corporation own the inventor's right to a living being? That's the problem—most laws surrounding this issue just don't make sense. According to the CFS, "Monsanto has often been allowed, and even encouraged, by U.S. legislators, regulators, and courts to use patent law as a weapon against the American farmer"[44]—and the American consumer, we would add. But that can—and must—change.

Biotech food consultant Don Westfall clarifies what we're up against. "The hope of the [biotech] industry is that over time, the market is so flooded that there's nothing you can do about it. You just sort of surrender."[45] Indeed, this seems likely given that trials of genetically modified tomatoes, rice, melons, lettuce, alfalfa, potatoes, strawberries, beets, squash, grapes, wheat, walnuts, sunflowers, apples, peppers, and tobacco are currently underway.[46] But they're not on the market yet. And what if they never are? What if we *don't* surrender?

Right now is a crucial time in the development of the biotech food industry. We are on the cusp of no return; once the genetic taint is too widespread, crop purity may be lost forever. But if we act now, there is still time to change our course.

Concerned farmers, consumers, and politicians envision a variety of ways in which we can halt the biotech industry, dismantle Monsanto's monopoly, and reclaim the integrity of our food sources. Kleese put it succinctly: "It comes down to, who owns the food system? Monsanto owns the seed; they own the food system from seed to plate. Is that okay with you?"[47]

Political Action

If we decide it's *not* okay, we must pressure the government to enact legislation to stem the tide of genetic engineering. As you can read in the Food Corporations and GM Policy sidebar (see pages 135–136), a number of large food corporations, such as Nestlé and Kellogg, sell only GMO–free products in Europe, where the growth and sale of GMOs are prohibited.

If it can happen there, it can happen here.

There are many potential avenues to restrict the legal power of biotech giants like Monsanto. Ideally, the Patent Act could be amended so that sexually reproducing plants would no longer be patentable, and the Plant Variety Protection Act could be altered to exclude genetically modified plants. Since Monsanto is obviously not able to control the spread of these seeds or the altered genes they contain, it would make sense for them not to have sole rights over them.

Alternatively, more-conservative changes could be made. For example, the Patent Act could be amended to decriminalize saving GM seed or the accidental possession, use, or sale of it. Or, avoiding government legislation entirely, Monsanto's technology agreement itself could simply be modified to hold the corporation, rather than farmers, liable for the dispersal of the seeds.

However, any of these changes would require action by Congress, which is difficult (though not impossible) to achieve. As a more attainable means of opposing biotechnology, the CFS and other analysts instead encourage regional action. "Given the lobbying power of the biotechnology industry, it is extremely unlikely that Congress would take such action in the foreseeable future," the CFS concludes, but "state bans are more feasible … [and] county-wide bans are very viable."[48]

Indeed, several counties in California have already passed voter initiatives to ban the cultivation of genetically modified crops in their domain. Meanwhile, the entire state has succeeded in prohibiting the sale of GM fish and rice.[49] In Maine, a statewide coalition called GE Free Maine works to organize farmer pledges and town resolutions against genetically modified crops.[50] These regional successes demonstrate that until a national policy is established, local change is certainly possible.

Consumer Action

Politics aside, farmers and companies that buy seed have vital choices to make as to which seed producers and vendors they choose to support. As we say in regard to many topics in this book, consumers' buying habits have a huge sway over corporate policy, and consequently, government policy. Selective buying could turn things around. Some American seed companies are taking a stand right now.

Fedco Seeds is one business that's resisting the biotech takeover. In 2005, Monsanto announced their buyout of Seminis, one of Fedco's key seed suppliers. "The Monsanto buyout presented us with a serious ethical dilemma," the company explained in their 2006 catalog. "Many of our consumers have depended on Seminis' good genetics. [Yet] however much we may think we require these varieties in the short run, they come at a devastating social cost, ultimately the complete alienation of sower from seed."[51]

Alarmed by growing corporate control of the seed and food industries, and concerned by uninvestigated health effects of GM food, Fedco polled their customers: Should they stop buying from Seminis and take a stand against Monsanto? Or should they continue to buy rare seed varieties that are available nowhere else?

"We received an unprecedented response." They reported, "54.8 percent voted for us to drop the Seminis/Monsanto line immediately, and an additional 17 percent to phase it out over time."[52] One customer conceded that "it's a hard thing to fight a Monsanto when we're so deeply embedded in a system that produces Monsantos. Sort of like Jefferson hating slavery while owning slaves." Another, however, defiantly declared, "Buyer's choice is real democracy. We, the buyers, either keep them in business or put them out of business."

This is true whether you're buying the seeds, the food, or both. Fedco ultimately chose to stop business with Seminis and is currently working to find alternatives and replacements for the forfeited seeds. "We do so," they conclude, "because Monsanto epitomizes the road down which we no longer choose to go: the road that leads to our complete surrender of control ... of our food system."[53]

If you, too, wish to economically boycott Monsanto, the only way to be sure is to buy certified organic corn, cotton, soy, and canola. The United States is one of the few countries in the world that does not require labeling of genetically modified ingredients, but the USDA's standards for organic food do prohibit the use of GMOs. Although organic food may be contaminated with GM content, at least it does not financially support the Monsanto corporation.

Notes

1. Center for Food Safety, *Monsanto vs. U.S. Farmers Report* www.centerforfoodsafety.org/Monsantovsusfarmersreport.cfm.
2. Center for Food Safety, "The Hidden Health Hazards of Genetically Engineered Foods," *Food Safety Review* 1 (spring 2000).
3. Rebecca Spector and Andrew Kimbrell, "Genetically Engineered Food and Agriculture in California: Issue Background," *California Food and Agriculture Report Card*, Center for Food Safety.
4. Daniel Charles, *Lords of the Harvest: Biotech, Big Money, and the Future of Food* (New York: Perseus Book Group, 2001).
5. Margaret Mellon and J. Rissler, "Gone to Seed: Transgenic Contaminants in the Traditional Seed Supply," Union of Concerned Scientists, February 24, 2004, www.ucsusa.org/food_and_environment/genetic_engineering/gone-to-seed.html.
6. Ibid.
7. Center for Food Safety, *Monsanto vs. U.S. Farmers Report*.
8. G. R. Squire, G. S. Begg, and M. Askew, "The Potential for Oilseed Rape Feral (Volunteer) Weeds to Cause Impurities in Later Oilseed Rape Crops," Department for Environment, Food and Rural Affairs, August 2003, www.defra.gov.uk/environment/gm/research/pdf/epg_rg0114.pdf.
9. Fedco seed catalog, www.fedcoseeds.com/.
10. Lidia S. Watrud, E. Henry Lee, Anne Fairbrother, Connie Burdick, Jay R. Reichman, Mike Bollman, Marjorie Storm, George King, and Peter K. Van de Water, "Evidence for Landscape-Level, Pollen-Mediated Gene Glow from Genetically Modified Creeping Bentgrass with CP4 EPSPS As a Marker," *Proceedings of the National Academy of Science*, 101(40): 14533–8.
11. Monsanto, Technology Use Agreement, www.monsanto.com/.
12. Richard Weiss, "Seeds of Discord: Monsanto's Gene Police Raise Alarm on Farmers' Rights, Rural Tradition," *The Washington Post*, February 3, 1999, A6.
13. Center for Food Safety, *Monsanto vs. U.S. Farmers Report*.
14. Ibid
15. Ibid.
16. Ibid.
17. Ibid.
18. Charles, *Lords of the Harvest*.
19. Ibid.
20. Center for Food Safety, "Genetically Engineered Foods and the Environment: A Catastrophe in the Making." *Food Safety Review* 3 (spring 2002).
21. Rebecca Spector and Andrew Kimbrell, "Executive Summary," *California Food and Agriculture Report Card*, Center for Food Safety (emphasis added).
22. Weiss, "Seeds of Discord."
23. Fedco seed catalog.
24. Ibid.
25. Center for Food Safety, *Monsanto vs. U.S. Farmers Report*.

26. Center for Food Safety, "Genetically Engineered Foods."

27. Charles Benbrook, "Genetically Engineered Crops and Pesticide Use in the United States: The First Nine Years," October 2004, www.biotech-info.net/Full_version_first _nine.pdf.

28. Center for Food Safety, "Genetically Engineered Foods."

29. Center for Food Safety, "The Hidden Health Hazards."

30. A. N. Mayeno and G. J. Gleich, "Eosinophilia Myalgia Syndrome and Tryptophan Production: A Cautionary Tale," *Tibtech*, 12 (1994): 346–352.

31. Center for Food Safety, "The Hidden Health Hazards."

32. Ibid.

33. Julie A. Nordlee, et al., "Identification of a Brazil-Nut Allergen in Transgenic Soybeansm" *The New England Journal of Medicine* 334 (March 14, 1996): 688–692.

34. Michael Hansen and Jean Halloran, "Why We Need Labeling of GE Food," Consumers International, Consumer Policy Institute, April 1998.

35. "The Impact of Genetic Modification on Agriculture, Food and Health—Interim Statement," British Medical Association, May 1999, cited in "The Hidden Health Hazards."

36. Spector and Kimbrell, "Genetically Engineered Food and Agriculture in California."

37. Ibid.

38. Center for Food Safety, "Genetically Modified Crops and Foods: Worldwide Regulation, Prohibition, and Production," November 2005, www.centerforfoodsafety .org/genetical5.cfm.

39. Lyle F. Friesen, Alison G. Nelson, Rene C. Van Acker, "Evidence of Contamination of Pedigreed Canola (*Brassica napus*) Seedlots in Western Canada with Genetically Engineered Herbicide Resistance Traits," *Agronomy Journal* 95 (2003): 1342–1347.

40. Mellon and Rissler, "Gone to Seed."

41. "North Dakota Organic Farmers Worry About Biotech Contamination," *Cropchoice News*, February 6, 2001.

42. Squire, Begg, and Askew, "The Potential for Oilseed Rape Feral (Volunteer) Weeds to Cause Impurities in Later Oilseed Rape Crops."

43. Center for Food Safety, "The Hidden Health Hazards," (emphasis added).

44. Center for Food Safety, *Monsanto vs. U.S. Farmers Report.*

45. Stewart Laidlaw, "Starlink Fallout Could Cost Billions," *Toronto Star,* January 9, 2001.

46. Spector and Kimbrell, "Genetically Engineered Food and Agriculture in California."

47. Tony Kleese, personal communication, October 7, 2005.

48. Center for Food Safety, *Monsanto vs. U.S. Farmers Report.*

49. Spector and Kimbrell, "Executive Summary."

50. GE Free Maine, www.gefreemaine.org.

51. Fedco seed catalog.

52. Ibid.

53. Ibid.

More Advantages of Buying Organic

The USDA organic certification program protects consumers and wildlife from much more than genetic modification and all of its ramifications. The organic label also protects us from more-familiar hazards, such as the application of chemical herbicides, pesticides, and fertilizers. When applied to crops, these chemicals disperse into woodlands and streams where they impact nontargeted plants, wildlife, and humans. The U.S. Geological Survey has found pesticide residues in nearly every body of water in the country.[1]

Pesticides and herbicides can accumulate in soil and damage soil quality by killing microorganisms that convert organic matter into soil. This diminishes nutrient levels and water retention, often leading farmers to use more chemical fertilizers to maintain the same level of production. Runoff from chemical fertilizers, together with runoff from livestock waste, is the leading source of nutrient pollution in our surface waters and wells, often leading to fish kills and loss of biodiversity. Many chemical fertilizers also leave trace cadmium and uranium in soils and water. Both of these elements are toxic and carcinogenic to humans and wildlife.[2]

Buying organic is one way to avoid contributing to these problems. According to the USDA's organic guidelines, "Organic food is produced by farmers who emphasize the use of renewable resources and the conservation of soil and water to enhance environmental quality for future generations. Organic meat, poultry, eggs, and dairy products come from animals that are given no antibiotics or growth hormones. Organic food is produced without using most conventional pesticides; petroleum-based fertilizers or sewage sludge-based fertilizers; bioengineering; or ionizing radiation.[3]

Organic agriculture is not newfangled nonsense; it's actually old-school farming in disguise. Until recently, all food was grown organically because chemical fertilizers, pesticides, and herbicides did not exist. In fact, DDT from the 1960s is considered the first modern pesticide; before this time, farmers relied on organic variants. Chrysanthemum flowers, for instance, provide organic compounds called pyrethrins that function as natural insecticides and can be applied to fields. However, pyrethrins are biodegradable and break down with exposure to the sun, so there is no bioaccumulation. They are far less harmful to mammals and birds than many synthetic insecticides. Pyrethrins have been in use for generations around the world and are used successfully by organic farmers in the United States today.[4]

Choosing organic food is easy because, unlike

many other food labels, organic labeling is regulated by the USDA, which has created four categories of organic foods. It's important to know what they all mean because the titles can be deceiving.

- 100 percent Organic—Every ingredient in this product must be certified organic, as well as all the facilities that handle the product before it comes to you. None of the ingredients can be genetically modified.
- Organic—At least 95 percent of the ingredients in this product are certified organic and not genetically modified.
- Made with Organic Ingredients—At least 70 percent of the ingredients in this product are certified organic and not genetically modified.[5]
- All natural, hormone free, or cage free—These labels can mean anything. Any product with less than 70 percent organic ingredients is not regulated, so the producers can label it as they wish. Check the list of ingredients; if any of them are organic, it will say so there.

Notes

1. Rebecca Spector and Andrew Kimbrell, "Executive Summary," *California Food and Agriculture Report Card*, Center for Food Safety.
2. G. C. Jahn, "Effect of Soil Nutrients on the Growth, Survival, and Fecundity of Insect Pests of Rice: An Overview and a Theory of Pest Outbreaks with Consideration of Research Approaches," *Multitrophic Interactions in Soil and Integrated Control*, International Organization for Biological Control/West Palaearctic Regional Section, Bulletin 27 (1): 115–122 (2005).
3. U.S. Department of Agriculture, Government Printing Office, "Agriculture Fact Book 2001–2002," www.usda.gov/factbook/chapter1.htm, or order a hard copy from http://bookstore.gpo.gov/.
4. "What Is Pyrethrum?" PyGanic, McLaughlin Gormley King Company, 2005, www.pyganic.com/tpl_pyrethrum.asp (accessed December 16, 2007).
5. "Labeling and Marketing Information," The National Organic Program, October 2002, www.ams.usda.gov/nop/Fact Sheets/LabelingE.html (accessed November 24, 2006).

Food Corporations and GM Policy

Because the government does not regulate the use of genetically modified ingredients, food suppliers are free to determine their own GM policy. Some companies follow the U.S. Department of Agriculture's example in accepting all of the Food and Drug Administration's approved GM ingredients. Other suppliers decline to specify their GM guidelines,

leaving consumers to guess. Some responsible companies, however, have opted to draft a more stringent GM policy of their own. These vary by company and are detailed below. If you wish to avoid GM ingredients, it is best to choose organic products or those with a clearly defined GM policy.[1]

Food Suppliers that defer to the U.S. Department of Agriculture and Food and Drug Administration's policy on genetically modified foods:

- Albertsons
- Cargill, Inc.
- Coca-Cola (Dannon, Fruitopia, Nestea, Sprite)
- Dole Food Company
- General Mills (Betty Crocker, Cascadian Farms, Cheerios, Green Giant, Häagen-Dazs, Pillsbury, Yoplait)
- Kellogg (Carr's, Cheez-It, Famous Amos, Kashi, Keebler, Morningstar Farms, Nutri-Grain)
- Kraft (A1 Steak Sauce, Breyer's, Breakerstone, Country Time Lemonade, Jell-O, Kool-Aid, Maxwell House, Minute Rice, Miracle Whip, Post, Stove Top Stuffing, Velveeta)
- Kroger
- Land O'Lakes
- PepsiCo (Frito-Lay [see below], Gatorade, Quaker Foods, Tropicana)
- ConAgra (Hunt's Healthy Choice, La Choy, Manwich, Orville Redenbacher, Pam, Parkay, Peter Pan, SlimJim)
- Nestlé U.S.A and Canada (Carnation, Coffee-mate, Juicy Juice, Kern's Nectar, PowerBar, Stouffer's, Taster's Choice)
- Safeway
- Sara Lee (Ball Park, Bimbo, Hanes, Hillshire Farms, Jimmy Dean, Playtex, Sara Lee)
- Unilever North America (Ben & Jerry's, Hellmann's, Lipton, Knorr, Slim-Fast, Wishbone)

Food Suppliers with no policy available on genetically modified foods:

- Anheuser-Busch (Budweiser, Michelob, O'Doul's, Busch)—Although they did threaten to boycott Missouri rice in 2005 if genetically engineered rice was grown in the state
- Campbell's Soup
- Dean Foods (Alta Dena, Berkeley Farms, Horizon Organic, Meadow Gold, Silk)
- Mars (M&Ms, Mars, Milky Way, Skittles, Starburst, Three Musketeers, Twix, Seeds of Change, Uncle Ben's Rice)
- Smithfield Foods (Farmland, John Morrell, Stefano, Virginia's Choice)

- Tyson (Bonici, Corn King, Jordan's, Iowan Ham, Lady Aster, Russer, Thorn Apple Valley, Weaver Wright)

Food Suppliers that have set their own policy regarding genetically modified foods:

- Amy's Kitchen—Requires proof from suppliers that ingredients are free from genetically modified foods
- Barbara's Bakery (Alpen, Grainfield's, Nature's Choice, Weetabix)—Reviews the genetically modified status of each ingredient
- Campbell's Soup Europe—No genetically modified ingredients are in their products sold in Europe
- Fantastic Goods—Tests its products for genetically modified organisms
- Frito-Lay—Contracted farmers are told not to plant genetically modified corn
- Hain Celestial Group (Celestial Seasonings, Garden of Eatin', Earth's Best, Soy Dream)—Prioritizes non–genetically modified ingredients and labels many products "non-GMO"
- Heinz—(Bagel Bites, Boston Market, Classico, Linda McCartney's, Ore-Ida, Smart Ones)—Seeks to avoid genetically engineered ingredients
- J.M. Smucker Beverage Company (Crisco, Jif, R. W. Knudsen, Smucker's)—No genetically modified foods in products labeled "natural"
- Kellogg Europe—No genetically modified ingredients are in their products sold in Europe
- Nestlé Europe—No genetically modified ingredients are in their products sold in Europe
- Newman's Own Organic—Prioritizes non–genetically modified ingredients and supports a moratorium on genetically modified foods
- Spectrum—Prioritizes non–genetically modified ingredients
- Trader Joe's—No genetically modified ingredients are in store brand products
- Whole Foods—No genetically modified ingredients are in store brand products
- Wild Oats—No genetically modified ingredients are in store brand products

Note

1. Rebecca Spector, "Report Card on Genetically Engineered Food and Agriculture: State of the State," *California Food and Agriculture Report Card*, Center for Food Safety.

Giant Meats
Turning Corn into Beef:
A System Designed to Self-Destruct

It Starts Out Good

"It's just so peaceful, watching them graze," said the cattle rancher we interviewed recently. We agreed. Her small herd of grazing Hereford beef cattle, with three or four nursing calves, provided a scene of deep serenity. Even though, personally, we would rather see a woodland of native trees and undisturbed wildlife than a cow pasture, a contented cow on a grassy hillside is a peaceful sight. Some kind of cultural conditioning, we guess.

Relatively speaking, beef *calves* have a pretty good life. Eighty percent of hogs and 99 percent of poultry in the United States spend their entire lives in crowded confinement sheds in which tens of thousands of animals are packed into each building. The floor of such a shed is covered with accumulated waste, which gets all over the animals and causes "hock burns" and "breast blisters" in chickens. The waste creates fumes that are unhealthy for neighbors, livestock, and farmers. Then there's the problem of leaking waste lagoons, which we'll get to in a bit.

On the Range, Where the Living Is Easy

Why do animal advocates agree that beef cattle have an easy beginning relative to hogs and chickens? Because beef calves spend their first six or seven months on the range with their mothers, nursing and beginning to graze in much the same way that they have in this country for decades.

But after the first six or seven months, things go downhill quickly.

The Downhill Slide to the Feedlot

After six or seven months of roaming the range, beef calves are weaned and separated from their mothers. It would make sense to think that, hereafter, they would consume a diet of grasses—the food their bodies are equipped to handle. But that doesn't happen in conventional operations. After the peaceful beginning, the penny-shaving mentality that has saturated the pork and poultry industry takes over.

Here in the United States, the usual procedure is to wean beef cattle to eat a diet dominated by corn. This practice started after World War II. With the development of petrochemical fertilizers, powerful pumps for irrigation, and new hybrid corn seeds, corn was abundant and cheap. Farmers began feeding the surplus to their livestock. They were pleased that supplementing the animals' diets with corn made them gain weight faster. But over the decades, supplementing the diet has morphed into a diet that's 60 to 85 percent corn for most beef cattle.[1, 2] A little corn was tolerable for cattle; heavy doses fed to young cattle can be hell.

But these days the conventional corporate meat industry is all about profits for shareholders. Federal subsidies have made the price of corn even lower than the cost of growing it. In addition to being extremely cheap, corn is compact, thus it's easier and cheaper to transport than hay or other bulky forage. Another big advantage is that corn-fed cattle can be kept confined in close quarters, meaning that more animals can be finished (grown to slaughter weight) on a small amount of land.

A Lucrative Business

But for cattle owners, perhaps the most important benefit of raising corn-fed cattle is that they gain an average of three pounds a day, while grass-finished cattle gain an average of only one pound a day.[3] Since meat is sold by the pound, heavier animals bring owners more money. Also, the upkeep of an animal as big as a steer is expensive, even in the less-than-luxurious conditions of a cattle feedlot, and faster growing cattle have fewer maintenance expenses because their lives are shorter.

We called a cattle specialist at the University of Nebraska, Dr. Galen Erickson, to learn more about the relative financial merits of corn-feeding versus grass-feeding from a rancher's or a feedlot owner's perspective. A growing number of consumers are seeking grass-finished or pastured animal products because of health and environmental benefits, but Erickson doesn't recommend to feedlots that they switch to grass-feeding because corn-feeding is more lucrative. "Grass-fed cattle are lighter; 1,200 pounds versus 1,400 pounds," said Dr. Erickson. "So to make a living, you have to be paid for the difference. If you can raise a steer to 1,400 pounds on corn and sell it for 80¢ per pound, then you'd have to sell the 1,200-pound grass-finished steer for 96¢ per pound to make the same amount of money."

What's a Feedlot Like?

So, for the vast majority of American beef cattle, it's off to the feedlot within a few weeks after they're weaned for a diet of corn and more corn. The youngsters are usually transported by truck because there are no government regulations on how often they must be fed and watered on trucks. (Train travel, on the other hand, is regulated and thus more expensive.)

A feedlot can be a massive operation, with as many as 200,000 head of cattle.[4] According to the USDA, 80 to 90 percent of cattle are from large feedlots.[5] Most are young steers, or castrated males. The rest are heifers, or young females that have never given birth. Feedlots are all over the United States, but most large operations are on the Great Plains from Nebraska and Colorado down to Texas.[6]

A feedlot is a loud and bewildering expanse of stinking muck and bawling animals. Newly arrived calves are herded from the trucks to the muddy, barren pens for the duration of their stay. The gray mud, a hoof-churned pudding of feces and urine, is smeared and clotted on the animals' coats. This becomes an issue inside the slaughterhouse later on, when the cattle must be skinned without contaminating the meat.

The young cattle spend several months at the feedlot gaining weight. Most are slaughtered at the age of twelve to fourteen months.[7] The feeding troughs, or "bunks," are always full, to encourage eating. In addition to speeding weight gain, the corn in the diet causes the cattle's muscles to become marbled with fat. Corn also gives the meat a particular taste that Americans have grown accustomed to.

Corn-feeding is clearly more profitable, but it's not pleasant or natural for the cattle, and so it takes some training, called backgrounding, to get them to tolerate it. Just after weaning, the calves are fed hay and other forage (chopped plants). If the forage has been fermented to preserve it, it's called silage. The corn is gradually mixed in in increasing amounts. An article in *Feedlot Magazine* recommends "step up" increments of corn in the diet, from 55 to 65 to 75 to 85 percent corn over a period of three to four weeks.[8] The corn is hard on a cattle's digestive system; it causes the contents of the stomach to be more acidic. So even though the young animals are eased into the new diet, the excess acid can make the cattle very sick. This is a fact openly acknowledged within the industry by both cattle experts and feedlot operators.

"The Beef Cattle Handbook," a reference document for feedlot managers, describes "subacute acidosis," a term for the symptoms that afflict cattle on a typical feedlot diet high in corn. "Animals with this condition," the handbook says, "are plagued with diarrhea, go off their feed, pant, salivate excessively, kick at their bellies, and eat dirt." The handbook goes on to say, "Nearly every animal in the feedlot will experience subacute acidosis at least once during the feeding period." The manual then reassures readers that this is "an important natural function in adapting to high-grain finishing rations."[9]

A Dead Steer

What causes this acidic condition in the animals' stomachs? During normal digestion, bacteria in the stomach of cattle produce acids. Grasses are high in tough cellulose and require a lot of chewing (rumination) and a lot of stomach acid in order to be broken down and digested. When the animals ruminate, they produce a high volume of saliva that neutralizes the acidity. But a feedlot diet of corn is lower in roughage than a diet of grasses, so the animals do not ruminate or chew as long, nor produce as much saliva. The net result is acid indigestion.

Over time, the excess acid can cause more than discomfort, panting, and kicking. It can lead to inflammation and ulcers in the wall of a steer's stomach. Bacteria can pass through the ulcers into the bloodstream and travel to the liver, where they can cause infection and abscesses. We called a cattle feedlot specialist at a Midwestern university to ask about the frequency of liver abscesses in cattle. He estimated that 10 percent of feedlot cattle develop liver infections. "The Beef Cattle Handbook" reports an incidence of 15 percent.[10]

If there's subacute acidosis, is there also acute acidosis? Yes, there is. The syndrome has a range of symptoms, from mild to severe. According to *Feedlot Magazine*, "acute acidosis is easy to identify: a dead steer."[11]

What Else Are They Eating?

If the bulk of the diet is corn, what's the remaining 15 to 45 percent of a feedlot steer's diet? We posed this question to a couple of feedlot specialists at agricultural state universities. They told us that the remainder of the diet is a combination of roughage, protein supplements, vitamins, synthetic hormones, antibiotics, and ionophores, which can function like antibiotics. Some of these items have implications for our own health and for the health of our environment.

Roughage and Ruminants

The nature of the roughage depends on what's available locally for a cheap price— alfalfa hay, sorghum, or corn silage are common choices. Roughage is necessary because, like grass, it's high in cellulose, so it's really the only part of the diet that truly fits the animals' digestive physiology.

The Infamous Protein Supplements

Feedlot cattle are given protein supplements because corn is mostly starch. The particular supplement offered depends on what's available locally. In the Midwest, where corn is common and plentiful, the by-products of the manufacture of corn syrup or corn ethanol are often used, such as corn gluten and corn distillers' grain. In the South, cottonseed meal is a common protein supplement. Soybean meal is another option, but more expensive. These may not sound high in protein, but they are, ranging from 20 percent for the corn gluten to 50 percent for the soybean meal.

There's another common source of protein for cattle: even though cattle are herbivores, many are fed ground-up animals and animal wastes.

One Expert Hung Up on Me

If you've read much about the meat industry, you've probably read that livestock are often fed pellets made from other livestock. We called a number of people at meatpacking companies and universities to try to find out just what is eating what. But no one seemed to want to talk about livestock that are eating other livestock. One animal-science professor did tell me that cattle are routinely fed tallow, which is beef fat. But he said this is not a problem because the tallow has been "purified." He didn't elaborate on what that means, other than that the fat is free of infective agents for diseases such as mad cow disease, or bovine spongiform encephalopathy. He wouldn't say more than that, and hung up on me in midquestion.

Another agricultural professor, a beef specialist, was more willing, though cautious. And he didn't want his name used. He told us that it's common practice to feed slaughterhouse scraps to livestock. He said the scraps fall into three categories: meat and bonemeal, tallow, and blood meal. He told us that in 1997, the USDA banned the feeding of meat and bonemeal from a cattle slaughterhouse to cattle because the infective agent for mad cow disease can be transmitted from steer to steer in this way. This ban, he said, is called the "Food Ban Rule" in the industry. He also said, as another precaution against the transmission of diseases, that it is no longer legal to use as feed the bodies of animals that died spontaneously before slaughter. Any animal whose tissue will be used as food, for humans or animals, must be "ambulatory"—still able to walk—before death. But outside of these two bans, any livestock body part, tissue, or fluid can be fed to any other kind of livestock. Beef tallow and blood meal can be fed to beef cattle. The professor said that no one wants to admit to feeding animal products to their livestock. Ranchers, feedlot operators, meat companies, no one. They keep it quiet because consumers don't like it.

Livestock Munching Livestock

We found someone at the National Chicken Council who was willing to talk to us openly about animal by-products in livestock feed, though he also didn't want his name used. He confirmed that the Food Ban Rule forbids feeding cattle meat and bonemeal to cattle. But he said that cattle are often fed poultry by-products. The feeding of poultry to cattle is most common in places where feedlots and poultry co-occur in large numbers. Let's see … feedlots are in the Midwest, poultry are in the South, so that must mean where the Midwest and South overlap. Yep, Texas and Oklahoma are two states where the cattle feedlot "protein supplement" is often poultry by-products, which means slaughterhouse scraps—heads, feet, skin, organs, bones, fat, ground up, in pellet form. He also commented that "ruminants benefit from the cellulose in feather meal," meaning ground up poultry feathers. Feeding feather meal to cattle is quite common, he said. We asked about poultry litter, the scrapings from the floor of poultry sheds that is mostly composed of poultry feces and spilled poultry feed. He told us that, yes, cattle and other livestock are at times fed poultry litter and feces, but not as commonly as they're fed feather meal and poultry scraps from the slaughterhouse.

Well, that's a relief. At least cattle are not being fed cattle-slaughterhouse scraps, at least not cattle meat and bonemeal scraps. What with mad cow disease and all. But wait a minute. The man from the National Chicken Council did tell us that 75 percent of our country's poultry are fed meat and bonemeal from cattle slaughterhouses. "Meat and bone-meal have a lot of protein, a lot of vitamins and minerals," he said. But ... if cattle are eating poultry that ate cattle, is that a problem in regard to transmitting mad cow disease? "Oh, no," he said. "It is permitted. It's safe. Scientists have tried to infect chickens with BSE and the chickens don't get it."

Yes, but if the poultry by-products contain ground up chicken *stomachs* and *intestines*, which they do, what if some cattle bonemeal is still in the chicken's gut when it's ground up to make cattle feed? And what about the spilled poultry feed in the poultry litter, the pellets made from cattle meat and bonemeal? As you may know, eating cattle bones and meat from around the bones is by far the most likely transmission vector for mad cow disease. Not good.

Cows Eating Cows ... Wrapped in Poultry

We asked one of the Midwestern university cattle consultants about this. He confirmed that cattle meat and bonemeal from slaughterhouses is routinely fed to poultry, and that chicken litter containing feces and spilled pellets is fed to cattle. He seemed to share our concern about the possible recycling of the BSE infective proteins, or prions, from cattle through poultry, back to the cattle. He said, "It's expected that feeding chicken litter to ruminants will be banned. They've been discussing it for a year or more." Further on in the conversation, he reiterated this. When we asked him point blank if the infective proteins could survive travel through a chicken's digestive track, he said he didn't know. After a moment's pause, he added that the proteins "are quite resistant to breakdown."

Hormones and Antibiotics in Meat

Hormone implants are also routinely given to feedlot cattle. Revlar is a common brand of synthetic estrogen; it is implanted in the skin behind the ear. In addition, daily doses of antibiotics are routine for almost all mass-produced livestock, including cattle. The antibiotics are mixed with the corn, roughage, vitamins, protein supplements, and other feed ingredients before all of it is pumped into the troughs. The American Medical Association has issued repeated warnings about the overuse of antibiotics because bacteria develop immunity to them. In the United States, humans consume 3 million pounds of antibiotics per year. Sounds like a lot—no wonder we read articles in the newspaper telling us not to overdo it with the antibiotics. But, oddly, those articles never seem to mention that livestock in the United States receive *25 million pounds* of antibiotics per year. And these are not different antibiotics "just for animals," but the same erythromycins and streptomycins that are prescribed to the

American public to treat infections.

The motive for this misuse is that antibiotics promote weight gain in livestock, a powerful inducement for feedlot managers. In addition, antibiotics suppress or delay the liver disease that results from eating too much corn.

Feedlot management is a race between growth to slaughter weight and erosion of the digestive system. A good manager sees to it that growth wins and the animal reaches slaughter weight before it succumbs to disease.

Brainers and Liver Abscesses

A safer way to keep liver disease at bay would be to reduce the amount of corn fed to cattle, since it's the corn that's causing the health problems. "The Beef Cattle Handbook" states that as long as cattle are finished on corn, acidosis will be an important problem, leading to sudden death, brainers, rumenitis, liver abscesses, and so on.[12] A brainer is a central nervous system disturbance, or in feedlot parlance, an animal that has such a disturbance, which is usually fatal.

European countries have banned the practice of routinely feeding livestock subtherapeutic doses of antibiotics; the bans have had no adverse effects on their meat industries. But the giant American meatpacking corporations resist any ban. They want the extra dollars from the added weight gain.

Fat and More Fat

The corn diet causes health problems for beef consumers as well as for cattle. As noted above, corn adds to the amount of fat in beef, and it's well-known now that eating animal fat increases cholesterol levels. Fat is also high in calories, and 60 percent of Americans are overweight or obese.

Strain 0157 Is Deadly

Corn-fed beef can also be contaminated with deadly bacteria, most notably E. coli. Most strains of E. coli are harmless. In fact, all of us have E. coli in our intestines, with no ill effects. But one strain of E. coli is deadly—E. coli 0157. The acidic conditions in the stomachs of corn-fed cattle encourage the growth of this strain. It's so toxic that eating just a few cells of E. coli 0157 can kill a human. The United States has seen occasional outbreaks of E. coli 0157 poisoning during which several people in one town will become extremely ill and a few may die. Since children eat more than half the hamburgers sold in the United States, the victims are often children. The poisoning is usually traced to a single hamburger restaurant that has a batch of meat with E. coli in it.

In the past, this dangerous E. coli strain from cows could not survive in the human digestive tract because of the pH, or acidity, of our stomachs. But because a corn diet increases the acidity of cattle's stomachs, the pH of their stomachs becomes similar to our own. So the cattle's dangerous E. coli have adapted to a more acidic stomach and can now survive in our stomachs too.

How do the E. coli get from the cattle's digestive tracks to our stomachs? During the slaughter and processing of a bovine, the anus is tied shut before the animal is eviscerated so that the contents of the stomach and intestines won't spill freely onto the floor, the workers, and the carcass. But that doesn't stop the transmission of E. coli. Back at the feedlot, the animals' coats were continuously splattered with feces and fecal bacteria. Although carcasses are skinned before they're cut up and are sprayed with disinfectant and steam, bits of waste still stick to the workers' gloves, coats, boots, knives, saws, and hooks. Inevitably, the meat is contaminated with feces to some degree—it's impossible to get rid of every speck, especially when the dangling carcasses are moving along the processing trolley, from worker to worker, at breakneck speed. And a small proportion of the fecal contamination will still contain living E. coli cells. That's why the industry has turned to irradiating meat. Radiation kills the bacteria on any contaminated meat. But not all meat is irradiated, so sometimes E. coli gets through and winds up in somebody's hamburger.

If cattle are taken off the corn diet for five days prior to slaughter, and fed hay or silage instead, their stomachs return to the more alkaline, normal pH that kills the acid-adapted E. coli. Any remaining E. coli would not be able to survive in our own stomachs, so would not be a threat to us.[13] Although this precautionary step of switching feed prior to slaughter seems logical, most feedlots are not implementing the practice because it might cost a few ounces in weight gain.

An Environmental Downside: Manure Galore

One steer generates fifty to sixty pounds of urine and manure every day. What happens to it? The muck in feedlots is scraped up periodically and pushed into mounds in the pens. Then, anywhere from once a month to once a year, the mounds are moved to waste lagoons, which are open cesspools as large as ten acres each. These pools of liquefied feces and urine surround the feedlot. The untreated waste is sprayed on cropfields to make room for more. It also leaks and spills. Many states allow a million gallons of leakage per year for every three acres of lagoon. Although some of the waste is absorbed by crops, much of it finds its way downhill, polluting our surface waters and groundwaters with nitrates and phosphates, and with fecal bacteria—some of which have developed immunity to common antibiotics.

One steer generates fifty to sixty pounds of waste per day.

Corn Creates More Problems

According to the USDA, corn that is grown to feed cattle accounts for more than 40 percent of all the commercial fertilizer and herbicides applied to U.S. crops.[14] Why is that bad? Chemical fertilizers are the primary source of nitrates and phosphates that pollute surface and groundwater, resulting in fish kills, contaminated wells, and disrupted ecosystems. Toxic herbicides such as atrazine also wash into our water from cornfields, a concern for wildlife as well as human communities.[15]

Another problem is the vast amount of water consumed by growing corn. Corn is a thirsty crop. Almost half of all corn grown in the United States is irrigated, most of it in Midwestern states that draw both irrigation water and municipal water from the shrinking Ogallala aquifer.[16] This is a major factor in the further depletion of the aquifer, a serious problem with no solution in sight.

Corn for cattle creates an unhappy picture all the way around—for the animals, for consumers, for the environment. For everyone except the feedlot operators and the meatpackers, who are making more money with the corn system. But the economics are relative. If *no one* fed corn or other grains to cattle, if *all* cattle were grass finished, then the playing field would be level. Americans would grow accustomed to paying more for their beef and would come to enjoy the taste of grass-finished beef. Many ranchers even say that they object to modern feedlot practices, but they do what they feel they must in order to stay competitive.

So, What's the Solution?

The most effective solution is for all of us to eat less beef and fewer animal products overall. But if you are going to eat them, you can choose products that have less negative impact. That could be grass-finished beef, organic animal products, or locally produced animal products.

The term *grass-finished* is applied primarily to cattle because cattle are ruminants whose natural diet is grass, while poultry and hogs are omnivorous. Almost anyone raising cattle can claim their animals are "grass-*fed*" or "pastured" since virtually all cattle spend their first few months at pasture. If you want to be sure that cattle was not corn-fed or grain-fed later in life but subsisted entirely on grasses (which can include dried hay), look for a grass-finished label on your beef products.

Tough grasses, including hay, are the appropriate diet for cattle and other ruminants. Cattle process corn much too quickly, which causes serious digestive problems.

By purchasing grass-finished beef, you are almost certainly not supporting a feedlot—grazing is not possible in such close quarters. Grass-finished cattle are less likely than feedlot animals to have received hormone implants or daily antibiotics. From a nutritional perspective, grass-finished beef has about one-third the fat of corn-fed beef,[17] and a six-ounce serving of grass-finished beef has 100 fewer calories than corn-fed beef.[18] Promoters of grass-finished beef point out that it is higher in certain nutrients than corn-fed beef, such as omega-3 fatty acids, vitamin E, and conjugated linoleic acid, or CLA. Omega-3s have been shown to decrease the risk of high blood pressure and death from heart attack or stroke.[19] Research also suggests that a diet rich in omega-3s and CLAs may help reduce the risk of cancer.[20] Jo Robinson's website, www.eatwild.com, is a good source of information on the nutritional advantages of grass-finished animal products over mass-produced products.

Environmentally, grass finishing has a number of merits over finishing at feedlots. Livestock at pasture are less likely to generate the waste-management problems that afflict feedlots and factory farms because there are no waste lagoons to leak and spill. The waste can naturally assimilate into the soil if the animals are widely spaced enough. Modest amounts of animal waste can actually enhance soil quality.

Another environmental benefit is that grass-finished cattle are not eating corn and thus aren't associated with the intensive use of chemical fertilizers.

But grazing livestock are not environmentally harmless. Pastured cattle with access to streams can destroy stream ecosystems by trampling, eroding, and churning stream banks and streambeds, as well as leaving waste in streams. Eighty percent of streams in the United States have been negatively impacted by livestock.[21] The United Nations (UN) estimates that livestock across the globe are responsible for 55 percent of erosion and sedimentation of surface waters.[22] Responsible livestock owners are increasingly providing alternative water sources for pastured animals and are creating buffers around streams with livestock-proof fencing—though livestock owners in developing nations are less likely to have the resources to do so.

Livestock and Land Use

Most of us would rather have a pasture in our backyard than a feedlot or a factory farm, but a forest is better than either one. Livestock are using more and more land around the globe. According to the UN, grazing livestock now occupy 26 percent of the ice-free terrestrial surface of the planet. If you include the area required to raise feed crops for livestock (including hay for grass-finished animals in winter), livestock production accounts for *70 percent* of all agricultural land.[23]

In addition, raising livestock, pastured or not, is an inefficient use of land when compared to raising plant-based foods. This is particularly pertinent right now, when the human population is projected to increase by 39 percent by the year 2050.[24] The amount of land required to feed 100 people on animal products could feed at least 400 people on plant-based foods alone.

How does using so much land for livestock affect global biodiversity? Not in a good way. Livestock now account for 20 percent of the total terrestrial animal biomass. Virtually all of the earth's land surface that is now devoted to livestock and their feed was once habitat for wildlife.[25] According to the UN, "the livestock sector may well be the leading player in the reduction of biodiversity, since it is the major driver of deforestation, as well as one of the leading drivers of land degradation, pollution, climate change, overfishing, sedimentation of coastal areas and facilitation of invasions by alien species."[26] These assessments include grass-finished cattle, as well as livestock raised organically and livestock products marketed locally.

How does grass-finished beef compare to organic meats? Animals raised organically

Farms and feedlots that raise large numbers of tightly packed animals have waste-management issues such as the pollution of nearby streams and wells.

cannot be given hormones or fed antibiotics routinely. Their feed crops must be grown without synthetic pesticides and petrochemical fertilizers, so their flesh (and milk and eggs) are free of these chemicals, as are the fields where their feed is grown. Animals whose products are certified organic cannot be fed carcasses or litter of other animals, thereby protecting you from mad cow disease.

But in cases where organic livestock are raised in large numbers and in crowded conditions, the farms may still have waste-management problems that pollute nearby streams and groundwater. Some dairies that market organic products have been known to keep their cows in conditions scarcely, if at all, more humane than conventional dairies. (Inhumane conditions at dairies can include continuous confinement on concrete floors, with little or no access to pasture.) Still, all things considered, animal products that are certified organic are greener and more humane choices than products from animals finished in conventional feedlots or factory farms.

As consumers learn more about agricultural methods, the market for grass-finished beef and organic meat is increasing. We will get what we demand. If consumers of animal products demand humane and eco-friendly providers, then such providers will find the financial and regulatory support they need. As consumer interest in sustainable methods grows, the opportunities for conscientious and responsible farmers to develop viable livelihoods will improve.

Local

For many consumers and producers, buying and eating locally raised products has become a more powerful inducement than either grass-finished or organic. See Local Food (page 162) to learn why many foodists are demanding local produce and animal products.

Notes

1. Kate Clancy, PhD, "Greener Pastures: How Grass-Fed Beef and Milk Contribute to Healthy Eating," Union of Concerned Scientists, 10, www.ucsusa.org/food_and _environment/sustainable_food/greener-pastures.html.
2. Teres Gatz-Lambert, "Subacute Acidosis: An Often Unobserved Thief," *Feedlot Magazine* 105 (June 7, 2000), and from personal communication with cattle specialists at Midwestern agricultural universities.
3. Bill Niman and Janet Fletcher, *The Niman Ranch Cookbook* (Berkeley, CA: Ten Speed Press, 2005).
4. Ibid.
5. Economic Research Service, *Cattle: Background*, Washington, DC: United States Department of Agriculture, 2004), www.ers.usda.gov/Briefing/Cattle/Background .htm (accessed March 26, 2006).
6. "Agricultural Alternatives: Feeding Beef Cattle," Small-Scale and Part-Time Farming Project at Penn State, 2001, http://agalternatives.aers.psu.edu/livestock/feeding _beef_cattle/feeding_beef_cattle. pdf (accessed March 12, 2006).
7. Niman and Fletcher, *The Niman Ranch Cookbook*, 37.
8. Gatz-Lambert, "Subacute Acidosis."
9. Rick Stock, PhD, and Robert Britton, PhD, "Beef Cattle Handbook," www.iowabeefcenter.org/pdfs/ bch/03500.pdf.
10. Ibid.
11. Gatz-Lambert, "Subacute Acidosis."
12. "Agricultural Alternatives: Feeding Beef Cattle."
13. J. B. Russell and J. L. Rychlik, Factors That Alter Rumen Microbial Ecology, *Science* 292 (2001):1119–1122.
14. L. A. Christensen, "Soil, Nutrient, and Water Management Systems Used in U.S. Corn Production," Agriculture Information Bulletin 744, 2002, Washington, DC: United States Department of Agriculture Economic Research Service, cited in Kate Clancy, PhD, "Greener Pastures: How Grass-Fed Beef and Milk Contribute to Healthy Eating," Union of Concerned Scientists, page 13, www.ucsusa.org/food_and_environment/ sustainable_food/greener-pastures.html.
15. Clancy, "Greener Pastures."
16. "Irrigation and Water Use: Questions and Answers," 2000, Washington, DC: United States Department of Agriculture Economic Research Service, www.ers.usda .gov/Briefing/WaterUse/Questions/qa4.htm (accessed March 26, 2006).
17. Jo Robinson, *Why Grass-Fed Is Best: The Surprising Benefits of Grass-Fed Meat, Eggs, and Dairy Products* (Vashon Island, WA: Vashon Island Press, 2000).
18. "Health Benefits of Pasture Raised Food," Sustainable Table, www.sustainabletable.org/issues/pasture/ pastured2.html (accessed March 8, 2006).
19. F. B. Hu, M. J. Stampfer, et al., "Dietary Intake of Alpha-Linolenic Acid and Risk of Fatal Ischemic Heart Disease Among Women," *American Journal of Clinical Nutrition* 69 (1999), no. 5, 890–897.
20. Robinson, *Why Grass-Fed Is Best*.
21. A. J. Belsky, A. Matzke, and S. Uselman, "Survey of Livestock Influences on Stream and Riparian Ecosystems in the Western United States," *Journal of Soil and Water Conservation* 54 (1999): 419–431.
22. H. Steinfeld, P. Gerber, T. Wassenaar, V. Castel, M. Rosales, and C. de Haan, "Livestock's Long Shadow: Environmental Issues and Options," The United Nations Food and Agriculture Organization Executive Summary, 2007, www.fao.org/docrep/010/a0701e/a0701e00.htm.
23. Ibid.
24. International Data Base, www.census.gov/ipc/www/idb/ worldpopinfo.html.
25. H. Steinfeld, et al., "Livestock's Long Shadow."
26. Ibid.

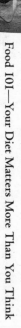

Community Voice

Nicolette Hahn Niman, Cattle Rancher: You Are What They Eat

Nicolette Hahn Niman is an environmental attorney, frequent contributor to *The New York Times*, and cattle rancher in Bolinas, California. Niman Ranch sells pastured and humanely raised meats.

"Because we raise cattle, my husband and I are often asked how safe it is to eat meat. After the Department of Agriculture recently confirmed another mad cow case in the United States, we got a lot more questions. We first reassure people that the risk in the U.S. to humans from mad cow disease is probably extremely small. Then we explain that they can eliminate any risk of exposure to the disease by eating only beef from animals that were never fed any meat by-products, the only known way for an animal to catch the illness.

"On our ranch, we believe the old adage that 'you are what you eat.' But it's no great leap to take a step back to the animals in our food chain and realize that we are what *they* eat too. Consequently, our cattle consume only mother's milk, grass, and hay, and, at the final stages of their lives, some grains, alfalfa, and molasses. We base their diet on what they'd eat in nature. And we never feed anything that could be toxic to them, let alone to human beings.

"This may not sound radical, but it's quite different from the way most food animals are fed today. And although the list of feed ingredients would surprise most consumers, the companies that provide us with fish, meat, egg, and dairy products do not have to tell us anything about the feeds they use. A 2004 *St. Paul Pioneer Press* article on the animal feed industry called it 'a $25 billion-a-year industry that's operated as a nearly invisible link in the U.S. food chain.'

"In fact, feed ingredients are closely guarded secrets. I learned this while working as a lawyer for an environmental organization combating water and air pollution from industrial-style hog operations. We found that no one involved in raising the animals really knew what was in the feed. The farmers just used whatever was provided by the meat companies with which they were contracting. In his book *The Meat You Eat*, Ken Midkiff documents that every major sector of the animal food industry asserts that its feeds are 'proprietary trade secrets.'

"A closer look at what's actually being fed to animals reveals a lot of bizarre stuff that most of us would not want in our food chain. This is most likely the real reason feed ingredients are such carefully protected secrets.

"For example, meat by-products, ground-up bones, and chicken feathers are added to many animal feeds. Until a 1997 FDA prohibition, much of the conventional beef and dairy industry had been using ground-up cattle parts as feed even though cattle are strict herbivores in nature. In 2004, after a case of mad cow was discovered in the U.S., FDA expanded the scope of banned products from cattle feed, but still failed to outlaw adding cattle blood and other meat by-products, such as chicken feathers and feet. Bonemeal and slaughterhouse wastes are still fed to many pigs, chickens, and salmon. Because these animal parts may carry diseases, the Consumers Union argues that the FDA should also ban the feeding of all animal remains to food animals.

"Arsenic is commonly fed to chickens and sometimes to hogs. These industries say they use arsenic to 'improve feed efficiency' (reduce feed costs).* But arsenic can get into the environment because most animal manure is eventually spread onto crop land. Researchers at Johns Hopkins University School of Public Health have studied the consequences of adding arsenic to poultry feed and believe that it may pose a cancer risk to humans and could contaminate soils and drinking water. Europe has outlawed arsenic in animal feeds because of these kinds of environmental and human health concerns.

"Antibiotics are routinely fed to food animals to stimulate faster growth. Due to industry secrecy, official figures for this use are unavailable, but the Union of Concerned Scientists has estimated that 25 million pounds of antibiotics—*half the antibiotics used in this country annually*—are put in animal feeds to stimulate growth. A June 2005 report by the organization Environmental Defense confirms that this use continues virtually unabated despite growing public objections.

"Such rampant usage has alarmed health organizations, who warn that it is contributing to the rise of antibiotic-resistant disease strains. The Centers for Disease Control and Prevention, the American Medical Association, and the World Health Organization, among others, have called on the livestock industry to drastically reduce its antibiotics use. The European Union banned many antibiotics in animal feeds in 1997.

"Poultry manure is often mixed into cattle and hog rations. After the 2003 mad cow scare and because of disease-transmission concerns, the FDA announced it would ban chicken waste from cattle feed. But beef industry lobbyists resisted, and the FDA backed off the proposal. This is still being allowed today. In justifying its about-face, the FDA explained that putting chicken manure in cattle feed should be continued because it's an important disposal method for the chicken industry.

"Dyes are added to feeds for fish and egg-laying hens. One is cantaxathin, a reddish pigment that is added to farmed salmon feed (even "organically" farmed salmon) to make the (otherwise gray) flesh pink, and to confined-hen feed, to make (otherwise too pale) egg yolks yellow. Cantaxathin was marketed, then withdrawn, as a human tanning pill in Great Britain in the 1980s.

---

* Arsenic in the form of roxarsone is commonly fed to broiler chickens to combat intestinal parasites and thereby accelerate growth. In 2006, the Institute for Agriculture and Trade Policy tested poultry samples and reported that 55 of 155 samples of supermarket chicken and all ninety fast-food chicken samples contained measurable levels of arsenic.[1] The public also ingests arsenic from the poultry industry in drinking water. Most of the arsenic fed to livestock is excreted by the animals and is dispersed when manure is sprayed onto agricultural fields. The National Academies reported to Congress in 2001 that "arsenic causes cancer in humans at doses that are close to the drinking water concentrations that occur in the United States."[2] Arsenic in meat can be avoided by buying USDA–certified organic meats. Livestock raised by federal organic certification standards may not be fed arsenic.

"We never feed any of these substances to our cattle because we know that what our animals eat affects both the food we produce and the natural environment. On top of that, we believe that most people simply do not want chemicals, drugs, and slaughterhouse wastes in their food chain. Many such commonly used feed additives should probably be banned altogether.

"But at least consumers should be able to decide for themselves whether to eat products from animals that were fed things like meat by-products, arsenic, and antibiotics. It's time for the food industry to make this information available to the public. Each of us can start to make this happen by simply asking retailers and restaurants the question 'What was this animal fed?'

Notes

1. John Vandiver, "Arsenic: Chicken Feed Effects Questioned: Researchers Study Health, Environmental Impact from Use of Arsenic," (Maryland) *Daily Times*, January 4, 2004.
2. Institute for Agriculture and Trade Policy, "Consumers Beware: Dangerous Levels of Arsenic Found in Non-Organic Chicken," April 2006, www.organicconsumers.org/food safety/arsenic060405.cfm

Pork and Poultry Go Industrial— The Exploitation of Workers, Consumers, Land and Animals

Americans eat more meat per capita than people in any other country in the world—a whopping 248 pounds of meat per person per year, evenly distributed between beef, pork, and poultry.[1] We are encouraged to do so by fast-food chains, such as Pizza Hut with their Meat Lover's Pizza and Hardee's with their Monster Thickburger of bacon, beef—and 107 grams of fat. "Not a burger for tree-huggers," said Hardee's CEO Andrew Puzder.[2] The Center for Science in the Public Interest agreed, calling the Thickburger "food porn."[3] But regardless of its critics, the Thickburger had the desired effect on Hardee's restaurants, inflating sales by almost 8 percent in 2004.[4]

Fast food is just the beginning. Main-stream shoppers for the family dinner table are also manipulated at supermarket meat counters by companies such as Tyson, with their warm and fuzzy slogan, "Tyson. It's what your family deserves."

Although Americans lead the pack in meat consumption, other industrialized nations are making inroads, consuming on average 176 pounds of meat per person per year.[5] People in developing nations eat only a third that much, with an average consumption of 66 pounds of meat per year per person.[6] If you eliminate rapidly developing China from the last category, the number drops considerably.

Long Ago, In a Galaxy Far, Far Away ...
Traditionally, people around the globe have subsisted on a diet of primarily grains, beans, and other vegetable protein. Meat has been regarded as an occasional luxury for special days or served as a small garnish or side dish. Even in the United States—eighty years ago—meat was not expected at every meal. It was too expensive, too hard to come by. In many rural parts of the world, that perspective continues. Beans and tortillas are staples in rural Latin America, lentils and chapatis in India, soy and rice in many other parts of Asia.

But globalization, lower meat prices, and urbanization worldwide are changing all that. With the elimination of trade barriers, prosperous American companies such as Tyson, McDonald's, and Kentucky Fried Chicken are free to market their wares to developing nations around the world. As that happens, consumption patterns around the world are changing, for better or worse. Diets high in animal protein have become a near-universal aspiration.

Corporations Are Sociopathic, Yet Protected by Law

As you contemplate this changing global market, consider a point so aptly made in the documentary film *The Corporation*.[7] The vast majority of corporations have one goal, and one goal only: to maximize profits for the shareholders, and they'll typically use whatever means possible to achieve that goal. As the film documented so well, corporations typically behave like sociopaths, self-serving people who lack a conscience. Yet, although their behavior is unscrupulous, corporations have all the rights and protections of individuals under U.S. law.

The first example that comes to my mind is the heavy marketing of infant formula in impoverished nations during the 1960s, 1970s, and 1980s. The product contributed to infant mortality due to improper use by mothers who couldn't read the instructions or lacked access to clean water, yet the incident brought millions of dollars to manufacturers of the formula.[8] This formula issue continues today, although the World Health Organization and the United Nations have reduced the extent of corporate marketing. Additional examples of international corporate exploits abound as the automotive industry, the timber industry, and the meat industry stampede into potential new markets in the world's developing nations.

More and More Meat

Global meat production has increased more than fivefold since 1950.[9] It is projected to increase 2 percent annually through 2015.[10] Where is the current growth occurring? In the rich, industrialized nations of the world that already consume most of the world's goods? No, the market for meat in these nations is close to saturated, with little opportunity for expansion.

The biggest American meat corporations are now drooling over the largely untapped markets of developing nations, particularly Asia, Latin America, and Africa. In the next decade, meat consumption in these countries is expected to grow 2.7 percent, compared to only 0.6 percent in industrialized nations.[11]

Among developing nations, there's a wide discrepancy in meat consumption per country, depending on their rate of economic growth and their population density.

Take a Gander at China

India, Indonesia, Pakistan, Bangladesh, and Nigeria—densely populated countries with slowly developing economies—consume an average of only eleven pounds of meat per person per year.[12] Other developing countries with more rapidly growing economies consume much more, particularly China, at ninety-seven pounds of meat per person per year, a figure which has *doubled* since 1983.[13]

China now has a population of 1.3 billion people, compared to roughly 303 million in the United States (as of 2008). China's total consumption of meat in 2004, 63 million tons, far surpassed the 37 million tons consumed in the United States the same year.[14] China alone produces and consumes half the world's hogs. Brazil is the world's largest producer of beef and the second largest consumer of beef, after the United States. The United States leads the world in poultry production and consumption.[15]

What's Behind this Growing Clamor for Flesh?

What's going on in these developing nations to bring about the rapid growth in their meat consumption? The growth is due to urbanization and rising incomes, along with the Westernization of their cultural aspirations. The infiltration of Western standards is facilitated by television, movies, music, and especially by increased global advertising and marketing. Marketing by whom? American meat corporations and fast-food companies, such as Tyson, Smithfield, Perdue, ConAgra, Goldkist, McDonald's, Pizza Hut, and so on. If you've done any traveling outside of the United States, you've probably seen American fast-food restaurants. I remember a gaudy McDonald's in the center of a quaint pedestrian plaza in one Latin American city. Local vendors attempted to sell fresh papaya and mango outside, but the local children scampered up and down the promenade proudly displaying the McDonald's wrappers on their cheeseburgers. We imagine they did not know that *70 percent* of previously forested land in the Amazon is now occupied by cattle pastures. And much of the remaining 30 percent has been cleared to raise livestock feed crops.

If meat consumption is rapidly expanding around the world, where else are animals being raised? What about poultry and hogs? Are there more and more backyard flocks and barnyard pigpens? Maybe. But any expansion in backyard herds and flocks is dwarfed by the explosive and malignant spread of America's factory farm model.

Hogs and Poultry Raised on Factory Farms

Here in the United States, more than 80 percent of hogs[16] and 99 percent of poultry[17] are raised on factory farms, where tens of thousands of animals are crammed into each warehouse-like building, packed so tightly that they are unable to even stretch their limbs—all for the purpose of saving space and increasing profits for the corporations like Smithfield and Tyson that own them. As with feedlot cattle, warehoused poultry and hogs have diets supplemented with antibiotics, slaughterhouse scraps, fecal wastes, and other additives to maximize growth rates. Their social and physical needs are ignored for the sake of whittling down production costs.

Contract Farmers Get a Raw Deal

Although the great majority of U.S. hogs and poultry are owned by big meatpacking corporations, they are not raised by their owners, but by farmers who work under contract to the corporations. This system is referred to within the industry as vertical integration. A company such as Perdue, ConAgra, or Tyson owns not only the animals, but the feed mills, hatcheries, slaughterhouses—everything *except* the farmers' land and the buildings that house the growing animals. This leaves the farmers responsible for any lawsuits over environmental damages from the odors or the leaking lagoons where liquefied manure is stored. The system also saves the company from having to spend money on land and construction. The corporation integrates the tasks of each arm of production, employing drivers and catchers to move the animals from one stage of production to the next.

How a Tyson Complex Works

For example, Tyson has thirty-three poultry complexes and two hog complexes over an area of thirteen states,[18] mostly in the Southeast where labor is cheap, union representation is low, and environmental laws that might impede waste storage tend to be slack. Each Tyson poultry complex has at its center a hub consisting of a feed mill, hatchery, and slaughterhouse/processing plant that serve all the contracted farmers within a fifty-mile radius.[19] A single complex includes about 200 farms operating under contract. Each farm has from one to several warehouse-like buildings for raising either broiler chickens, breeder chickens, or hogs. The buildings are windowless metal sheds, longer than a football field, with automated food and water dispensers. For the broiler business, Tyson workers deliver chicks from the hub's hatchery to the long, automated buildings that the farmer has had constructed at his own expense. Each building costs around $200,000, so the farmer is paying a huge mortgage for the buildings—in most cases, with his family's land as collateral. The farmer manages the birds' care while they're on his farm, although, as mentioned above, he never owns them. Tyson provides

the feed and the antibiotics and other chemicals added to the water, but the farmer has to pay the heating and cooling costs and electric bills, which run in the thousands of dollars. When the chicks have grown into 6- or 7-pound broiler chickens, Tyson employees arrive at the farm to round up all 24,000 or so chickens in each building and take them to the hub's processing plant. The farmer is paid a flat fee regardless of the current market. He can earn bonuses, though, by saving the company money in different ways. For example, he might use less feed and still achieve the desired weight gain per bird. One way to do this is to install huge cooling fans at his own expense; birds that are less stressed by summer heat gain more weight per unit of feed.

The farmers we interviewed were friendly hosts when we visited and were conscientious about their work. All had inherited their farms from their parents in the days before animals were packed so tightly and shuffled so indifferently through their automated life stages. The parts of these farms that were under the farmers' control were spic-and-span. Inside the buildings, though, where conditions and densities are dictated by the company, the chickens were crammed neck to neck, with burns on their breasts and rumps from resting on accumulated fecal matter that was inches deep. We never did quite figure out how these kindly country folks compartmentalized the prescribed animal-care methods in their own minds. We suppose they write it off mentally as "the American way," or "the corporate way," or perhaps "progress." But progress for whom? Shareholders, certainly. But not for the farmers, not for the animals, and not for the American public who eat the animals.

What's Leftover for the Farm Family?

Said a former poultry farmer that we interviewed, "A poultry house today will cost on the average $180,000 to $200,000 just to build. But one building of chickens won't feed your family. In fact, four of them won't feed your family. Eight buildings might barely feed your family in the typical income of $40,000 or $50,000 that you'd like to have with two or three children. So four or eight times $200,000 for the buildings—that leaves you a million or a million and a half dollars in debt. But, if you have eight chicken houses, then you've got to have one or two hired helpers, too, and you're paying their salaries. What's left over for the family?"

Poultry farmers under contract to corporations are not getting rich, even though they work seven days a week, Sundays and holidays, from dawn to "dark-thirty," as one farmer told us.

Factory-farmed hogs raised under contract to a corporation aren't making anybody rich either, although the income for a hog farmer might be better than that of a chicken farmer. Hogs are often raised on three different factory farms. One handles pregnant and nursing sows, a stage called farrowing. Another farm might raise young pigs, called feeder pigs, for the three months or so after weaning. And a third farm might take care of finishing, or raising the pigs up to their slaughter weight of 250 to 280 pounds, at twenty-five weeks of age. A few hog farms keep the animals through all

stages, from "farrowing to finishing." We visited one for our research for *Veggie Revolution*.[20] But these all-in-one farms are unusual.

How Did All This Get Started?

Factory farms are fairly new on the scene. One hundred years ago, most livestock were raised on small family farms. Farm animals were kept alive longer then and spent most of their lives outdoors. Because they lived longer and farmers had fewer of them, the animals were raised with greater respect for their long-term physical and social needs. It wasn't practical to keep livestock cooped up because crowded animals couldn't graze or forage adequately and were too prone to illness and injury.

Industrialized Meat

But that all changed during the 1900s. Ironically, the change began here in the United States, in the land of wide-open spaces. Lots of space, yes, but we're also the land of business opportunities. The practice of raising hundreds of chickens indoors began during the 1920s when Cecile Steele of the Delmarva peninsula in Maryland accidentally received a shipment of 500 chickens rather than the 50 she had ordered for her backyard flock of layers. Rather than send them back, she built a shed for them and made a nice profit selling them for 62¢ a pound. At that time, broiler chickens and hens that laid table eggs were not distinct breeds as they are today. Steele's neighbors admired her methods, and the practice spread throughout the area around her, making the Delmarva peninsula the center of U.S. broiler production until just after Word War II.[21]

John Tyson took another major step toward industrializing the poultry business when he drove 500 chickens from Arkansas to a slaughterhouse in Chicago in 1936. According to Stuart Laidlaw, that decision broke the traditional bond between chicken farmers and local processing plants.[22] Tyson's drive to Chicago opened the doors to competitive pricing; slaughterhouses and meatpacking companies no longer had to buy the birds closest to them, but could shop around for the cheapest birds. This created a huge incentive for growers to reduce their expenses, which eventually led to the penny-pinching system we have today. On today's corporate factory farms, everything is secondary to the corporate priority of shaving production costs. *Everything* is secondary, including animal comfort, food safety, workers' rights and safety, environmental standards, farmers' financial welfare, and the rural way of life.

Tyson didn't stop after his landmark load of chickens. He devised new ways to raise large numbers of chickens in one place with fewer expenses per bird, built hatcheries with nearby feed mills, and eventually built his own meatpacking plants.

Breeders began developing new breeds of broiler chickens that would need less feed but could grow faster and develop bigger breast muscles because the white breast meat sells for a higher price in the marketplace than other parts of the chicken. Before 1946, it took an average of sixteen weeks to produce a 3.7-pound broiler.[23] Today, on a Tyson broiler farm, it takes only seven to eight weeks to produce a six-pound broiler with meaty breasts—with much less feed.[24] This "superior growth" is due to selective breeding, crowding that eliminates exercise, and growth-enhancing food additives.

The Downside of Huge Breasts

But breeding for large breasts and fast growth has disadvantages. Breasts grow so large and so fast that the standard broiler breed has trouble walking as it nears maturity. Feed must be carefully balanced to prevent overgrowth of the breast muscles. Still, the massive weight gain sometimes deforms the leg bones, crippling the bird so that it can't reach the automatic feed and water dispensers—a flaw that proves to be fatal. For this reason, said one chicken farmer we interviewed, poultry farmers must walk the length of *each* shed five times *every day* trolling for dead birds—while breathing fecal and feather dust and ammonia. This task takes hours, which accounts for the high rate of respiratory illness in poultry farmers.

Pork Goes Corporate

Deformed birds and coughing farmers were no impediment to the proliferation of corporate poultry farms—profits were too compelling for corporations to be deterred by such details. As the cash began to flow in poultry land, the pork industry took notice. Starting in the 1960s, pork companies began to adopt the vertical integration system that made chicken farming so profitable. Small family farms were bought up and consolidated into confined animal feeding operations, or

CAFOs, an industry term for factory farms that confine tens of thousands of animals in each building.

Like the poultry farms that preceded them, hog CAFOs maximize profits for the corporation through high volume and faster production. In 1950, there were 2 million pig farms in the United States producing about 80 million hogs per year. The number of *hogs* hasn't changed much over the last fifty-six years; our country today produces about 100 million hogs per year. But the number of *hog farms* has changed dramatically over the same time period—from 2 million down to only 73,000.[25] The drastic reduction is due to consolidation and the use of automated confinement buildings that each hold tens of thousands of animals.

Visiting a Factory Hog Farm

We visited a factory hog farm last year, a facility for 40,000 hogs. All the hogs, on this farm and all factory hog farms, spend their entire lives in darkened, windowless buildings, with automated food and water dispensers. They are either crowded together in indoor pens with wire mesh floors, or isolated in crates so small that the animals can't turn around. We saw sows in tiny farrowing crates, each animal pinned in place with a grate of metal bars, unable to take a single step in any direction. The air was so foul with accumulated feces and urine that our clothes and hair reeked for hours afterward, until we could get home to scrub ourselves, our coats, our shoes, and our bags. We even had to clean our notebooks and cameras to eliminate the stink.

The hog waste that drops through the slatted floors of a confinement building is periodically flushed through big pipes to an outdoor lagoon of liquefied manure. A single lagoon can cover ten acres, an environmental nightmare. Whether leaked, spilled, sprayed, or illegally dumped, much of the waste is inevitably washed into the nearest body of water, where it travels downstream and downriver, killing aquatic life along the way and sometimes snuffing out tourist businesses along rivers and coastal estuaries.[26]

The Export of Our Corporate Food Model

Given Tyson's aggressive trailblazing in meat production, you won't be surprised to learn that Tyson Foods now bills itself as "the largest provider of protein products on the planet." Tyson Foods is indeed the world's largest meat and poultry company, with 2004 sales of *$26.4 billion*. Many of their profits are garnered abroad. This American company now has operations in Argentina, Brazil, China, India, Indonesia, Japan, Mexico, the Netherlands, the Philippines, Russia, Spain, the United Kingdom, and Venezuela.[27]

But, although Tyson is the world's biggest, it's not alone. Four other giant multinational agribusiness companies, Goldkist, Pilgrim's Pride, ConAgra Poultry, and Perdue Farms, join Tyson in dominating the production and processing of chicken meat in the United States and, with Tyson, are about to dominate the world supply.[28]

Tyson Draws a Bead on China

China is the epicenter of the meat industry's expansion, the fantasy frontier of America's agribiz corporations. In 1997, Tyson Foods entered an agreement with Kerry Holding Limited, a Hong Kong–based subsidiary of the Kuok Group, to investigate locating poultry complexes throughout China, each designed to process half a million birds per week. In March of 2005, at a food summit in Chicago, a Tyson executive said that Tyson saw its investments in China as laying the "foundation for profits in coming years."[29]

Is anyone surprised at that? China is fertile ground for profit-taking. With more than 1.3 billion people, the world's most populous nation already produces and consumes more meat than any other country. As noted before, their per capita consumption of meat and milk has doubled in the last couple of decades—but the surge has not yet peaked. Although China already has about 14,000 factory farms, these farms are producing only 15 percent of the country's pork and chicken.[30] The land is rife with opportunities for more corporate confinement operations. Many of the existing poultry CAFOs in China and throughout Asia are owned by American companies. Others are owned domestically, but model their means of production on the system so profitably exemplified by Tyson, et al.

Are We Doing Them Any Favors?

Is Tyson a company with a history of good labor relations? Environmental stewardship? Human Rights Watch, a nonprofit that investigates worker rights, concluded no on both counts. Tyson and giant meatpacking corporations in general have a history of low wages, dangerous working conditions, and repeated violations of environmental regulations. Human Rights Watch published a 2004 report on conditions in a Tyson chicken-processing plant in Arkansas and in Smithfield's infamous pork-processing plant in North Carolina.[31] *Processing plant* is an industry euphemism for the building(s) where livestock from a company's CAFOs are slaughtered, cut up, and packaged. It's well documented that slaughterhouse work has death and injury rates higher than any other industry.[32] Workers must contend with sharp blades as carcasses are rapidly moved along a processing line. Slaughterhouse workers are also exposed to caustic chemicals that are used for cleaning, often without protective gear. The Human Rights Watch report noted that production-line speedups, with frequent reductions in numbers of workers, are often causes of injuries. The workforce in slaughterhouses is largely composed of ill-trained immigrants, many of whom are undocumented. Managers in these processing plants often react to worker complaints about production speedups, safety violations, or injuries with deportation threats, calls to immigration officials, or firings.[33]

Community Voice

One Tyson Worker Describes His Experience

"Tyson always gets rid of workers who protest or who speak up for others. When they jumped from thirty-two chickens a minute to forty-two, a lot of people protested. The company came right out and asked who the leaders were. Then they fired them. They told us, 'If you don't like it, there's the door. There's another 800 applicants waiting to take your job.' They are the biggest company, so what they do goes for the rest."[1]

Note

1. "Blood, Sweat, and Fear: Workers' Rights in U.S. Meat and Poultry Plants," Human Rights Watch, 2004, 175, www.hrw.org/reports/2005/usa0105/usa0105.pdf.

Tyson also fiercely resists efforts to unionize workers. According to William Engdahl of Global Research, Tyson and other industry giants have consistently worked to block unionization and drive out any existing unions from their meatpacking facilities. "In 1993, the National Labor Relations Board found Tyson Foods guilty of unlawfully directing and controlling a union expulsion at its Dardanelle, Arkansas, plant. The company interrogated workers about their union sympathies and illegally promised wage increases, bonuses, and other benefits if workers voted to get rid of the union. In 1995, Tyson was found guilty of illegally eliminating a union in one acquired company, Holly Farms. Tyson management coercively interrogated workers about their union sympathies, threatened to arrest workers exercising their lawful rights, threatened union supporters with firing if they remained loyal to the union, and fired fifty-one workers for supporting the union."[34]

One Tyson chicken farmer we interviewed recollected for us the takeover of his former employer, Holly Farms, by Tyson. Holly Farms, he said, had a profit-sharing plan that provided periodic bonuses for the farmers. It also gave the farmers a feeling that the company cared something about their welfare. But Tyson did away with the profit-sharing bonuses during the buyout. "You don't get to be the world's biggest by being Mr. Nice Guy," said the farmer.

Several farmers we interviewed said that all meatpacking companies compete with one another for Wal-Mart's business, in particular, because Wal-Mart has so many retail outlets in the United States and does such a high volume of business. Wal-Mart is Tyson's biggest customer. In order to get Wal-Mart's business, or any supermarket's business, a meatpacker has to offer them the cheapest wholesale meat. So all big meat corporations are focused on cutting their own production costs. Cutting costs gets retail deals and maximizes profits—for the stockholders and the executives. After all, that's the goal. Workers are last in line. Well, no. Animals are last in line. Then workers. Or which is it?

Environmental Stewards?

What about the environmental stewardship angle? Are these corporations doing a better job there? Mary Edwards of Calhoun, Kentucky, is in a position to know. Edwards said she and her late husband built a house on thirty-seven acres in 1995, only to have it surrounded by Tyson chicken sheds within a few years.

"I stay in my house because of the smell and dust; I don't have my kids over to grill out," she said. "When they turn those fans on, you can see the dust and dirt coming out of those chicken barns in the afternoon. It gets on my car and my house and inside my house."

Edwards was a plaintiff in a suit against Tyson filed by the Sierra Club over ammonia emissions from its factory chicken farms. Did Tyson take responsibility for the emissions? No, the corporation responded that the farmers who raise Tyson's chickens, under contract to the corporation, are legally responsible for all environmental damages. The court disagreed, finding both the corporation and farmers liable.[35]

What about water safety? In 2005, Oklahoma attorney general Drew Edmondson sued fourteen poultry farms, three run by Tyson, accusing them of fouling Oklahoma waters with the waste from millions of chickens and turkeys. Edmondson pointed out that nitrates and phosphates from the runoff of poultry waste fuel the overgrowth of algae, which clogs rivers and streams, and depletes streams of oxygen as it decays, thereby killing fish.

He remembers when, as an Oklahoma college student, he could stand chest high in the Illinois River and still see his toes. "I've seen it change," Edmondson said. "It's nice to have green land. It's not so nice to have green rivers."[36]

According to Environmental Defense and other environmental groups, factory farms, like feedlots, pollute not only our rivers and streams with excess nutrients, but also our groundwater and drinking water. While ingesting phosphorus is not dangerous to human health, high levels of nitrates are and

can even be fatal to infants.[37]

Although Tyson is known mainly for its poultry operations, the company also raises hogs. But the world's largest pork corporation is Smithfield. This corporation operates the planet's biggest hog-processing plant, in the tiny town of Tar Heel, North Carolina, on the banks of the much-abused Cape Fear River. The Smithfield plant slaughters and packages 32,000 to 35,000 hogs a day, at breakneck speed, and is notorious for its environmental and labor abuses.

Nothing Could Be Finer Than to Be in Carolina

Why did Smithfield locate the world's largest pork-processing plant in North Carolina? The meat industry has homed in on the Southeast because of lax environmental-protection laws, for one thing. In 1992, when Smithfield constructed the Tar Heel plant, the plant was seen as an employment and business opportunity for the state. But during the 1990s, when the number of hogs in North Carolina ballooned to exceed the number of people, a series of deadly hurricanes caused several massive lagoon spills and drowned thousands of trapped hogs. Since then, environmental oversight has improved somewhat.

But environmental laxity was just one piece of the lucrative puzzle for Smithfield. The corporation also chose North Carolina because the state has the lowest rate of unionization in the country. With only 3.8 percent of the state's workforce having union representation, North Carolina provides cheap labor for meat corporations whose top priority is cutting production costs.[38] However, other states across the Southeast and Midwest are not far behind. Nationwide, nonunionized workers are far less likely to demand a livable wage, insurance and health benefits, protection from hazardous working conditions, and other costly workers' rights. Nothing could be finer for a pork corporation with money on its mind.

But Why the Tiny Town of Tar Heel?

"Smithfield knew what they were doing," said Randy Tiffey, a senior representative with United Food and Commercial Workers. "They came to a place with the highest poverty rate and highest unemployment in the state," he said. "People here think $8 an hour is really making it because now they can get a double-wide for $30,000."[39]

The meat industry's workforce is not only without union representation, it is also increasingly foreign-born. As noted above in the remarks about Tyson, foreign workers are often undocumented, vulnerable to threats of deportation, and, consequently, are much more accepting of dangerous and abusive working conditions and low wages. Between the 1990 and 2000 census, North Carolina has seen a 273.2 percent increase in the numbers of immigrants who become residents, the highest rate of increase in the country. Seventy-two percent of the state's foreign-born population are from Mexico.[40] This growth in immigration has paralleled the growth of the meat industry in the state; the number of hogs in the state quadrupled in the 1990s.[41] Eighty-five percent of the 6,000 employees in Smithfield's Tar Heel plant are ethnic minorities, and more than half are Latino.[42] Smith-

field and other meatpacking companies find it easy to exploit and intimidate Latino workers, many of whom cannot speak English.

Just as in Tyson processing plants, unionization is discouraged by Smithfield. According to a document from Duke University, Smithfield was found by the National Labor Relations Board to have committed "egregious and pervasive" federal labor law violations at the Tar Heel slaughterhouse in the 1990s, including the firing of workers without reason.[43] The plant has also been fined several times for serious worker safety violations since it opened in 1992.[44]

José Sauceda, a Mexican immigrant, told a government panel that his supervisors at Smithfield's Tar Heel plant "were really hard on the workers, especially the immigrants who don't speak English. My supervisor was making us work faster and faster; get out the product. I was rushing and I reached for a loin and I got my hand caught in the saw."[45]

Smithfield Abroad

Like Tyson, Smithfield Foods is eager to promote and partake of the booming market for meat around the globe. In addition to dominating the pork market, Smithfield is the world's fifth largest beef packer, with more than $10 billion in total annual sales. The company already has plants in China, Canada, Mexico, and Europe.[46] But, given what we know about Smithfield's operations in the United States, is this a company that other nations will want to welcome?

In the spring of 2005, I had the opportunity to accompany Diane and Marlene

Halverson of the Animal Welfare Institute (AWI) on a tour of sustainable hog farms. During our drive between farms one day, Diane told me about AWI's campaign to keep Smithfield out of Poland. Poland! I was surprised. She said Bobby Kennedy Jr., president of the Waterkeeper Alliance and a fierce opponent of factory farming, had accompanied her and other AWI representatives to Poland to meet with farming activists there in an effort to block Smithfield's foreign expansion.

The Iowa of Europe

Why does Smithfield have its sights set on Poland? In 1998, Smithfield Foods president Joseph Luter III told *National Hog Farmer* magazine that he wanted to make Poland "the Iowa of Europe."[47] Iowa has the largest hog population of any state in the United States, followed by North Carolina. Poland, as it turns out, has cheap labor and lax environmental laws, just like Iowa and North Carolina. And Smithfield already has a local subsidiary in Poland, Animex, with twenty-nine huge hog farms up and running. Is Animex doing a good job so far? According to a 2005 Worldwatch document,[48] indiscriminate waste disposal is causing problems for local residents. The small town of Wiekowice complained that hog waste near an elementary school caused students to vomit and faint. The influx of Smithfield's hogs into the Polish market has caused a drop in hog prices, which has been a disaster for small hog farmers. Smithfield is unaffected; grocery store prices for Smithfield products have remained the same.

The Animal Welfare Institute, together with Polish union leaders, is working to convince the Polish government to resist factory farming.

Are Smithfield and Tyson going to be conscientious and accountable neighbors in overseas communities, enriching the lives of workers, and safeguarding the environment? Will they improve our international relations, generating goodwill toward Americans? What do you think?

Are these the kinds of companies whose activities we want to support with our consumer dollars? For us, it's not a difficult decision to make.

Notes

1. Lester R. Brown, "China Replacing the United States as World's Leading Consumer," Earth Policy Institute, February 16, 2005, www.earth-policy.org/Updates/Update45.htm (accessed March 14, 2006).
2. "Hardee's Hails Burger as 'Monument to Decadence,'" *USA Today*, November 15, 2004, www.usatoday.com/money/industries/food/2004-11-15-hardees_x.htm (accessed March 17, 2006).
3. Ibid.
4. Ibid.
5. Food and Agriculture Organization of the United Nations, http://faostat.fao.org, cited in Danielle Nierenberg, "Meat Production and Consumption Grow," Vital Signs 2003, Part I, 29, Worldwatch Institute, May 2003, www.worldwatch.org/pubs/vs/2003, reprinted at www.mindfully.org/Food/2003/Meat-Production-WorldwideMay03.htm (accessed January 11, 2006).
6. Food and Agriculture Organization of the United Nations, http://faostat.fao.org, cited in Danielle Nierenberg, "Happier Meals: Rethinking the Global Meat Industry," Worldwatch Paper 171, September 2005, 10.
7. Mark Achbar, Jennifer Abbot, and Joel Bakan, "The Corporation," Zeitgeist Films, 2005.
8. "Infant Formula: Hawking Disaster in the Third World," *The Multinational Monitor*, no. 4 (April 1987), http://multinationalmonitor.org/hyper/issues/1987/04/formula.html, and Richard M. Harley, "Bottle-Feeding, Good or Bad? UN Agency Takes Critical Vote," *Christian Science Monitor*, May 18, 1981, www.csmonitor.com/1981/0518/051835.html.

9. Food and Agriculture Organization of the United Nations, http://faostat.fao.org, and Nierenberg, "Happier Meals," 9.

10. David Brough, "World Meat Demand to Rise, Animal Disease Fears—FAO." Reuters News Service, August 28, 2002, www.planetark.org/dailynewsstory.cfm/news ide/17468/story.htm (accessed January 11, 2006).

11. Ibid.

12. Paul Appleby, "A Global Stampede to the Meat Counter," October 1998, www.ivu.org/oxveg/Publications/Oven/Articles_General/wi_meat.html.

13. Nierenberg, "Happier Meals," 38.

14. Brown, "China Replacing the United States."

15. Food and Agriculture Organization of the United Nations, http://faostat.fao.org, cited in Nierenberg, "Meat Production and consumption grow."

16. "What Is a Factory Farm?" Grace Factory Farm Project, www.factoryfarm.org/topics/hogs/ (accessed March 15, 2006).

17. "Kids' Farm at the National Zoo Deceives Children, Promotes Myth of the 'Happy Farm Animal,'" Compassion Over Killing, March 19, 2006. www.cok.net/feat/kids farm.php (accessed March 19, 2006).

18. Tyson Foods, Inc., Company Information, Growers—Complexes, www.tysonfoodsinc.com/AboutTyson/CompanyInformation/GrowersComplexes.aspx (accessed March 19, 2006).

19. Sally Kneidel and Sara Kate Kneidel, *Veggie Revolution: Smart Choices for a Healthy Body and a Healthy Planet* (Golden, CO: Fulcrum, 2005).

20. Ibid.

21. Nierenberg. "Happier Meals," 14.

22. Stuart Laidlaw, *Secret Ingredients: The Brave New World of Industrial Farming* (Toronto, Ontario: McClelland and Stewart, 2004), cited in Nierenberg, "Happier Meals," 14.

23. Nierenberg, "Happier Meals," 15.

24. Kneidel and Kneidel, *Veggie Revolution*.

25. National Agricultural Statistics Service, United States Department of Agriculture, "Volume I, Chapter I: US National Level Data," *2002 Census of Agriculture*, www.nass.usda.gov/census02/volume1/us/index1.htm, cited in Nierenberg, "Happier Meals," 17.

26. JoAnn Burkholder, et al., "Impacts to a Coastal River and Estuary from Rupture of a Large Swine Waste Holding Lagoon," *Journal of Environmental Quality* 26 (1997): 1451–1466.

27. Tyson Foods, Inc., 2004 Annual Report, 2, http://media.corporate-ir.net/media_files/irol/65/65476/reports/ar04.pdf (accessed March 21, 2006).

28. Tyson Foods, Inc., About Tyson, Our Locations, www.tyson.com/Corporate/AboutTyson/Locations/Tyson LocationMap.pdf (accessed December 9, 2007).

29. F. William Engdahl, "Bird Flu and Chicken Factory Farms: Profit Bonanza for U.S. Agribusiness," Centre for Research on Globalization, November 27, 2005, www .globalresearch.ca/index.php?context=viewArticle&code =ENG20051127&articleId=1333 (accessed January 15, 2006).

30. Ibid.

31. Nierenberg, "Happier Meals," 38.

32. "Blood, Sweat, and Fear: Workers' Rights in U.S. Meat and Poultry Plants," Human Rights Watch, 2004, 175, www.hrw.org/reports/2005/usa0105/usa0105.pdf.

33. Eric Schlosser, *Fast Food Nation* (New York: Harper Perennial, 2005).

34. Ibid., 90.

35. Engdahl, "Bird Flu and Chicken Factory Farms."

36. James Bruggers and James Malone, "Judge: Tyson Shares Farm Responsibility: Ruling May Have Impact beyond W. Kentucky," *The Courier Journal*, www.factoryfarming .com/environment_TYSON.htm (accessed March 18, 2006).

37. "Arkansas Poultry Companies Accused of Water Pollution," *USA Today*, July 24, 2005, www.usatoday.com/news/nation/2005-07-24-poulty-pollution_x.htm (accessed March 18, 2006).

38. Kneidel and Kneidel, *Veggie Revolution*.

39. Elizabeth Jordan, "The State of Working North Carolina," Report by North Carolina Justice Center, 2004, 27, as quoted in "Hog Farming: Workers and Jobs," North Carolina in the Global Economy, Fall 2004, www .soc.duke.edu/NC_GlobalEconomy/hog/workers.php (accessed December 9, 2007).

40. Kristal Brent Zook, "Hog Tied: Battling It Out (Again) at Smithfield Foods," *Amnesty International Magazine*, Amnesty International USA, www.amnestyusa.org/Winter_2003/HogTied_Battling_it_Out_again_at_Smithfield_Foods/page.do?id=1105525&n1=2&n2=19&n3=429 (accessed March 18, 2006).

41. "Hog Farming: Workers and Jobs," North Carolina in the Global Economy.

42. Pat Stith, Joby Warrick, and Melanie Sill, "Boss Hog: North Carolina's Pork Revolution," (Raleigh, North Carolina) *News and Observer*, February 1995, 19, 21, 22, 24, and 26, www.pulitzer.org/year/1996/public-service/works/about.html (accessed August 29, 2006).

43. Zook, "Hog Tied."

44. "Hog farming: Workers and Jobs," North Carolina in the Global Economy.

45. Ibid.

46. Zook, "Hog Tied."

47. Dale Miller, "Straight Talk from Smithfield's Joe Luter," *National Hog Farmer*, May 1, 2000. http://nationalhog farmer.com/mag/farming_straight_talk_smithfields/.

48. Nierenberg, "Happier Meals."

Farmers and Foodies
Seeking Solutions
Local Food

One way to avoid supporting the exploits of giant meatpackers is to buy animal products only from local farmers who use sustainable methods. For many environmentalists concerned with food, buying local is more important than buying organic. Just how does buying local benefit consumers, the environment, and communites?

Environmental scientists today agree that global climate change is the biggest challenge to our planet; many feel it's the biggest challenge we've ever faced. The United States has contributed more greenhouse gases, the cause of global warming, to our atmosphere than any other country. Our coal-fired power plants are a major source of greenhouse gases, as are our gas-guzzling transportation choices. But a United Nations report concluded that our food choices contribute more to greenhouse gases and climate change than do our transportation choices.[1] Much of that is due to deforestation for livestock pastures and livestock feed crops, particularly in Latin America; those cheap foreign feed crops are often fed to *our* livestock. Other sizable sources of food-related greenhouse gases include the transport of American-grown feed crops to factory farms and feedlots, the transport of animals from one stage of production to another, and the energy-intensive transport of refrigerated animal products from packing plants to markets. When we buy local animal products, we circumvent at least some of that transportation, although the source of the feed crops for livestock can be a problem even when livestock are raised locally.

Eating a plant-based diet of organically and locally grown produce is the most sustainable food choice we can make. Richard Pirog of Iowa State University examined the fuel consumption and greenhouse-gas emissions of a local food system where farmers sell to nearby markets and food travels an average of just forty-five miles. He calculated that carbon dioxide emissions were five to seventeen times less, and fuel consumption was four to seventeen times less, than in a continent-wide distribution system.[2]

But it's not all about greenhouse gases. Local food has other advantages as well. All of the owners of small farms that we interviewed for this book and for *Veggie Revolution* market their products, whether meat or vegetable, locally. They believe strongly that local food systems contribute to strong communities. When we buy locally produced food, we are supporting our own neighbors and our own local economy.

Notes

1. H. Steinfeld, P. Gerber, T. Wassenaar, V. Castel, M. Rosales, and C. de Haan, "Livestock's Long Shadow: Environmental Issues and Options," The United Nations Food and Agriculture Organization Executive Summary, 2007, www.fao.org/docrep/010/a0701e/a0701e00.htm.
2. Neal Pierce, "Consume the Right Lesson from Spinach Scare," *Charlotte Observer*, October 14, 2006.

Jonathan McCarthy: What Does *Local* Mean?

Jonathan McCarthy is a food activist and produce manager at a food co-op that buys from local growers.

"*Local* isn't simply an indication that food is grown nearby. After all, Tyson and Smithfield foods can be considered locally grown in some parts of the country. Rather, *local* is used to mean food that comes directly from the farmers rather than from a corporation, farmers who live close enough to deliver the food in person. In such cases, consumers can talk to the growers themselves, develop relationships with them, and learn about their growing methods and business practices.

"It's important to be able to talk to growers because there's more to know about farms than whether or not they are certified organic. Certifiers for fair trade are beginning to appear, but only for a few crops, such as cocoa, coffee, bananas, and various other tropical fruits. To become certified organic, a farm doesn't have to pay fair wages to laborers and doesn't have to treat them fairly. Large organic farms in California and Florida rely on Latin American workers who often labor under exploitive conditions and are vulnerable to deportation threats. All vegetables sold in produce sections are picked by hand. *All* of them. When food is marketed close to its source and is labeled as such, a shopper can have more confidence that the situation is fair for laborers because the farm is more easily visited and inspected by consumers.

"Since local farms can communicate directly with their buyers, a relationship of trust develops. For this reason, many farms with fair, sustainable, and organic practices are not certified organic. They may practice farming methods that are even stricter than the National Organic Program requirements for organic certification. There simply is no label for small farms, family farms, and direct-marketing farms because they are so diverse in their methods.

"By buying local, you not only support your local economy, choose less shipping, and support fair labor practices, but you also tend to eat seasonally. Vegetables have particular seasons in which they grow best. If you live in my city and eat fresh tomatoes or cucumbers in any months other than July through November, then they have been shipped from distant lands or grown with the aid of fuel for heating a greenhouse. Seasonal and local eating has the lowest environmental impact of all. Does this mean you might have to make some sacrifices and eat greens all spring? Not necessarily—if you learn the bounty of each season, unfamiliar crops, and how to prepare and enjoy all of those. And by buying primarily from local farmers, you make it more economically feasible for farmers to offer produce in the so-called off season, when local food is often hard to find. When farmers find it more profitable to grow all winter, we will all enjoy better food all winter. Buying locally-grown produce benefits us all."

Eliza MacLean's Gourmet Hogs

A Melodious Din of Snorts, Bleats, and Grunts

We've interviewed a lot of farmers, but none have intrigued or inspired me more than Eliza MacLean. Her willowy frame and long sun-streaked hair don't fit the stereotype of a southern hog farmer, nor does the purple school bus parked beside her farmhouse. But as we wandered around the eleven-acre Cane Creek Farm with MacLean in her muck boots and denim overalls, her arms and shoulders strong and tanned, the whole scene began to make perfect sense. A farm is a busy place, and MacLean thrives on the activity. She draws her energy from the hogs and other

Eliza MacLean's Cane Creek Farm and purple school bus.

animals whom she loves tenderly, from the enormous, bristly haired Clyde, to the little goat she's bottle-feeding. She also appreciates the harmony of a well-balanced farm, how the dung enhances her crops, while the vegetable waste nourishes her menagerie of contented livestock. MacLean understands and values the connection between the quality of an animal's living space and diet and the quality of its meat.

Like all farmers, MacLean hurtles through chores from dawn 'til dusk, but regardless of the task, she remains committed to her principles of compassion and sustainability. In addition, she's an astute entrepreneur, carving a unique niche in the booming market for artisan meats.[1] Meanwhile, she gets to raise her young son and daughter in a child's wonderland of miniature donkeys, pygmy goats, kittens, and spotted piglets, with a pleasing backdrop of grunts, squeals, bleats, and brays.

Eliza MacLean murmurs a kind word to one of her goats.

The farm includes a rustic store inside the barn from which MacLean sells farm products on Saturday mornings, mostly pork. "People will come and buy a cooler full and stock their freezer, then I'll see them like four months later," she told us.

MacLean got her start as an academic, earning a graduate degree in environmental toxicology from Duke University, then found a job as herd manager for pigs at North Carolina A&T University. She loved the work and knew she wanted a farm of her own. "Pigs are so smart and funny, they're fascinating. And when I saw this farm, I totally fell in love with it. It's probably the hardest work I've ever done, but my passion maintains itself. I get up every morning psyched to start a new day. I know I can do some good; I know I can make the animals happy. I also know that every effort I make here has ramifications all the way up to New York City."

It's clear that MacLean's relationship with her animals is very personal. As we go from chore to chore on the farm, feeding animals, checking on litters, filling troughs with water, she interrupts her commentary every couple of minutes to greet a particular kitten or piglet or goat, pointing out individuals who've had particularly illustrious histories.

"I Jumped Out of the Way Just in Time"

"Do I have the prettiest barn cats you ever saw?" MacLean asked as we approached the open barn door. She stooped to pick up a cat who ran out to greet her. "When this little cat was about eight weeks old, I ran over her with the truck. I heard her squeal and looked behind me, and I saw her twirling around—I almost vomited. I jumped out of the truck and screamed for my cousin, and she goes, 'The truck! The truck!' and I jumped out of the way just in time. I'd left it in neutral and it rolled straight back into the barn and tacoed that door. It was just a total brain fart! Anyway, I convalesced her in the house for two months, and she turned out to be the most obscenely sweet, affectionate kitten, and now she's fine."

She murmured to the kitty, rubbing it behind the ears, then put it down and headed into the barn to check on the nursing sows. The doors to the barn and all the stalls were open, so the lounging sows and their youngsters were free to move about, indoors or out. We tagged along behind MacLean, pausing to look at a particular sow.

Nuked by a Copperhead

"This sow right here, the small one, two years old, she got nuked by a copperhead this year. Her jaw swelled up so much, it almost turned inside out, and it's never quite gone back." The sow looks okay to me, lying on the ground outside her stall, her piglets nursing.

MacLean explains that usually sows with very young piglets choose to stay in their stalls with bedding, but it's been so hot, they plop down outside the stalls instead. The sows' milk comes in better when they're not heat stressed, so she lets them pick their own comfort zone.

As we move on, MacLean pauses over a youngster ambling across our path. "Why will this pig just not gain weight? He's the runt of the litter. He could run over there and be with his mother, but he just doesn't."

She stops to speak softly to another young piglet. "This one was a hand-fed runt; we still feed him occasionally," she tells us.

During summer, Eliza MacLean's sows relax outside their bedded stalls where the air is cooler.

A runt that won't nurse well is hand-fed on Eliza MacLean's farm.

A moment later, she admires another piglet scampering after his siblings. "I'm amazed at the stripes on this little guy. You're so cute!"

As we make our way through this area of nursing sows and young piglets, she comments on the physical differences between the pigs—stripes or spots, upright ears, floppy ears, pointed snouts, barrel-shaped bodies, long, low bodies. She loves breeding the animals, seeing what she'll get. Many of her animals are rare breeds, from the goats and donkeys, which she breeds and sells as show animals, to the rare hog breeds, such as Tamworths, Old Spots, and the now-famous Ossabaws.

Four-Footed Olive Trees

"I think I partly got into hog farming because of rare breeds," MacLean told us. "I already had rare-breed donkeys, goats, and ducks, and I did an exhibition for American Livestock Breeds Conservancy where I fell on Chuck Talbott and the Tamworth hogs."

Ossabaw hogs, such as MacLean's, are prized for having more omega-3 oils in their meat than other breeds of hogs.

Talbott, a professor formerly at North Carolina A&T State University, is a specialist in the production of upscale pork on small farms.[2]

After she had the Tamworths, MacLean was one of two farmers selected by Talbott and Pete Kaminsky to raise an extremely rare breed of hogs from Ossabaw, a small island off the Georgia coast. These black-and-white spotted pigs, distinguished by their long snouts, long legs, and small, barrel-shaped bodies, are descendents of Iberian pigs that escaped from the early Spanish settlers. They are highly prized for the taste of their meat. Kaminsky, in a *New York Times* article about artisan pork, raved about the "long-cured, translucently pink Iberico ham, glistening with droplets of amber fat" that he tasted in Spain. "The flavor—salty, sweet, nutty, slightly funky—was as complex as a mature pinot noir."[3]

The nutritional quality of their fat is also highly valued. The meat of the Iberian hogs and their Ossabaw descendants has more monounsaturated fat and omega-3 oil (the good oils found in olive oil) than that of other breeds, leading Spaniards to call it the "four-footed olive tree."[4]

The challenge in marketing the Ossabaw meat is that the fat breaks down quickly in transit. MacLean has crossbred her Ossabaws with Farmers Hybrid hogs, a standard hybrid of five breeds popular for its thriftiness and traditional size. By crossbreeding, MacLean hopes to create a unique hybrid that retains great flavor and good quality fat and is more stable during transport.[5] So far, she seems to be succeeding. Her specialty pork is in high demand; MacLean sells to markets as far away as New York City.

She Gives Them a Good Life

MacLean loves her animals, but she's not conflicted about raising them for the meat market.

"It's sort of a counterintuitive thought to be saving a rare breed by actually eating it, and people take issue with that. But there isn't a huge use for them; I'm not gonna be able to sell them to people as pets."

MacLean provides the highest quality of care any pig might expect—except for the one bad day at the end, the day they're delivered to the slaughterhouse. But until that day, MacLean's hogs are able to do all the things that hogs like to do. They can wander freely, run, play, and sleep together, cool themselves in mud. She feeds them a high-quality mixed feed with barley, and no antibiotics or hormones. They also get vegetable scraps and end-of-season plants from her organic garden. Along with a healthy dose of daily TLC. All the grown hogs have names she knows well. And she seems to recognize even the piglets, most of which won't stick around very long.

Unlike factory-farmed animals, MacLean's hogs are able to keep themselves clean. "They'll choose a dunging area that's away from their sleeping area. Pigs are the cleanest livestock animal; they'll never urinate and defecate where they sleep. They can't stand that, even though they love to lie around in mud. People don't realize that about hogs.

"If we're gonna be carnivores, we really should treat the animals, especially the higher ones, with respect, and give them the things that they would normally try to find in a natural setting," MacLean continued. "They're grateful, and we're grateful, and it immediately transfers into the quality and the taste of the meat. And it's not a difficult thing to harvest an animal knowing that you played God and you put it on the ground and you gave it a good life. Personally, I couldn't do it if I were doing it any other way."

Our Bodies and Breast Milk

MacLean's farming methods are better for consumers as well as the animals. "I believe we owe it to ourselves not to introduce into our bodies and our breast milk all the antibiotics and chemicals that conventional growers now use. I mean, they [big meatpacking corporations] don't care about people's health or the animals or the land. I care very much about all three of those things, and you can see that in the way I run my farm."

Corn Is a Clogger

MacLean is adamant about the importance of an animal's diet in creating a tasty and healthy meat product. "It's important to feed animals well. Corn tends to be a clogger. Even if you start with good quality fat, you can feed an animal the wrong way. If you start with a chicken and you put it inside with no sunlight, feed it the nasty conventional diet of corn and animal waste, you're gonna get high cholesterol. Whereas if you take that same chicken and let it eat grass and bugs and run around and eat a clean feed, your eggs will have half the cholesterol. It's the same with these pigs. You can do yourself a total disservice by feeding them wrong, even if they start out with the potential to be, you know, almost good for you."

Sustainable Methods Are Good For Hogs and Agricultural Land

MacLean is able to provide the hogs with a good quality of life and maintain the health of her fields because she has a relatively small number of hogs—less than 200 at any particular time. She has only twenty-five breeding sows, a few boars, and the rest are their offspring, which are generally sold at less than seven months of age. The standard slaughter age for hogs is about twenty-five weeks. Having so few hogs is key to having ample space for the animals to wander. She rotates groups of pigs among pastures of timothy alfalfa, fescue, and clover, allowing the grasses time to recover between rotations. During winter, she provides temporary huts with bedding in the pastures for shelter. MacLean explains, "They'll all sleep together in the hut, and they'll have clean grass to graze on, and not have pneumonia and parasite issues to deal with. It won't be a swamp; our soil and water conservation people are happy about that. It solves every problem—it creates a clean environment for the animal, it doesn't allow runoff to my neighbors, I don't lose topsoil literally to the wind, it provides a food source and a fiber source that's important to a lactating female, and it teaches the little pigs starting at three weeks to eat fibrous material."

In addition to rotating her pigs among healthy pastures, MacLean also moves groups of pigs into crop fields after a particular crop has been harvested to clean up the leftover plant waste. In the crop fields, as well as in the pastures, the pigs fertilize the soil as they forage. With low numbers of hogs, MacLean has no waste-management problems. Manure is worked into the soil naturally. "The typical color of soil here is red, but it's gone to chocolate brown in two years from bedding and manure. There is no better fertilizer than pig poop," said MacLean. "The growers that have been doing organic veggies for twenty years in this area cannot believe that my produce rivals theirs. Without really knowing what the hell I'm doing. It's the fertilizer—the pig poop."

Eliza MacLean refills a watering trough for hogs that are cleaning up leftover plant matter in a harvested crop field.

"This may sound sort of hippyish, or whatever," said MacLean, "but I really do think that our consumer-driven world is why we have hurricanes like Katrina and Rita. I studied biogeochemistry, I have a degree in environmental toxicology, I do understand how it really works. I believe we are in an accelerated state of unbelievable natural disasters because of our environment, and if we all just took the time to slow down a little bit and do more on our own land and with our own time to feed our neighbors, things would be better."

MacLean is doing her part.

As we walked around her farm, I thought about the wretched, crowded hogs we had seen earlier on our tour of an automated factory farm. The hogs in such facilities never see outdoors except for the day they're shuffled along a chute from the warehouse where they were raised to the truck that takes them to slaughter. At the factory farm, there was no human in sight, no one to pick up the dead piglet on the walkway, no one period, other than the fellow who showed us around ... and he was only there to show us around.

But MacLean's pigs enjoy another world, tidying her harvested tomato fields in the warm October sun, rooting out the tasty remnants. We watched, enamored with the whole scene, as MacLean climbed over the fence to fill a trough with clean drinking water. I stooped down to scratch a dog's ears and heard MacLean whoop. We looked up in time to see her riding one of the big boars like a bull rider at a rodeo! The ride lasted only a few seconds before she was tossed into the dirt. No harm done. She patted the Old Spot boar; he gave her an indignant snort.

Restaurants and Farmers Markets

MacLean markets her meats in several ways. She sells directly to consumers from her small farm store and at local farmers markets. She sells to high-end local restaurants as well, where diners pay top dollar for trendy Ossabaw pork with its omega-3 oils.

She also works with a distributor who sells her fashionable meat to niche markets in New York City for several dollars per pound. Organic meat and sustainably raised meat is growing more popular among conscientious and gourmet consumers. MacLean's meat has been praised in print by a variety of food writers, fanning the flames of its popularity among true connoisseurs who seem willing to pay whatever it costs.

Eliza MacLean takes a spur-of-the-moment ride on a startled boar.

A Rep for Niman Ranch

At the time we interviewed MacLean, she was also working as a regional rep for Niman Ranch, a California-based company that markets humanely and sustainably raised meats. She sold breeding stock to their farmers and helped them manage their herds. But since our interview, Niman Ranch has pulled out of North Carolina. The company, owned by Bill and Nicolette Hahn Niman, started small, but now provides meat nationally to the Whole Foods Market natural-foods chain and Chipotle Grills, as well as other specialized or niche markets.

Niman Ranch's pork operations have received a seal of approval from the Animal Welfare Institute, an organization that has developed humane animal-husbandry protocols for pork and for cattle. All hog farmers who sell to Niman Ranch must follow the standards of the AWI, which include these key provisions, among others:

Curious pastured piglets have a life worth living on a farm approved by the Animal Welfare Institute.

- Pigs must be raised on true family farms—farms that are family owned and operated and the farmers own the animals.
- All pigs must live in pasture or roomy, deeply bedded pens.
- Pigs must be allowed to engage in natural behaviors, such as nest building, and must be housed in groups, not in isolation.
- No farrowing crates and no gestation crates are allowed at any time.
- Pigs are fed only natural grains and other feeds fit for human consumption. No antibiotics, no hormones, and no meat by-products are allowed.
- Liquefied manure systems are prohibited.

Said MacLean of her former employer, "Niman Ranch has taken something to a national level that logistically was very difficult. Any farmer can choose to raise hogs for Niman Ranch as long as they do it in a humane manner. The standards are set by Marlene and Diane Halverson at the AWI. The standards make sense, and the meat is better quality because the animals are happier, and, really, that's the end of the story. They're just not stamped out like car batteries in a liquid-manure indoor system that is really the most evil thing I've ever seen done to an animal. Factory hog farms are as bad as chicken houses. Pigs are so intelligent and their dignity is bred right out of them. It's worse than an Irish setter that's been inbred. They make the most schizy, nasty, hyperactive, nervous pigs that step on their young and smush them through the slats of the hog house. Why is anybody eating meat like that? All for the sake of the corporate owner and mass production making him a buck. It's the worst-case scenario. There's nothing good about it."

MacLean's work with Niman Ranch included troubleshooting for local farmers who provided meat for the company. She was "somewhere between their mama and their vet," said MacLean, who at one time received 50 to 100 calls a day from North Carolina's Niman Ranch farmers.

She only rarely sold her own pork to Niman Ranch because she's willing to put in the time to sell it directly to retailers and consumers, who pay much more.

"Why don't all pork farmers sell to retailers directly?" I ask MacLean.

"Because if you're a farmer who raises corn and soybeans and pigs, you've got your work cut out for you simply managing those systems, filling the water, doing the feed, every day. The last thing you want to do is go solicit yourself to a restaurant and say, 'I have the best pork you've ever tasted.' Very few farmers want to take the time to do that. They're not entrepreneurial. They're animal people; they're not marketing people. I'm trying to do both because I'm trying to keep my system small. I want to keep the high-end product that I sell for a good price, but also not leave my humble roots. I want to make enough on the high-end places that I can still give my rural friends a barter deal for fixing my plumbing.

"Niman Ranch pays a very good price for a market hog, but I can sell my meat for several multiples of that. I mark it way up because I'm packaging a product of beautiful pork chops that are sliced and labeled with

my farm on it. I take it directly to the farmers market. It's fresh, not frozen. People buy the meat they might get in an upscale restaurant; they can go home and cook it for themselves.

"I do high-end, a couple hogs here, a couple hogs there, shoulders for someone's wedding, shanks for a caterer down the road, because my profit margin is bigger per item that I sell. But if I were a large-scale producer, I would want a market like Niman's because I would deliver 120 head of hogs and get a check for $14,000, or something like that. (That's totally off the top of my head, I don't know about the math.) But if you're raising them for a wholesale market like that, that's then going to stock stores and do the packaging, you're protected by them. You stand behind their label; they stand behind you. It's a nice relationship. But you really need, for that system to be profitable on a family farm, at least fifty sows. I sneak by with twenty-five sows, and the only reason I have that many is because a bunch of them are the small breeds."

Although MacLean's entrepreneurial efforts have moved her to a different level, she believes, as we do, that Niman Ranch is a part of a more-sustainable solution for the masses, and she is happy to be a part of their system.

I find myself often thinking of MacLean's farm—when I'm tired, or stressed, or fed up with the flotsam of everyday suburban life. I share her love of animals, and even though I'm a vegetarian, I understand her perspective. I, too, want to wander among a menagerie of creatures every morning, fussing over the infirm, stroking kittens, patting piglets, playing God, and making animals happy. I'm totally with her in her drive to do that. But much bigger than that—I admire MacLean in the role she has played in modeling a new system of agriculture. I believe people will continue to eat meat as long as it's possible to do so. MacLean is treading a new frontier, figuring out how we can do it without trashing streams and agricultural land and without torturing animals. She's kind to her livestock, and she does everything a hog farmer can to protect our air and water, the health of her customers, the welfare of wildlife downstream from her farm. And what a farm it is, with its purple school bus in the yard, its blue-eyed dwarf goats, convalesced kittens, miniature donkeys, spotted pigs, and the most harmonious melody of grunts, snorts, and squeals I've ever heard.

—Sally

Notes

1. "Pork Futures," *Food and Wine* (November 2004), 188–195, 230–232, as quoted in "Hog Heaven: Pork Sausage from Cane Creek," www.globalprovince.com/bestoftriangle.htm (accessed October 7, 2005).
2. Susan Houston, "High on This Hog," *Raleigh News and Observer*, www.lanternrestaurant.com/pages/press/N&O_ossabaw.htm (accessed March 6, 2006).
3. Peter Kaminsky, "On the Trail of Fine Ham: First Plant an Acorn," *The New York Times*, October 6, 2004, DII, as quoted in "Hog Heaven: Pork sausage from Cane Creek."
4. Kaminsky, "On the Trail of Fine Ham."
5. Cat Moleski, "Cane Creek Farm: Handcrafted Hogs," *Weaver Street Market*, www.weaverstreetmarket.com/article/display.php?id=755 (accessed October 7, 2005).

Additional Resources

Peter Kaminsky, *Pig Perfect: Encounters with Remarkable Swine* (New York: Hyperion, 2006).

Cance Creek Farm, www.canecreekfarm.us.

The Animal Welfare Institute and Niman Ranch

The Animal Welfare Institute (AWI) logo is worth searching for. Unlike the bogus "Care Certified" stamp of the United Egg Producers,[1] and other such instances of companies certifying themselves, approval from the Animal Welfare Institute really means something. This is in part because the AWI is a third party without a vested interest in the industry they are regulating.

Sisters Diane and Marlene Halverson have developed a set of humane and environmentally sustainable standards and protocols for raising livestock so that the animals might have "a life worth living." Any company whose producers meet their standards can earn the AWI Approved seal.

While a number of small farms have sought and received the AWI's approval, their most public partnership is with Niman Ranch. Niman Ranch is one of the biggest environmental and humane meat companies in the country. They network with independent farmers around the country who raise animals on Niman Ranch's behalf.

To earn the approval of AWI, a farm must provide livestock with five basic freedoms:

- Freedom from hunger, thirst, and malnutrition
- Freedom from physical and thermal discomfort
- Freedom from pain, injury, and disease (including parasitic infections)
- Freedom to express normal behavior
- Freedom from fear and distress[2]

In addition, AWI has developed very specific requirements regarding space, food, comfort, social needs, and medical care for each type of farmed animal—such as the hog guidelines listed in the section Eliza MacLean's Gourmet Hogs. The specific requirements vary depending on the type of livestock.

We were able to travel with the Halversons to visit and inspect a number of hog farms that sell their products to Niman Ranch. On these AWI–approved farms, such as Eliza MacLean's, we saw for ourselves the difference these guidelines make. Having toured a factory hog farm in 2005, which we described in our book *Veggie Revolution*,[3] we were able to appreciate the animals' freedom and quality of life on these humane farms. On one Niman Ranch–network hog farm, we chased a gang of forty or fifty tiny piglets through pastures of deep, green grass, trying in vain to take pictures of them. Their mothers watched placidly from a giant mud wallow in the pasture. On another AWI–approved farm, we watched as sows made nests of twigs and leaves for giving birth, then nursed their tiny piglets in the chill morning air. We recalled the county "waste management" agent who had told us earlier that sows are perfectly happy as long as they're warm and fed—even when isolated in tiny and barren gestation crates, lying in feces, the air saturated with ammonia fumes. He said that sows' attraction to nesting materials is meaningless—a vestigial behavior that means nothing to them and has no bearing on their contentment or well-being. We wished we could show him these healthy, happy sows and piglets in their woodland nests.

Because Niman Ranch provides meat to high-profile establishments such as Whole Foods and Chipotle restaurants, their partnership with AWI provides crucial publicity for both parties. You can learn more about AWI's approval criteria on their website, www.awionline.org. They also provide a list of AWI–approved farms. For a list of retail locations that sell Niman Ranch products, go to www.niman-ranch.com and click on Restaurants.

Notes

1. Sally and Sara Kate Kneidel, *Veggie Revolution: Smart Choices for a Healthy Body and a Healthy Planet* (Golden, CO: Fulcrum, 2005).

2. Animal Wefaire Institute, www.awionline.org. (Click on Animals in Agriculture, then on Standards.)

3. Kneidel and Kneidel, *Veggie Revolution*.

Natalie, Cassie, and Mr. Denzel

"Tyson. It's what your family deserves." This is perhaps the most ironic corporate slogan ever coined. What have families across the world done to deserve labor abuses, polluted drinking water, and bruised, tasteless meat laced with antibiotics? These are all by-products of Tyson's cost-cutting production methods.

To Cassie Parsons, a farmer who raises pastured poultry, the difference between her broilers and the corporate product is "like night and day. The texture of our chicken is firmer," she explains, "and the flavor is amazing. When you're cooking it, you can see the difference in the drippings from the meat. Our chickens have thick, healthy bones. When I make stock from our birds' bones, I get a gallon per bird, versus only two cups from a conventional hen. And it's no wonder—those birds are very weak because they don't get enough light or space or the right feed. Their bones and body don't grow properly. In our broilers, the viscera—the hearts, lungs, and livers—are very different from a conventional bird. They tell the story of how the animal's been treated. In a conventional bird, the liver is faded and graying, as compared to these healthy livers, which are black, like they should be."

You wouldn't eat vegetables that were bruised, damaged, or discolored, and you shouldn't eat such meat either, believes Parsons. She and her partner, Natalie Veres, own and operate Grateful Growers Farm, one of just three organic farms in their rural county in North Carolina. Parsons and Veres have dedicated themselves to raising healthy meat,

Natalie Veres and Cassie Parsons raise pastured hogs, broilers, and laying hens. Demand for pastured animal products is rapidly growing.

eggs, and vegetables. Visiting a corporate factory farm, Parsons said, "took my breath away. It reaffirmed what we're doing completely."

What Parsons and Veres are doing is surprisingly simple: they raise not only broiler chickens, but also hogs and egg-laying hens, all in grassy pastures under the sweet southern sun. They also grow and sell organic produce.

At Grateful Growers Farm, the broiler hens reside in pastured chicken-wire enclosures. Each fenced enclosure is sturdy enough to protect seventy-five hens from predators. Because broilers grow bulkier than laying hens, they are less nimble and thus more vulnerable to foxes, weasels, birds of prey, and neighbors' dogs. Yet, the chicken-wire enclosures are light enough to be portable, and are moved to fresh ground on the field twice a day—with the chickens still enclosed. So the manure is distributed evenly around the pasture, and is easily broken down by soil organisms to fertilize the pasture. The feces of factory-farmed broilers, on the other hand, are cleaned out of their sheds only once every eighteen months. Breathing the heavy fecal dust trapped in these sheds is sickening for the birds as well as the unfortunate humans who look after—or consume—them. Veres and Parsons's broilers, meanwhile, are breathing fresh country air.

Footloose

The Grateful Growers' laying hens have lives of true luxury, as livestock go. In contrast to the million caged and tightly packed hens on the factory egg farm we toured, Veres and Parsons's layers are free to behave as laying hens

have in centuries past, before corporations confined them to battery cages.* These country hens have the run of the farm, foraging for insects and seeds wherever they like. But they choose to stick pretty close to the henhouse, under the watchful eyes of a protective, strutting rooster. As we chat with Veres and Parsons about farming methods, the hens move in and out of the woods near the henhouse, dust-bathing, preening, pecking, and snuggling down together in the leaves. Are they after the stray beams of sunlight? Or just satisfying the social urge to congregate? Either way, they look healthy and contented.

The leisurely layer hens are separated by only a fence from a boar called Denzel. Huge but mild-mannered, he roots for morsels in his spacious outdoor enclosure, then lies down for a nap. He can be particular about his cover while napping, using his snout to

Unlike layers raised in battery cages on corporate farms, the laying hens on Grateful Growers Farm have the run of the farm and adjacent woodlands.

---

* See our book *Veggie Revolution* for a description of our tour of a factory egg farm—a facility with more than a million laying hens.

toss loose dirt and straw just so across his shoulder and back before he relaxes into slumber. We can't help but recall the confined hogs on the factory farm with nothing in their tiny cages but feces.

Meanwhile, the hens wander back to their shed voluntarily; it's time to roost. They're all trained to lay their eggs inside. Veres and Parsons collect close to fifty eggs every day. These hens lay *beautiful* eggs, in shades of pale blue, green, and gold.

Grateful Growers is selling out of eggs, meat, and veggies as fast as they can produce them. The future is looking bright for these small farmers, as well as for their flocks and followers.

Can we all eat pastured broilers and eggs from pastured hens? Not right now—there isn't room for every twenty-five broiler chickens in America to have a pasture of their

Cassie Parsons can collect eggs without disturbing the hens. These pastured hens can come and go at will from their clean, spacious henhouse.

own. If every twenty-five layer hens had a tenth of an acre, then the 1,100,000 hens in one factory egg farm we visited would require 4,400 acres. Does this mean that small-scale farming is not feasible? Not at all; rather, it's our level of *demand* that's not sustainable. After all, America currently slaughters five times the number of chickens it did just forty years ago, and each of those birds weighs close to twice what the average bird weighed in 1960.[1] If we could eat less meat and fewer eggs, we would have the energy and resources to produce those goods in an ethical and sustainable way. Then all Americans who eat meat could choose pastured meat.

"The key to it all is educating the consumer," stresses Parsons, "going back to quality versus quantity." She would argue, and we would agree, that a small amount of a high-quality product is far better for the health of the planet, for the animals themselves, and for the consumer. *That's* what your family deserves.

Note

1. *U.S. Chicken and Turkey Slaughter*, "Changes in Poultry Demand," www.ers.usda.gov/publications/aer787/aer787b.pdf.

Food Conclusions and Recommendations

Although the problems with our food system are numerous and complex, the solutions are fairly straightforward.

When large corporations take over food production and distribution, accountability and transparency diminish. Corporations have far too much license to alter food production in ways that are unhealthy for consumers, for laborers, for land and water, and for livestock. Corporations are allowed not only to use penny-shaving and damaging methods to compete with each other, but are also allowed to conceal these methods and to actively deceive consumers about methods and product quality. Examples of deception include supermarket murals of livestock frolicking under shade trees, when in reality, those meats are from animals raised in filthy and crowded warehouses. Other examples include the lack of labeling for products that have been genetically modified, or lack of labeling for dairy products that contain hormones. Many supermarkets promote vegetables that may have been sprayed with a dozen pesticides and shipped 1,000 miles as "Farmers market" produce, suggesting to consumers that it's local and pesticide-free.

Some of the solutions to these problems involve seeking accountability and transparency. The easiest and most direct way to do this on your own is to buy from local producers you know. When you can, shop at farmers markets, buying directly from families that grew and produced the products. People who farm using sustainable and healthy methods welcome questions and usually welcome tours of their farms as well.

When you can't buy from farmers markets, ask your grocers to carry local, seasonal, and sustainably produced foods—and when they do, thank them by buying the products. Even better, tell your grocery manager why you're buying these products, and that you plan to shop there more often because of the green products the store offers.

When you can't find local foods, buy certified organic foods. Remember that organic certification is the best way to fight the genetic modification of all of our seeds because certification excludes genetically modified organisms. Again, ask your grocer to carry organic products.

We've learned that animal products in general are not very earth friendly, regardless of how they are raised. Even happy livestock raised on Old McDonald's Farm must have pastures to graze, or have feed grains that take up valuable farmland. Livestock and their feed currently occupy 30 percent of the world's useable land surface, and their feed crops require 70 percent of the world's agricultural land.[1] That is not a sustainable form of land use in a world that will hold 9.5 billion people (median estimate) within four or five decades.[2]

But if you must have animal products, try to eat fewer of them and choose them wisely. Some are certainly greener than others. The Sierra Club recommends pastured meat over organic meat. But either is preferable to meat from a conventional feedlot or from a factory farm. If you shop at a conventional supermarket, ask the meat and dairy manager where the meat, eggs, and dairy products come from. Ask that they carry animal products from small farms in your area that use sustainable methods. Better yet, ask around at local farmers markets for farms that raise small numbers of animals humanely and without waste lagoons. If you visit a farm, ask how they manage waste. If they have hoofed animals, ask if they have fencing and buffer zones along their streams to keep livestock out. Ask if the animals are given hormones or routine antibiotics.

Seafood seems to be growing in popularity, especially among the health conscious. We know many people who have moved from consuming beef and pork to seafood, feeling that it is somehow healthier and more eco-friendly than eating muscle meats from four-legged animals. Is it? It's true that fish does contain omega-3 oils, which some studies suggest are beneficial to heart health. Fish also lacks the saturated fats found in most other meats. The seafood industry would have us think that we all need to be eating fish to have healthy hearts. But this is hardly true.

The vast majority of seafood today contains environmental contaminants, from dyes to hormones, the scariest of which may be mercury. (See Seafood—Here's the Carch, pages 112–114.) And omega-3s are available from a variety of plant sources with no accompanying pollutants. But from our perspective, of greater concern than tainted seafood is the fact that the mass-fishing techniques employed today (such as longlines, gill nets, and blast fishing) are destroying marine ecosystems in ways from which they will never recover. For a thorough treatment of this topic, read *The End of the Line: How Overfishing Is Changing the World and What We* Eat.[3] If you feel that you must eat fish, consult the frequently updated guide to the lowest-impact seafood selections on the Oceans Alive website, www.oceansalive.org/home.cfm.

Finally, the healthiest selection of all, for yourself and your planet, is to grow your own food. Gardening is the most popular hobby in the United States, with good reason. All of us can take pride in ripe, red tomatoes or dark, leafy greens that we nurtured and harvested ourselves. There's something fundamentally satisfying about a homegrown meal.

Eventually, I think we will go back to the way things used to be, before megafood corporations took over food production and distribution. We'll revert to local food out of necessity if the country runs out of oil in thirty-five years and the transportation sector collapses, as many scientists predict.[4] But we can do it sooner rather than later—if we take matters into our own hands and buy selectively right now.

For more shopping assistance, see the appendix (page 229).

Notes

1. United Nations Food and Agriculture Organization, "Livestock's Long Shadow," 2007, www.fao.org/docrep/010/a0701e/a0701e00.htm.
2. International Data Base, U.S. Census Bureau, www.idb.gov.
3. Charles Clover, *The End of the Line: How Overfishing Is Changing the World and What We Eat* (New York: New Press, 2006).
4. James Howard Kunstler, *The Long Emergency: Surviving the End of Oil, Climate Change, and Other Converging Catastrophes of the Twenty-First Century* (New York: Grove Press, 2006).

Chapter Five

Choosing Green and Worker-Friendly Clothes

Clothe Yourself Mindfully

Clothes Are Crops Too

When most of us hear the word *organic*, we think of food. But, like food, our clothing fibers also come from crops and from farmed animals. Clothing fibers, too, can be certified organic by the United States Department of Agriculture (USDA). Whether used for food or clothes, crops that are certified organic must be grown without the use of toxic and persistent chemical pesticides and without chemical fertilizers. The pesticide restriction applies to more than you might think, such as parasite dips for animals that grow wool.

We used to believe that organic certification was all about avoiding chemicals in the food we eat, but we know now that the reasons for farming organically are much bigger than that. Chemical pesticides and fertilizers disperse into the environment, into our groundwater and drinking water, into rivers and habitats and wildlife. We know, too, that many farm laborers who have to handle chemically coated products suffer health disorders from prolonged exposure.

Chemical Farming Is Not Progress

We were talking to a biologist friend about all this, and he lamented the fact that we *have to* use chemical fertilizers and pesticides to grow enough food and fibers to feed and clothe the swelling human population. To him, that's just one of the many ugly costs of our rapid population growth. We share his sentiment, but his rationale is quite mistaken. The use of chemical fertilizers, herbicides, and pesticides is actually *destroying* our prospects of feeding and clothing all the 9 or 10 billion people who will inhabit the planet by 2050. (That's a 50 percent increase over today's world population of 6.5 billion.) We'd have a much better chance of providing for all these people indefinitely if we reverted to agriculture the way it used to be. Reliance on chemicals destroys soil over time, and devastated soil won't grow anything at all.

Organic Fibers Are Picking Up Steam

The organic label is growing more mainstream every day. Both organic food and organic clothing are steadily increasing their market share, although organic foods are still much more available locally than organic clothing is. Most of the organic clothing we've seen is available online and most of it is made of cotton.

According to 2003 USDA figures, organic foods are carried in at least 73 percent of conventional grocery stores and account for 1 to 2 percent of food sales, with a 20 percent annual increase in sales each year.[1]

At present, organic fibers occupy a smaller portion of the overall fiber market. Organic cotton has caught on the fastest, but still comprises only 0.3 percent of worldwide cotton production.[2]

Estimates of the rate of growth of the organic fiber market vary depending on what products are included—just cotton or all fibers, just clothing or all fiber products (such as sheets, tampons, and so on). All the estimates, however, are encouraging. In general, the market for organic fiber seems to be growing somewhere between 20 to 45 percent annually, perhaps faster than the market for organic food.[3,4] Even Wal-Mart offers organic cotton shirts these days.

Eco-Neutral, But Not Organic

We've learned while researching this section that many fibers touted as being environmentally friendly, such as hemp, bamboo, and linen, are not usually certified organic. The reasons for that are complex. Some are grown in developing nations where, vendors claim, third-party certifiers are harder to come by. But some fiber-producing plants seem to be less attractive to pests than cotton is and are less likely to require heavy doses of pesticides, even from conventional growers. Nonetheless, they are produced abroad, and we generally support local products when possible. In this section, we review the current status of all of these fibers, including fibers produced by animals, and attempt to weigh the pros and cons of each.

Agriculture and Manufacturing Are Separate Issues

We've learned that the growing of fibers and the manufacturing of garments are two entirely separate issues. The USDA organic fiber certification applies only to *how fiber is grown*. The certification doesn't apply to the postharvest processing of fibers and fabrics. (See Beware of Bleaches, Dyes, and Finishes, pages 185–188). The Organic Trade Association offers a separate organic labeling for products that conform to their fiber *processing* standards.[5] (Later on, we offer some recommendations from Lynda Grose, an industry consultant, about how to shop selectively with regard to manufacturing processes. See pages 186–188.)

In addition to environmental concerns, we also consider human rights issues in the textile industry. Sweatshops have gained notoriety in recent years, and the garment industry is perhaps the prime culprit for exploiting women and children as laborers in developing nations. What's a consumer to do? We've included information about labor issues, fair trade certification, and endorsements from human rights organizations such as Sweatshop Watch that will help you make informed and responsible decisions.

Notes

1. Catherine Greene and Carolyn Dimitri, "Organic Agriculture: Gaining Ground," United States Department of Agriculture, Economic Research Service, Amber Waves, February 2003, www.ers.usda.gov/amberwaves/feb03/findings/organicagriculture.htm.
2. Wendy Priesnitz, "Organic Fibers: Dress Yourself and Your Home in Style with a Conscience," www.life.ca/nl/97/fibers.html.
3. Organic Trade Association, "Sales of Organic Fiber Products Continue to Grow," www.ota.com/news/press/39.html (accessed April 18, 2006).
4. Priesnitz, "Organic Fibers."
5. Organic Trade Association, American Organic Standards for Fiber, www.ota.com/AmericanOrganicStandardsforFiber.html.

Seek Guilt-Free Cotton

What Are You Wearing?

Cotton is comfy. Advertised as the "natural" fiber, it *is* more natural than synthetics such as nylon or polyester. But, as some of you may know, cotton is one of the most pesticide-intensive crops there is. We've been hearing that for years, yet we went right on buying cotton underwear, jeans, T-shirts, and sweat-shirts. We didn't really understand until we started researching the agriculture of fibers and the manufacturing of textiles.

Conventional Cotton: An Ugly Story of Chemicals

It takes one pound of pesticides and fertilizers to produce enough conventional cotton to make just one T-shirt and one pair of jeans.[1]

Cotton uses 25 percent of the world's insecticides.[2] Here in the United States, cotton is second only to corn in the tonnage of pesticides sprayed.[3] (Corn is the mainstay of our livestock industry, fed to farmed animals that will be served up on the dinner table. And lately, even more corn is being grown to provide ethanol as a gasoline additive. See Biofuels for Gasoline Engines, pages 11–14, for more information.)

What about those pesticides on cotton? Five of the top nine pesticides used on cotton in California—cyanozine, dicofol, naled, propargite, and trifluralin—are Category I or Category II materials, the most toxic classifications.[4] The Environmental Protection Agency considers seven of the top fifteen pesticides used on cotton in the United States in 2000—acephate, dichloropropene, diuron, fluometuron, pendimethalin, tribufos, and

trifluralin—as "possible," "likely," "probable," or "known" carcinogens.[5] Like all chemicals, they're dispersed to some degree in the environment when they're sprayed on fields or crops. Residues are ingested by birds and other wildlife, including amphibians and fish in the streams and ponds in the runoff.

An Eco-Friendly Feminine-Hygiene Product

Have you ever thought about how much waste is created from the use of tampons and pads? The average American woman throws away 15,000 sanitary pads and tampons in her lifetime, adding up to 250 to 300 pounds of waste.[1] Multiplied by the 85 million menstruating women in North America, that's about 12 billion pads and 7 million tampons, plus their packaging, added to U.S. landfills per year![2] And some don't even make it that far. The Center for Marine Conservation collected over 170,000 tampon applicators alone in just one year from U.S. coastal areas.[3]

Women who are concerned about this waste, not to mention the health risks of lodging wads of non-organic, dioxin-laden cotton close to their reproductive organs, have turned to one of the best-kept secrets in women's health care: the menstrual cup. A rubber or silicone cup, which costs $35, can be emptied, washed, and reused for up to ten years. In that time, a woman spends more than $1,500 on pads and tampons!

If you're intrigued, check out www.keeper.com. Reviews posted by other users are so enthusiastic, you'd find them ridiculous—if you haven't tried it for yourself. Personally, I agree with my friend Rachel, who puts it simply: "Quite possibly the most useful device ever invented."

—Sadie

Notes
1. The Keeper, Inc., Interesting Facts, 2006, www.keeper.com/facts.html (accessed November 24, 2006).
2. Ibid.
3. "Inner Sanctum: The Hidden Price of Feminine Hygiene Products," *E Magazine* 12, no. 2 (March–April 2001).

Cotton for Dinner

Destructive as it is to have those chemicals in your surroundings, it's even worse to have them in your stomach. And yet two-thirds of the cotton crop winds up in our food chain.[6] Cottonseed oil is common in processed foods. Check those bags of cookies and crackers, the bottles of salad dressing. In addition, raw cottonseed is a common "protein supplement" for dairy cows and beef cattle; every livestock specialist we've talked to has confirmed this, from feedlot operators to food science professors.

Cotton Poisons Workers—and Wearers

The variety of toxic insecticides, herbicides, fungicides, and miticides sprayed on cotton kills and injures workers on cotton farms and in textile mills around the globe.[7] Ninety-one percent of cotton farm workers in India exposed to pesticides eight hours a day have some kind of health disorder.[8]

According to Green Choices, the pesticides, herbicides, and defoliants used in growing cotton typically remain in the fabric after finishing and are slowly released during the lifetime of the garment.[9]

What Does the Organic Label Mean for Cotton?

Cotton can be certified organic if it's grown without the chemical fertilizers and the toxic and persistent pesticides that are used in conventional cotton cultivation. Growing cotton without chemicals is a huge advantage for the environment, for laborers, and for consumers. It's a big step in the right direction, but isn't yet the perfect solution, since the USDA organic fiber certification applies only to how fiber is grown. It also costs 20 to 50 percent more.[10] The extra expense seems worthwhile when you know the reasons for choosing organic, but not many people do.

Organic Cotton, Benign Dyes, Protected Workers: Is Any Company Batting Three for Three?

Patagonia made the decision years ago to switch to 100 percent certified organic cotton for all of its cotton clothing.

Using organic cotton is commendable. We called Patagonia to see if they've made a similar commitment to using low-impact dyes. A customer-service representative told me that they have, although he was unable to elaborate.

We called again to ask where their cotton is grown and manufactured into clothing. A customer-service representative told us Texas, New Mexico, Arizona, Colorado, Missouri, and Ontario. She then directed us to a website that addressed this question, which said, "We manufacture goods in China, Mexico, Portugal, Thailand, the U.S., and other countries." Upon further questioning, she said that cotton is also grown in these overseas locations.

The Patagonia website said that their farms and factories adhere to the standards of the Fair Labor Association Code of Conduct.[11] That's good. Better than no code of conduct, which is the case for many sweatshops. But this code of conduct falls short of that recommended by many human rights organizations, such as Sweatshop Watch. It still allows the employment of workers as young as fourteen or fifteen, for up to sixty hours a week, six days a week, for the local minimum wage or the prevailing industry wage, which is often not a living wage.

American Apparel

A representative from the Sustainable Cotton Project suggested American Apparel to us. She said American Apparel's 100 percent organic cotton clothing is assembled in Los Angeles, although she wasn't sure where the fabric is woven. American Apparel has a reputation for fair treatment of its LA factory workers, many of whom are Latino, with free English as a Second Language classes, health benefits, free parking, bus passes, good lighting and ventilation, and so on. We called to ask if the workers are unionized, though, and were told by a worker named Freddie that they are not. Bus passes, yes. Fair wages, not sure. Representation in decision-making, no.

We called American Apparel again to ask where their cotton is grown and to confirm that the organic cotton is woven, cut, and assembled in Los Angeles. The customer-service representative who helped us, Patty, excused herself for a moment to find out. When she came back, she pleasantly informed me that, yes, the organic cotton clothing is woven and assembled in LA, but that she was not allowed to tell us where it was grown. "What?" we said. "You can't tell us? We've never had anyone say that before." But Patty did not yield. "No ma'am, I can't tell you. It's company policy." We thanked Patty and hung up.

Not to be deterred, we made a couple more phone calls until we located someone in a California nonprofit who told us assuredly that American Apparel cotton is grown in Turkey and Pakistan. We must say, the fact that the company is so determined to hide this information is more incriminating than the information itself.

Other Companies Selling 100 Percent Organic Items

Prana, Harmony, and Gaiam also sell some clothing that is 100 percent organic. Other providers can be found by searching on the Internet. If you want 100 percent organic cotton, look for the percent; many companies make blends. Nike makes a blend that's only 3 percent organic. Organic cotton underwear is available online at Natural Selections,[12] bgreen,[13] and Spiritex[14] and other vendors you can locate via the Internet.

The Winner

Maggie's Organics is the only company we found that sells 100 percent organic clothing that is manufactured by either a unionized or worker-owned factory. Maggie's Organics T-shirts and camisoles are made by a worker-owned co-op in Nicaragua called Maquiladora Mujeres.[15]

Maggie's socks are made in Burlington, North Carolina, by Willow Brook Hosiery, and their tights in Peru, neither site a worker-owned co-op. But the employee we spoke with told us that all their work sites conform to the requirements for fair trade certification, even though that certification is not at present available for clothing manufacturers. (See What Does *Fair Trade* Mean?, pages 203–204, for a list of the fair trade guidelines.) The Maggie's employee told us, too, that the bleaches and dyes for their cotton conform to the Organic Trade Association's guidelines for postharvest processing. Whew! It's great that they're doing this, but it's sad that they're the only company we could find that pays attention to organic production, nontoxic bleaches and dyes, as well as worker's rights.

Promotional Tees and Totes, 100 Percent Organic

Schools are huge consumers of cotton, with all those T-shirts, sweatshirts, and little shorts with cute statements printed on the bottom. Because these items are produced so abundantly, getting a school to choose organic has a much bigger impact than does one individual's decision.

In April of 2001, California State University at Chico became the first university in the nation to have a line of organic cotton collegiate apparel, through an arrangement with Patagonia.[16] Unfortunately, Patagonia is no longer able to provide that service. We called American Apparel one more time to see if they could, since they have organic tees that are manufactured in the United States. We were told that they do sell blank T-shirts starting at $12 and can recommend printers by zip code who can affix messages or logos onto them. There is even an American Apparel store in our city that sells this product.[17]

Lynda Grose, a consultant for the Sustainable Cotton Project, recommended Happy Home/Spiritex as a source of blank organic T-shirts for school club logos. She said to contact Daniel Sanders at daniel@spiritex.net.

So, What's the Best Cotton Solution?

For new 100 percent organic cotton T-shirts, Maggie's Organics is a socially and environmentally responsible option, perhaps the best option. American Apparel is another choice. It's not worker-owned or unionized, but at least the clothing is assembled in the United States rather than in an overseas sweatshop.

If you want to buy organic cotton clothing, ask the vendor about the bleaches and dyes they use. Ask the country of origin. Ask about sweatshops. At least let them know you care what kind of chemicals they use and how they treat their workers. No matter what you buy, let vendors know you prefer clothing grown and manufactured using eco-friendly methods in worker-friendly factories. Production follows customers. When we buy selectively, we shape tomorrow's market.

Notes

1. Sustainable Cotton, Cleaner Cotton campaign, www.sustainablecotton.org/html/manufacturers/manufacturers.html.
2. Sustainable Cotton, Care What You Wear campaign, www.sustainablecotton.org/html/consumers/cwyw_ddt.html.
3. Wendy Priesnitz, "Organic Fibers: Dress Yourself and Your Home in Style with a Conscience," www.life.ca/nl/97/fibers.html.
4. Sustainable Cotton, Care What You Wear campaign.
5. Priesnitz, "Organic Fibers."
6. Sustainable Cotton, Care What You Wear campaign.
7. "White Gold: The True Cost of Cotton: Uzbekistan, Cotton and the Crushing of a Nation," December 8, 2005, www.ejfoundation.org/pdf/white_gold_the_true_cost_of_cotton.pdf.
8. Sustainable Cotton, Care What You Wear campaign.
9. "Clothes," Green Choices, www.greenchoices.org/clothes.html.
10. Sustainable Cotton, Care What You Wear campaign, Frequently Asked Questions, www.sustainablecotton.org/html/consumers/cwyw_faq.html
11. Fair Labor Association, Workplace Code of Conduct, www.fairlabor.org/all/code/index.html.

12. Natural Selections & Organic Selections, http://organic
    selections.com/catalog/.
13. .bgreen, http://natureusa.net/.
14. Spiritex, www.spiritex.net.
15. Maggie's Functional Organics, www.organicconsumers
    .org/sponsors/maggies/www.organicclothes.com/story
    .asp.
16. Sustainable Cotton Project, Case Studies, www.sustaina
    blecotton.org/html/consumers/case_studies.html.
17. American Apparel, Store Locations, www.americanap
    parel.net/storelocations/.

Additional Resources

Organic Trade Association, Organic Cotton Facts, www.ota
    .com/organic/mt/organic_cotton.html.
The Organic Trade Association's North American Organic
    Fiber Standards: Post-Harvest Handling, Processing,
    Record Keeping, & Labeling, www.ota.com/American
    OrganicStandardsforFiber.html.

Secondhand Is Twice as Good

The average American buys forty-eight new clothing items every year and discards an almost equal number.[1] Most of the discards wind up in the landfill; about a quarter are recycled. Of the recycled, about half make it to thrift stores. The rest is sold to "rag graders" and subsequently sent to other countries as used clothing, or chopped up to make items such as blankets.[2]

Every so often, we stop and do an inventory of how many of the garments we're wearing came from our favorite thrift store, Community Thrift. At any given moment, we're usually clad in about 75 percent thrift store items or hand-me-downs. Being tightwads by nature, we would shop at thrift shops even if the organic and sweatshop issues didn't exist. But shopping secondhand is definitely green—perhaps the greenest choice you can make. Your thrift store purchases do not financially endorse the use of pesticides, sweatshops, dyes, bleaches. Rather, by getting as much use out of their products as possible, you're improving the efficiency of cotton fields. Shopping at thrift stores is also a rare but wonderful instance in which the best solution is also the cheapest.

True, some thrift store items were made with toxic dyes. We try to avoid those by not buying anything that will bleed in water. Meanwhile, we're happy to know that we're not funding corporations that are poisoning the environment or exploiting laborers to offer cheap new products. Instead, we're reducing, reusing, and recycling, keeping material out of the landfill, and funding a nonprofit with a humanitarian mission.

Notes

1. Worldwatch Institute, "Clothing: The High Price of
   Fashion," www.worldwatch.org/pubs/goodstuff/clothing.
2. Worldwise, General Information, www.worldwise.com/
   textiles.html.

Beware of Bleaches, Dyes, and Finishes

United States Department of Agriculture Stops Short

As mentioned above, the organic certification of fabrics and clothing by the USDA applies only to agricultural methods in growing the fibers, not to any postharvest treatments, such as bleaching and dyeing and the application of "easy care" finishes. But manufacturers who buy organically grown fibers are more likely to process the fiber or fabric with less-toxic dyes and fewer finishes than other manufacturers.[1] In addition, clothing vendors who seek organically grown fibers may seek sustainably processed fibers as well.

Although the USDA ignores chemicals

in fiber and fabric processing, the Organic Trade Association (OTA) has stepped in to fill the gap. The OTA offers postharvest organic certification for products that conform to their fiber processing standards. You can order a copy of the processing standards through OTA's website.[2] Or you can see a draft of the OTA standards in full, posted on the Maggie's Organics website.[3]

So, what are the specific concerns with regard to chemicals in the processing of clothing?

What Do *Easy Care* and *Permanent Press* Mean?

We've often sought out wrinkle-free cotton in the past; we hate ironing. But after learning what the wrinkle-free finishing process involves, we think we'll go back to ironing. To achieve wrinkle resistance, cotton fabrics are treated with a toxic formaldehyde-based resin. It doesn't wash out because then the wrinkle resistance would be lost. The finish combines the resin with the fiber so it can't be removed. Such garments are labeled *easy care, crease resistant, no-iron,* or *permanent press.*

According to Worldwise, symptoms from the inhalation of vapors associated with easy care finishes can include "coughing, swelling, and irritation of the throat, watery eyes, respiratory problems, headaches, rashes, tiredness, excessive thirst, nausea, disorientation, asthma attacks, and insomnia."[4]

Dyes Aren't All That Pretty

How many times has your white underwear come out of the wash tinted pink or grayish blue? If dyes come out in the wash, then they also come out in sweat and body oils and can be absorbed through the skin. Virtually all commercial dyes are petrochemicals; according to Worldwise, some contain heavy metals that are dumped as toxic waste.[5]

Like pesticides, these dyes can affect workers' health in textile mills. They also have a heavy impact on the environment because unfixed dyes are flushed out in mills' wastewater, and treatment plants often fail to remove them. So the dyes and dye fixatives often wind up in rivers.[6] In developing nations, where many textile mills are located these days, the dyes can often be piped raw and unfiltered directly into rivers, with no effort to extract them from the wastewater. From a corporate perspective, that's the beauty of overseas textile mills and sweatshops in impoverished nations—few labor laws to protect workers, few enforced environmental regulations, minimal governmental infrastructure to pay much attention to penny-shaving manufacturing processes.

How to Avoid the Worst Dyes and Bleaches

We called several online clothing vendors who sell organic cotton garments to ask about their dyes. Most told me that they use *low-impact dyes.* To better understand this term, we called Lynda Grose, a designer and an educator in sustainable fashion design at California College of the Arts. She is also a consultant for the Sustainable Cotton Project's Cleaner Cotton campaign. We asked Grose what the term means, and how consumers can avoid buying clothes made with dyes and bleaches that have a heavy environmental toll. We asked her to tell us what, specifically, to ask a vendor.

"I worked at Esprit in the early nineties, and we coined the term *low-impact dyes* when we developed the E-Collection, a line of eco-logically responsible clothing," Grose told us. She explained that widespread dye processes are environmentally damaging in four ways: excessive use of water, excessive use of energy to heat water, water pollution (fixation of dye to the cloth versus what's left in the water), and the use of toxic dyes.

To support garment producers who are using water and energy conservatively, Grose recommends asking for clothes that were dyed using the cold pad batch dyeing process. This process has a liquor to fabric ratio of four to one, which means a relatively small amount of water is used. Cold pad batch is also a room-temperature dyeing process, so no energy is used to heat a water bath. If they don't use this process, she said to then ask if they use a heat-exchange system, where the hot water from the spent dye bath flows through pipes and warms up incoming cold water to save energy.

To support producers who minimize their water pollution, Grose suggested seeking fabrics that were dyed with a high fixation rate. She mentioned Ciba Geigy's bifunctional reactive dyes, which adhere to cotton cloth at around 80 percent fixation, which is a good percentage. Most dyes for cotton are at 60 percent or even lower, so more dyestuff stays in the water. When the water is flushed down the drain, the dyes go with it. Grose said that there are also low-salt dyes now, which are an

improvement. So consumers can ask for these as well.

Regarding toxicity of dyes, some colors are worse than others. The OTA guidelines require that low-impact dyes cannot contain heavy metals, which make their way into drinking water and food sources and then build up in our bodies, with toxic effects. Heavy metals such as lead, mercury, and arsenic are dangerous because they bioaccumulate. This means that they build up in the bodies of living things, mostly in fatty tissue, faster than our bodies can break them down. Who knew that clothes could be poisonous?

Said Grose, "For those who are concerned about metals, steering clear of turquoise and Kelly green avoids the copper content. If you see a turquoise low-impact dye, there is cause for skepticism. Sulfur black is also an issue. Chromium dyes that are used for wool are an issue, including chrome black." If you want to be a careful consumer, said Grose, ask clothing vendors if there are any heavy metals in the dyestuffs they use. There are environmental restrictions on some metals, so their use may be waning.

There are two different kinds of bleaching, Grose told us, one preferable to the other. Hydrogen peroxide bleach is biodegradable and environmentally benign. Chlorine bleach is neither. It produces highly toxic dioxins,[7] which are known to be carcinogenic.[8] Chlorine bleach is typically used on hemp to change it from beige to white, ready for dyeing, Grose told us. But chlorine bleach is not widely used on cotton, which is already naturally white. Wool doesn't need chlorine either, although the prewash or shrink-proofing of wool involves chlorine chemistry. When asking about fabric processing, Grose said to ask if chlorine bleach was used.

What's the Deal with Dyes?

We asked a vendor of organic cotton clothing why his company doesn't use all-natural dyes and skip the synthetic dyes altogether. He said that would be nice, but the problem is that natural dyes often bleed into the washing machine, and they fade rapidly. In addition, the colors may not be very vivid or clear to begin with. In such cases, he said, customers tend to blame the color problems on the fact that the fabric is organic. That's completely unfounded, but the misconception steers them away from organic fabrics. Still, he said, it's possible to use synthetic dyes that conform to the OTA standards and thereby avoid using heavy metals.

For more information about what heavy metals are and their effects on human health, see the Lenntech website, www.lenntech .com/heavy-metals.htm.

Asking Sends a Message

We know from personal experience that it's not hard to ask vendors questions about their fabrics and their dyes. Call customer service, or ask in person. Even if they don't know or won't answer, your question gives them the message that consumers are considering these issues.

Notes

1. Worldwise, General Information, www.worldwise.com/ textiles.html.
2. Organic Trade Association, American Organic Standards for Fiber, www.ota.com/AmericanOrganicStandardsfor Fiber.html.
3. "Fiber: Post Harvest Handling, Processing, Record Keeping, and Labeling," *American Organic Standards*, The Organic Trade Assocation, www.maggiesorganics.com/pdfs/ standards.pdf.
4. Worldwise, General Information.
5. Ibid.
6. Green Choices, Clothes, www.greenchoices.org/index .php/impacts-2.
7. Ibid.
8. "Environmental Health Risks: Information on EPA's Draft Reassessment of Dioxins," www.gao.gov/new.items/ d02515.pdf.

Look for Organic Wool

Wool is a generic term for fibers spun from the fleece of more than 200 different breeds of sheep, and from the hair of angora rabbits, cashmere goats, camels, alpacas, llamas, and wild vicuñas.

Sheep produce most American wool. According to the USDA, wool production is declining slightly in the United States.[1] Many Americans are fed up with wool-munching moths and stinky mothballs.

Wool, despite its itchy reputation, *can* be an eco-friendly choice for clothing, although only a tiny fraction of the wool produced in the United States is certified organic. A very tiny fraction—only 0.05 percent.[2] Eighty percent of our organic wool comes from New Mexico. The rest is from Montana, Maine, Colorado, Ontario, Vermont, and New Jersey.[3] Dozens of sheep breeds supply our organic wool, including Border Leicester, Cheviot, Cormo, Dorset, Karakul, and Icelandic.[4]

In order for wool to be certified as organic, it must be produced according to standards for organic livestock production.

According to the Organic Trade Association, these requirements include:

- Livestock feed and forage used from the last third of gestation must be certified organic.
- The use of synthetic hormones and genetic engineering is prohibited.
- The use of synthetic pesticides (internal, external, and on pastures) is prohibited.
- Producers must encourage livestock health through good cultural and management practices.[5]

Pesticides are a big factor. More than 14,000 pounds of pesticides were applied to U.S. sheep in 2000 to control mange, mites, lice, flies, and other pests. Some of the animals get multiple applications. These pesticides are hazardous to human health and the environment, not to mention the sheep's health. The top three chemicals applied to sheep in 2005—fenvalerate, malathion, and permethrin—are all somewhat toxic to humans and very toxic to fish and amphibians, which are doused with the runoff. Malathion in particular is highly water soluble, so it is easily carried off in rain- or irrigation water.[6] The pesticides in sheep dips have been linked to various ailments in sheep farmers, including nervous-system damage,[7] anxiety, depression,[8] and aberrations in bone formation.[9]

Organic wool is more expensive than conventionally raised wool. There are several reasons for this, including certification costs, higher labor and production costs, a smaller volume of business, and better herd-management practices. In conventional farming of animals that produce fibers, animals can be crowded together to increase production per unit of land. But, according to the OTA, organic standards prohibit overgrazing.[10]

What about the processing of wool? As with cotton and other fabrics, wool-dyeing procedures can involve hazardous chemicals. Chromium, the carcinogenic heavy-metal pollutant featured in the movie *Erin Brockovich*,[11] is a component of chrome dyes that are used particularly for wool. Chlorine bleaching is sometimes used for wool and contributes to dioxin pollution, another known carcinogen.[12] As mentioned above, these chemicals are in wastewater from textile factories, and sewage treatment plants often fail to remove them before the water is released into rivers, even here in the United States. Some wool garments are made of unbleached and undyed wool, but not many. If you partake of chemically altered wool, tell vendors you prefer low-impact dyes and relatively harmless hydrogen peroxide bleach.

Notes

1. Leslie Meyer, Stephen MacDonald, and Robert Skinner, "Cotton and Wool Situation and Outlook Yearbook," United States Department of Agriculture, 2005, http://usda.mannlib.cornell.edu/reports/erssor/field/cws-bby/cws2005.pdf.
2. Meyer, MacDonald, and Skinner, "Cotton and Wool Situation and Outlook Yearbook," and Organic Trade Association, Wool and the Environment, www.ota.com/wool_environment.html.
3. Organic Trade Association, Organic Wool Fact Sheet, www.ota.com/organic/woolfactsheet.html.
4. Ibid.
5. Ibid.
6. Organic Trade Association, Wool and the Environment.
7. A. Pilkington, et al., "An Epidemiological Study of the Relations between Exposure to Organophosphate Pesticides and Indices of Chronic Peripheral Neuropathy and Neuropsychological Abnormalities in Sheep Farmers

and Dippers," *Occupational and Environmental Medicine* 58 (November 2001): 702–710.

8. Kelly Morris, "Risks Accumulate with Cumulative Sheep-Dip Exposure," *The Lancet* 354 (1999): 9173, 133.

9. J. E. Compston, et al., "Reduced Bone Formation after Exposure to Organophosphates," *The Lancet* 354 (1999): 9192, 1791.

10. Organic Trade Association, Organic Wool Fact Sheet.

11. "Chromium Risks May Have Been Withheld: Public Citizen Report Claims Industry Hid Lung Cancer Data," Associated Press, MSNBC, February 23, 2006, www .msnbc.msn.com/id/11527696/.

12. "Environmental Health Risks: Information on EPA's Draft Reassessment of Dioxins," www.gao.gov/new.items/ d02515.pdf.

Back Then, Everyone Wore Linen

I remember having a couple of linen dresses when I was a kid. The threads were lumpy and the dresses were a little scratchy, but my mom considered them my fancy dresses for some reason.

I don't have any linen today. After looking at online vendors of linen, I remember why— it's expensive! But as concern mounts over the volume of pesticides applied to conventional cotton, lists of alternative, plant-derived, greener fabrics keep turning up. Linen is often on those lists.

Western culture has a long history with linen. The word has historically meant fabric made from the fibers of the flax plant, *Linum usitatisimum*. Linen cloth made from flax dates back at least 4,000 years to Egypt; some sources say as far back as 10,000 years. During the Middle Ages, linen was the most common fabric in Europe. It's very durable and can withstand repeated, abrasive hand-scrubbing in hot water, which was the cleaning method of the time.

Before the invention of the cotton gin, just before 1800, almost all clothing in the United States was made of either wool or linen. As cheap cotton cloth grew in popularity during the mid-1800s, linen was eventually left in the dust.

Is Linen a Green Fabric?

The word *linen* today doesn't necessarily mean cloth made from the flax plant. The word is also used to mean items that used to be made of linen. Sheets and pillowcases are "bed linens;" tablecloths and napkins are "table linens." Underclothes made from any fabric may be called linen. Even uncut fabrics of cotton or silk or modal (made of beech wood chips) may be referred to as linen. If you search on the Internet for *linen*, most of your hits won't be linen from flax, which is not that widely marketed.

European Linen

Until the 1950s, most linen was produced in Europe.[1] Some of it still is, by companies belonging to the European Confederation of Linen and Hemp.[2] The label Masters of Linen is granted to European linen products that meet certain quality standards.[3] Most top-quality linen produced now is made into expensive table and bed linens, or materials for art and hand-weaving.[4]

Linen's Not Organic

The cultivation of flax does require some fertilizer, though less than cotton does, but generally needs little water and few pesticides.[5] According to Lynda Grose, most linen *is* bleached with chlorine bleach prior to dyeing.

The Linen House, a Masters of Linen certified label, said that "harmful dyestuffs are being replaced with new, nontoxic formulae."[6] One hopes they mean dyes without heavy metals. Since they refer only to *formulae* and not to the dyeing methods, they likely still use water-intensive and heat-intensive conventional procedures.

Linen also requires an additional process that cotton does not, called retting. This process breaks down the outer stem and strengthens the inner fiber core. "When field retted, the process benefits the environment," said Grose. "When water retted in vats, the biological load on the wastewater is high." In other words, the wastewater is not good for the environment. This information suggests a couple of questions you can put to vendors if you're considering buying linen: Was chlorine bleach used? And was it field retted or water retted?

The organic processing standards from the OTA also have some comments about different ways of retting linen and echo Grose's remarks.[7]

Like Hemp and Bamboo …

Today, much of the world's linen is produced not in Europe, but in China. Chinese garment production always raises the suspicion of sweatshops, until proven otherwise.

On the whole, linen is probably not a fabric worth seeking out. Although linen is a greener choice than conventional cotton, it still requires the use of some fertilizers and pesticides. It is also very expensive, in the range of $100 per garment, unless you compromise by buying from a nonunionized

factory in China. The only linen we'll be buying will be at the secondhand store.

Notes

1. Linen, http://en.wikipedia.org/wiki/Linen.
2. The Linen House, Masters of Linen, www.thelinenhouse.com/EN/AboutLinen_MastersOfLinen.htm.
3. Ibid.
4. Linen.
5. The Linen House, Ecological Aspects, www.thelinenhouse.com/EN/AboutLinen_EcologicalAspects.htm.
6. Ibid.
7. Organic Trade Association's American Organic Standards for Fiber: Post Harvest Handling, Processing, Record Keeping, & Labeling, www.ota.com/AmericanOrganicStandardsforFiber.html.

Controversial Hemp

"Hemp is the solar power of fabrics," writes Chris Borris in *Sierra* magazine. "Give hemp a chance."[1] That's a powerful statement. But does hemp warrant such a hearty endorsement? What is hemp, exactly?

Hemp fibers are derived from the same plant species that gives us marijuana, *Cannabis sativa*. But before you try to smoke that shirt, hemp textiles contain virtually no THC, or tetrahydrocannabinol, the psychoactive agent in marijuana. It's been bred out. Selective breeding of hemp since 1930 has created three different strains that vary in their THC levels and in other ways. The three strains are for fiber, for medicinal and recreational use, and for seeds that yield hemp oil. The plants grown for fiber are harvested before they flower, another factor that would forestall their use as a drug source were they otherwise suitable.

Out of the Stone Age …

Hemp has been in use for more than 10,000 years. We have Stone Age pottery from China imprinted with hemp fibers. Historically, it's been used for rope, sacks, carpet, nets, and so on. Hemp is up to four times stronger than cotton, and lasts twice as long.[2] But nowadays, ropes, sacks, carpets, and nets are usually made with other fibers. And hemp fiber has been reassigned to new uses, one of which is eco-friendly clothing.

Hemp is a great fabric for clothing because it's breathable and porous and traps body heat for extra warmth in cold weather. Yet the breathable character of this fiber also allows hemp fabrics to be very comfortable during hot summers.[3]

Lawrence Serbin of Hemp Traders, the world's largest supplier of hemp products,[4] told us that hemp fiber is also used to make nontoxic particleboard for construction. Hemp Traders sells the particleboard online, as well as clothing, and hemp seed oil for use as a biofuel in diesel engines. Because hemp's fibrous stalk is high in cellulose, it's a good source of cellulosic ethanol to blend with gasoline, and as a plastics ingredient.

Hemp Chokes Out Competitors

Hemp's number one eco-advantage is that it's resistant to insects, so it doesn't require the application of pesticides.[5] No herbicides are needed, either, for two reasons: "Hemp plants are cultivated closely spaced, which inhibits competing weeds, *and* it grows so fast that it chokes out other plants," said Serbin. In addition to these advantages, it grows so vigorously that no fertilizers are needed, and produces at least three times more fiber per acre than cotton plants, and the most per acre of any other fiber source.

That's a long list of superlatives for one plant. Serbin acknowledged that hemp crops are at times sprayed with fungicides if the weather is damp enough to encourage fungal growth.

Close spacing of the hemp plants has a benefit beyond inhibiting weeds—it causes the stalks to grow tall and slender, producing long fibers, among the world's longest naturally occurring soft fibers. The fibers are strong because of their high cellulose content. Hemp fibers are not only longer and stronger than cotton fibers, but also more absorbent and more insulating.

Hemp is grown for fibers mainly in China and Romania, Serbin told us. Some is grown in Poland and Hungary. Other sources we've consulted mention Russia, France, and Italy. But the hemp for Serbin's company Hemp Trader all comes from China. Hemp cultivation is illegal in the United States—for surprising reasons, as you'll read later in this chapter. Canada grows the strain of hemp that produces oil-rich seeds.

Is Hemp Organic?

Although most hemp crops are organically grown, more or less, few hemp clothes are advertised as such. This is because there are few certifying organizations in eastern Europe and Asia, where most hemp fiber is grown. We called another online vendor, Fair Hemp,[6] to ask for a more elaborate answer. We caught

Alex by cell phone in Paris, but he was willing to talk to us for a few minutes. The hemp for his company is also grown and manufactured into textiles in China. Alex said that there are a couple of Swedish or Dutch companies (CAI and Skal) that could, in theory, certify Chinese hemp as organic. But, he said, one is too expensive, and the other basically greenwashes big corporations like Nike with meaningless certifications. He said the small community of hemp vendors in the United States are working together toward a more meaningful and accessible certification.

Although hemp is not at present certified organic, Alex asserted that it is indeed grown cleanly and sustainably. "It's all grown on small family farms," said Alex. "The farmers bring it to market" in small amounts, where it's collected and taken to factories. Alex has seen the farms; he said he knows the farmers don't use pesticides—because "they can't afford pesticides."

Not Sure about Dyes

Sustainability consultant Grose told us that hemp, like linen and cotton, is often treated with chlorine bleach before dyeing. Chlorine bleach from factories can pollute the environment with carcinogenic dioxins.

We asked Serbin how his hemp textiles are dyed in China and if his dyes contain heavy metals such as chromium. "No," he said. "No one uses chromium anymore." It's too toxic. "What about petrochemicals?" we asked. He didn't really answer that, other than to say that his dyes are low-impact and that they are synthetics that mimic plant

products. If his dyes really are low-impact, as defined in the OTA postharvest organic guidelines, that's great because *low-impact* means no heavy metals.[7]

"Sure, Wages Are Low … But They're Not Sweatshops"

Serbin said he'd been to one of the Chinese factories that produce his textiles. "What was it like?" we asked him. It was "just a regular factory," he said. We asked him if the fibers or textiles were certified fair trade in any way. He said fair is whatever the producer and the buyer agree is fair. He remarked that the Chinese hemp factories he visited were new and were staffed by adults, not children. He acknowledged that the wages were low, but said that the standard of living is low there too. Wages are low in parts of Los Angeles as well, he said. He didn't know about the work hours, but said that these factories did not qualify as sweatshops.

We asked Alex of Fair Hemp, also based in Los Angeles, the same questions. He said that his company has Chinese employees who are onsite in the Chinese factory, always watching, as a means of quality control. They don't use child labor, and the wages are "equivalent to, usually better than, prevailing wages." The working conditions aren't hazardous, he said, because the material is organic, even if not certified so. So the workers don't have to handle fabric laden with toxic chemicals. Alex said he visited one hemp factory that makes garments for another American vendor he wouldn't name that was unheated in winter and quite cold inside. The workers had fingerless gloves. "I don't see how they could do the work with hands that cold," he commented.

Alex said that there is no fair trade certification of textiles, only of raw materials. As to exactly why his materials aren't certified fair trade, we're not sure we got that. But he was passionate on the subject of his hemp products and their environmental merits. He asserted fervently that growing hemp without pesticides is a boon for the workers' health and the health of their entire community, which has, as a consequence, clean or cleaner water, cleaner soils, and perhaps some surviving remnants of wildlife populations. He also said two or three times that he believes adamantly in using only 100 percent organic cotton in his hemp-cotton blends. His clothing line is all blended. Lots of green clothing lines, in fact, use blends that contain some conventional cotton. That's no good, he said, and we agree with him. It's like buying margarine that's 20 percent trans fat and thinking it's great because it's not 50 percent. Trans fats, no matter the quantity, are toxic, and so is pesticide-soaked cotton.

The Greedy Truth

In the midst of our textile research, we got a startling new perspective on hemp from an unexpected source. We happened to call a U.S. Forest Service scientist with a question on a different topic, for Chapter Six, about the timber industry. He was a chatty type, and we got into a discussion of pine plantations as factory farms and other sustainable agriculture issues. He told us that his dream is to buy 600 acres and plant them all in

hemp. He's waiting, he said, for the agriculture of hemp to be legalized in the United States. Then he plans to quit his job and pursue his plan.

We were a little surprised. But he then went on to tell us about how completely versatile hemp is and how valuable it would be if it were legal. He confirmed much of what Serbin had told us, but he went much further. Hemp, he said, is a much better source of fiber for paper than wood is. Hemp grows to maturity in one season and requires fewer chemicals to make it into paper. Hemp can be used instead of trees to make particleboard, as Serbin had mentioned too. It can provide oil that can be converted to biodiesel and can be used to make plastics that are biodegradable. Of course, it can also provide fiber for clothing and rope and sails and everything else fiber is used for. And it makes good paint. Hemp can even be used in foods.

"Why is it illegal then, if it's so great and it isn't psychoactive?" we asked.

He told us a startling story. In February of 1938, the magazine *Popular Mechanics* published an article about hemp as the "New Billion-Dollar Crop." About the same time, an issue of *Mechanical Engineering* published an article presenting hemp as "The Most Profitable and Desirable Crop That Can Be Grown."

Not everyone was pleased with that publicity. According to our conversation, a wealthy and powerful paper corporation that was heavily invested in forested land was quite alarmed. If hemp was a better source of fiber for paper and particleboard than trees, then their land would be devalued. They pressed to have it criminalized, and it has remained so until today.

Further research corroborated this information. The 1938 magazine articles and the surge in hemp's popularity at that time are real. The specific events leading to its criminalization are cloudy, however. Some sources agree with our Forest Service contact, that a paper-manufacturing corporation stood to lose billions. Others say the oil industry put the skids on hemp as a competing product. Or perhaps its association with marijuana incited the government's decision to squash hemp production. At any rate, it seems certain that hemp's potential to change the status quo threatened one powerful organization too many. Hemp has been successfully repressed for about sixty years, at great—and evidently unnecessary—costs to our forests, water, and workers.

Hemp Industries Association, a consortium of about 250 importers, manufacturers, wholesalers, and retailers, is pushing to have hemp cultivation legalized. According to the *Los Angeles Times*, "the North American market [for hemp] has in the past decade gone from virtually nothing to an estimated $200 million. Not bad under the circumstances, but still a pittance for a plant that could clothe and house us, build and fuel our cars, enhance our diets, and keep the front gate from squeaking."[8]

In Short

With such an endorsement, it's hard not to like hemp. Yes, it is at least sometimes bleached with chlorine bleach, a contributor to dioxin pollution. It is sometimes treated with fungicides, and it's not certified organic. But on the plus side, it needs little water, and almost no pesticides, herbicides, or fertilizer. It seems that most vendors who bother to promote a relatively obscure textile like hemp go a step farther and try to choose low-impact dyes, although that's not guaranteed.

Another benefit of hemp is that it could replace the timber industry. You'll see how important this is when you read the section on pine plantations (see page 212). Hemp could also provide oil for plastics and biodiesel. The consensus seems to be that it's extremely versatile and greener than the things it replaces. That's great.

Our main hesitation is the China factor. Although both hemp vendors we talked to condone their Chinese factories' labor practices, neither of them convinced us entirely of the laborers' well-being.

To clarify this issue, we called Sweatshop Watch, an organization whose members work to promote fair labor practices and healthy working conditions around the globe.[9] We talked to a woman named Sihle who confirmed our concerns about labor practices. She said that China does have minimum-wage laws, but the minimum wage is very low. Sweatshop Watch only approves businesses that are unionized or worker owned. As far as we can tell, that excludes the hemp factories we investigated.

Sihle said that in the United States, there is no fair trade certification for fibers or textiles right now, although the International Labor Rights Fund has published a recent report on the production of raw materials that are not sweat free. There was recently a sweat-free communities conference in Minnesota, she told us, of organizations like TransFair USA, the company that certifies coffees. Meanwhile, Fair Labor, a fair trade certifier in Europe, "is already doing some certification of clothing."

If hemp cultivation were legalized here, then the Chinese factories would become a nonissue. But in the meantime, will we be wearing hemp clothing? Probably not. Unless we get them secondhand.

Notes

1. Chris Borris, "The Hidden Life of Clothing," www
   .sierraclub.org/sierra/200407/hidden.asp.
2. Fair Hemp, www.fairhemp.com/.
3. Earth Creations, Fabrics, www.earthcreations.net/fabrics
   .asp.
4. Hemp Traders, www.hemptraders.com.
5. Earth Creations.
6. Fair Hemp.
7. "Fiber: Post Harvest Handling, Processing, Record
   Keeping, and Labeling," *American Organic Standards*, The
   Organic Trade Assocation, www.maggiesorganics.com/
   pdfs/standards.pdf.
8. Lee Green, "The Demonized Seed," *Los Angeles Times*, January 18, 2004, www.votehemp.com/PDF/articles/1-18
   -04_LATimes.pdf.
9. Fair Labor, www.fairlabor.org

Additional Resource

Doug Yurchey, "The Marijuana Conspiracy—The Real Reason Hemp is Illegal," *The Illuminati News*, 2005, www.illuminati-news.com/marijuana-conspiracy.htm.

The Straight Scoop on Synthetic Clothing

Recycled Pop Bottles

Since 1993, sportswear company Patagonia has offered clothing made from recycled synthetics. The product line changes each season, but seems to always include some jackets and vests made from 100 percent postconsumer recycled (PCR) polyester. I called their customer service number and was told that some of their Synchilla garments are made, at least in part, from recycled soda bottles. And their current line of Capilene long underwear is made from 54 to 64 percent recycled polyester.[1]

Recycling is good—making polyester fiber from recycled garments saves both energy and materials. Still, it's not 100 percent green. The processing of recycled polyester still produces toxic waste that must be disposed of properly.[2] But is any clothing purchase 100 percent green? No—well, except for vintage clothes that would otherwise wind up in the landfill.

Rayon

Rayon is thought of as a synthetic, but is actually a seminatural fiber made of cellulose, taken from cotton linters, old cotton rags, paper, and wood pulp. According to Worldwise, the cellulose is broken down with petrochemicals in a toxic process and reformed into threads.[3] As mentioned in the bamboo section that follows, an industry consultant told us that rayon is made from a chemical process that is "highly polluting, involving hydrogen disulfide emissions." Lyocell, sold under the name of Tencel, is a similar fabric made of cellulose by way of a less-toxic process. The

Sierra Club reports that lyocell is not as prone to wrinkling as cotton, rayon, or linen.[4] Modal is another type of rayon made from beech wood cellulose.

Nylon and Acrylic

Nonrenewable synthetic fibers such as acrylic and nylon are made of nonrenewable crude oil, don't biodegrade, and can't be recycled. And according to Worldwise, manufacturing them produces toxic waste.[5] Nix that option.

What to Do?

For synthetic fleece or outerwear, we recommend calling Patagonia and asking about items made of recycled materials. We found that we needed help in locating the full array of recycled garments on their website as they are scattered about in different sections. Even if their recycled items aren't always 100 percent recycled and aren't always postconsumer recycled, the company is making a much better than average effort. All their cotton is 100 percent organic. In addition, they recently constructed a new building to meet Leadership in Energy and Environmental Design green building certification standards, which shows a more comprehensive approach to sustainable business. We like their attitude.

If Patagonia doesn't have what you need in a synthetic item, or if it costs too much, try a secondhand store. The last four fleece items we bought came from used-clothing stores and were in excellent condition.

Notes
1. Patagonia, www.patagonia.com.
2. Chris Borris, "The Hidden Life of Clothing," *Sierra* magazine 89, no. 4 (Jul/Aug 2004), 26, www.sierraclub.org/sierra/greenclothing/index.asp.
3. Worldwise, Textiles, www.worldwise.com/textiles.html.
4. Borris, "The Hidden Life of Clothing."
5. Worldwise, Textiles.

From Bamboo to Blouses

Bamboo is a new fabric heralded as green by its vendors. It's as soft as cotton, with a gentle sheen like silk. Bamboo clothes can handle dryers and ironing and will resist wrinkling if pulled from the dryer immediately. Bamboo fabric air-dries faster than cotton.

Just How Green Is It?

Bamboo is both grown and manufactured in China. We could not determine whether it's cultivated entirely without pesticides and fertilizers, but, apparently, it doesn't require the volume of pesticides used in conventional cotton cultivation. Bamboo Textile in Los Angeles seems to be one of the leading providers of bamboo clothing in the United States.[1] Their website states, "Bamboo's natural growth habits allow it to reproduce in abundance without the use of fertilizers and without the need for pesticides." That sounds hopeful, yet evasive. Why don't they just say, "We don't use pesticides," if, indeed, they don't?

Shirts of Bamboo, another well-established vendor of bamboo clothing, makes a similar claim. "Bamboo ... is grown without pesticides or chemicals, is 100 percent biodegradeable, and is naturally regenerative," the website says. It never explicitly says *their* bamboo is grown without pesticides.[2]

We called Bamboo Textiles several times and left messages, but were unable to reach anyone. And so we asked the hemp providers with factories in China, mentioned in the previous section about hemp, for information about the manufacturing process for bamboo fibers in China.

Bamboo Showers

Lawrence Serbin of Hemp Traders was willing to answer a question or two about bamboo. Of course, we expected that his answers might be biased since he sells competing hemp products. But we asked anyway. Serbin said that bamboo is not a natural fiber like hemp or cotton because there is no usable fiber in the bamboo itself. Rather, the bamboo is ground up and treated with chemicals that turn it into a liquid pulp. Then the liquid is shot out from something like a showerhead. The extruded streams of liquid harden into the fibers that are woven together to make bamboo fabric.

We asked Grose, our sustainable textiles consultant, about the environmental aspects of bamboo. She told us that bamboo is a sustainable alternative for hardwood floors in the construction industry, which we discovered in our visit to the Martin household (see pages 60–61). "However," Grose said, "rendering bamboo from a plant to a yarn is a chemical process, the same process for conventional rayon. It's highly polluting, involving hydrogen disulfide emissions. Rayon and bamboo are regenerated cellulose fibers and are man-made. Most marketing touts bamboo as a natural fiber. That's true for bamboo

hardwood floors, but not for textiles."

This information was corroborated by the Bamboo Textile website. "Stalks of bamboo are essentially crushed and pulped to separate the natural fibers. The fibers are then mixed with the lowest impacted chemicals to convert the plant fiber into textile quality fiber. As with many textiles, the process to make bamboo into fiber uses caustic soda. There are, however, alternatives that are more environmentally friendly."[3] The site doesn't mention whether the company is using the more environmentally friendly alternatives. The information given doesn't seem to contradict Serbin's comments.

Stay Tuned for More Information on Waste Dumping

Factories in developing nations such as China are notorious for dumping toxins, such as dye residues, into streams and rivers, or spewing foul clouds, unfiltered, into the air. We were eager to find a denial of such polluting practices in the purportedly green bamboo industry. Unfortunately, we didn't find one. Instead, the Bamboo Textile website says vaguely, "We are currently researching the answer to this question. Please stay tuned."[4]

Their information on cultivation and harvesting practices is equally vague. "Crop rotation and intercropping ... are not common practices integrated with bamboo plantation management. Our factory in China is utilizing the best harvesting practices to ensure a long-term supply of bamboo fiber."[5] Such a statement communicates no useful information at all.

Labor and Sweatshop Matters

What we learned about labor practices in bamboo factories also failed to impress. At least some bamboo producers, including Bamboo Textile[6] and Shirts of Bamboo,[7] claim to aspire to the SA 8000 labor standards developed by Social Accountability International. These stipulate the following workers' rights:

- Child Labor: No workers under the age of fifteen; minimum lowered to fourteen for countries operating under the ILO Convention 138 developing-country exception; remediation of any child found to be working

- Forced Labor: No forced labor, including prison or debt bondage labor; no lodging of deposits or identity papers by employers or outside recruiters

- Health and Safety: Provide a safe and healthy work environment; take steps to prevent injuries; regular health and safety worker training; system to detect threats to health and safety; access to bathrooms and potable water

- Freedom of Association and Right to Collective Bargaining: Respect the right to form and join trade unions and bargain collectively; where law prohibits these freedoms, facilitate parallel means of association and bargaining

- Discrimination: No discrimination based on race, caste, origin, religion, disability, gender, sexual orientation, union or political affiliation, or age; no sexual harassment

- Discipline: No corporal punishment, mental or physical coercion or verbal abuse

- Working Hours: Comply with the applicable law but, in any event, no more than forty-eight hours per week with at least one day off for every seven-day period; voluntary overtime paid at a premium rate and not to exceed twelve hours per week on a regular basis; overtime may be mandatory if part of a collective bargaining agreement

- Compensation: Wages paid for a standard work week must meet the legal and industry standards and be sufficient to meet the basic need of workers and their families; no disciplinary deductions

- Management Systems: Facilities seeking to gain and maintain certification must go beyond simple compliance to integrate the standard into their management systems and practices.[8]

As you see, these could be worse, but they could be better too. According to these standards, it's okay to hire fourteen- or fifteen-year-olds to work six days per week, up to sixty hours per week (including the permissible overtime), and wages must equal the industry standard. As for industry standard, Worldwatch reports clothing-industry salaries of 15¢ per hour in Indonesia, and 85¢ per hour in Mexico.[9] In short, the SA 8000 standards are far from fair and satisfactory. Again, as Sihle at Sweatshop Watch said, in order to be sure a garment factory is not a sweatshop, the factory should be unionized or a worker-owned co-op.[10] It looks like most bamboo factories have a long way to go.

Not Worth It

Bamboo has at least one good point in that it seems to require few or even no pesticides, and perhaps little fertilizer as well. But other than that, we see no particular reason to buy it. The hydrogen disulfide emissions associated with the manufacturing process are a turn-off. But the labor situation is worse. We don't want to support a factory that can hire a fourteen-year-old to work sixty hours a week.

Secondhand clothing continues to look like the best choice for the environment and avoids supporting exploitive labor practices.

Notes

1. Bamboo Textile, www.bambooclothes.com.
2. Shirts of Bamboo, www.shirtsofbamboo.com/information.php?info_id=1.
3. Bamboo Textile.
4. Ibid.
5. Ibid.
6. Ibid.
7. Shirts of Bamboo.
8. Overview of SA 8000, SA 8000 Elements, www.sa-intl.org/index.cfm?fuseaction=page.viewPage&pageID=473&parentID=4.
9. "Clothing: The High Price of Fashion," Worldwatch Institute, www.worldwatch.org/pubs/goodstuff/clothing.
10. Sweatshop Watch, www.sweatshopwatch.org.

Beware of Animal Body Parts

Since 1970, more than 90 percent of the world's wild rhinos have been slaughtered for one reason: the superstitious belief that their horns have medicinal value.[1] Rhinos are among hundreds of species whose populations are declining due to demand for their body parts in traditional medicines. Traditional remedies made of plants may have some real effect on diseases or symptoms; animal body parts virtually never do.

Tigers and bears are two other well-known animals that are extremely threatened by the demand for their body parts for medicines. As China depletes the native bear populations of Asia to obtain bear bile, suppliers turn elsewhere to look for this highly valuable

fluid. At present, the American black bear is the most numerous bear species on the planet, but this species is increasingly targeted by smugglers hoping to cash in on the demand for bear bile in China. Because black bears live in remote areas, killing them and smuggling their gall bladders, or the contents thereof, out of the United States is relatively easy.

The market for traditional Chinese medicines is flourishing here in the United States as well. According to TRAFFIC International, the world's largest wildlife trade monitoring network, certain traditional Chinese medicine products are more available in North America than in China. A survey by TRAFFIC of 110 traditional Chinese medicine shops in seven cities found that 49 percent of the shops offered for sale at least one product that contained a protected species.[2]

Community Voice
Alligator on a Stick: Animal Souvenirs

On a recent trip to the South Carolina coast with my friends, we stopped at Bargain Beachwear on Highway 17 to look for clothes. Among the thousands of random objects in this outlet store were many unfortunate animals—dead and alive. Alligator heads were a featured item, as well as alligator feet or claws attached to a wooden handle so that consumers could hold the handle and pretend to "claw" people like a real alligator. There was a wire cage full of hermit crabs, all of which had shells dyed neon colors. The floor of the cage was made of wide-holed mesh; the crabs could barely move across the mesh because the gaps were so big; most of them were stuck. One of the women who worked there said that she was the only one who was not too squeamish to clean the cage. They also sold live frogs in small containers; the containers held about one cup of water. The frogs were advertised as requiring almost no cleaning or maintenance. On the floor of the shop were fake cats that looked real enough, curled in a sleeping posture. They had about 200 of these, made to lie on the floor of your house, so you could fool visitors into thinking you had a real cat. Upon closer inspection, I discovered that the cats' fur was made of rabbits' fur. Who knows how many rabbits were killed for this ridiculousness. For about a dollar, the outlet also sold puffer fish, inflated to full capacity and solidified with some invisible goo. Fake eyes had been placed over their original bulging sockets. Also for sale, overlooked in their relative insignificance, were endless numbers of dead and dried starfish, sea horses, and other sea life. Each little carcass was embossed with a posh Myrtle Beach design—a perfect token of how we've exploited this once-beautiful coastal ecosystem.

—Alan Kneidel

What You Can Do

Americans like to shop. We bring home foreign jewelry, carvings, shoes, shawls, leathers, musical instruments—all of which can be made from animal tusks, horns, wool, and skins of threatened animals. Whether you're shopping in your hometown or across the planet, pay attention to what you buy.[3, 4, 5] When you choose leather, fur, or wool, read the label, ask questions, and ask for documentation that the object did not come from a protected or endangered animal. Better yet, avoid gifts or souvenirs made from animal parts. If you buy wood products or ornamental plants such as orchids, ask the proprietor about the source. Americans consume 60 percent of the world's harvested mahogany trees for furniture—57,000 trees per year.[6] When you see anything questionable, tell the shop owner of your concern. For more detailed guidance about specific products, download a brochure from the World Wildlife Fund. During the 1970s, the World Wildlife Fund and the World Conservation Union founded TRAFFIC. Take their brochures with you when you shop.[7, 8] Their website also has a wealth of information about global traffic in wild animals and plants.[9]

Notes

1. World Wildlife Fund, Wildlife Trade, www.worldwildlife.org/trade/index.cfm (accessed December 2, 2006).
2. Traffic Network, Traffic North America (the wildlife trade-monitoring network), www.traffic.org/network/network6_2.htm. 4. "Sturgeon and Paddlefish," Traffic Network, CITES, www.traffic.org/copII/briefingroom/sturgeon.html.
3. "Buyer Beware: Don't Bring Home a Suitcase Full of Trouble," World Wildlife Fund, Wildlife Trade, Buyer Beware, www.worldwildlife.org/buyerbeware/.
4. "Be a Souvenir Sleuth!" World Wildlife Fund, Wildlife Trade, Buyer Beware, www.worldwildlife.org/buyerbeware/tourist_shop.cfm.
5. "Be a Pharmaceutical Flatfoot!" World Wildlife Fund, Wildlife Trade, Buyer Beware, www.worldwildlife.org/buyerbeware/pharmacy.cfm.
6. "Mahogany Matters: The U.S. Market for Big-Leafed Mahogany and Its Implications for the Conservation of the Species," Traffic Network, Mahogany and CITES, www.traffic.org/mahogany/us.html (accessed December 2, 2006).
7. "Buyer Beware" brochure, World Wildlife Fund, Wildlife Trade, www.worldwildlife.org/trade/pubs/FinalGeneralBuyerBeware.pdf.
8. "Buyer Beware Caribbean" brochure, World Wildlife Fund, Wildlife Trade, www.worldwildlife.org/trade/pubs/caribbean_buyer_beware.pdf.
9. World Wildlife Fund, Wildlife Trade, TRAFFIC, www.worldwildlife.org/trade/traffic.cfm.

Beware of Furs

Fur trim is often referred by garment makers as a by-product so that potential buyers won't feel responsible for the animal's death.

Trim is not a by-product. More animals are killed for fur trim than for garments made entirely of fur.

According to the Animal Protection Institute, a staggering 50 million animals are violently killed each year for their fur.[1]

Some are grabbed by painful traps. Others spend their lives in crowded and filthy conditions on fur farms across the globe before being slaughtered. The Canadian government sanctions the clubbing of hundreds of thousands of seals for fur, many just weeks old. These are the facts that the fur industry tries to conceal from consumers.

Like meatpacking companies and other industries that abuse animals, the fur industry employs legions of public relations experts to mislead consumers. The industry fights legislation that would force them to use truthful labels.

Since most Americans oppose the killing of animals for fur, fur vendors must help customers disconnect animals' suffering from their fur products. This includes dying fur unnatural colors, trimming or braiding it, labeling it as "fabric." Fur trim is actually experiencing a surge in sales both here and abroad—due to the successfully deceptive marketing. Fur is increasingly found on toys and gimmicks these days.

Be an informed consumer. Recognize deceptive marketing: any and all fur is the skin of an animal that was brutally killed to provide it.

Because it's often hard to tell fake fur from real, wearing fake fur may send a message to everyone you meet that you approve of the fur industry. To avoid encouraging the popularity of fur in any way, avoid all furs, fake or real. But if you must have fur, use the test below to figure out if garment has faux fur or real.

Is That Fur Real or Fake?

Here's a quick guide courtesy of The Animal Protection Institute and the Fur Free Alliance[2] to help you tell the difference between real and fake fur on the rack:

The Feel Test
• Feel the difference by rolling the hairs between the finger and thumb.
• Genuine Fur: Feels smooth and soft, easily rolls between the fingers.
• Fake Fur: Feels coarse.

The Look Test
• Blow on the hairs so that they divide, and look at the base.
• Genuine Fur: Often made up of several layers of thin, almost curly hairs that form a dense underwool through which the longer hairs stick out. The hairs remain attached to the leather (skin).
• Fake Fur: Simpler in structure, individual hairs are often the same length and are even in color.

The Pin Test
• Drive a pin through the base where the fur is attached.
• Genuine Fur: The leather resists; the pin is hard to push through.
• Fake Fur: The pin goes through the base easily.

The Burn Test
• Carefully pull a few hairs from the fur and hold them to a flame.
• Genuine Fur: Singes and smells like human hair.
• Fake Fur: Melts and smells like burnt plastic and forms small plastic balls at the ends that feel hard between the finger and thumb.[3]

Notes

1. Animal Protection Institute, www.api4animals.org/a5d_fashion.php.
2. Ban Cruel Traps, www.BanCruelTraps.com.
3. "Is That Fur Real or Fake?" Animal Protection Institute, www.api4animals.org/articles.php?p=453&more=1.

What Does *Fair Trade* Mean?

If you ask five people what *fair trade* means, you'll get five different answers. Essentially, a fair trade product is one produced by workers who are not children or slaves, are treated fairly, receive a living wage, and work under conditions that are healthy for themselves, their communities, and the environment. Fair trade is an antidote to the modern global economy, "where profits rule and small-scale producers are left out of the bargaining process, and farmers, craft producers, and other workers are often left without resources or hope for their future."[1] Fair trade provides exploited and marginalized producers, mostly in developing nations, with a way to earn a living and maintain their traditional lifestyles with dignity. The concept of fair trade applies to a range of goods, from agricultural products from the global South like coffee, chocolate, tea, bananas, and clothing, to handcrafts, household items, and decorative arts.

At present, fair trade labeling is used mostly for foods and handcrafts, but labor organizations worldwide are seeking to expand the labeling to include more clothing and eventually all farmed and manufactured items.

Global Exchange, an international organization that promotes fair trade, lists the following principles of fair trade:

- Producers receive a fair price—a living wage—that covers the cost of production and facilitates social development.
- For commodities, farmers receive a stable, minimum price.
- Forced labor and exploitative child labor are not allowed.
- Buyers and producers trade under direct, long-term relationships.
- Producers have access to financial and technical assistance.
- Sustainable production techniques are encouraged.
- Working conditions are healthy and safe.
- Equal employment opportunities are provided for all.
- All aspects of trade and production are open to public accountability.[2]

Certification and Labeling

Products that are produced under these conditions can be identified by the Fair Trade Certified label or the Fair Trade Federation logo on a product. The Fair Trade Certified system involves nonprofit organizations in seventeen different countries, all of which are affiliated with Fairtrade Labelling Organizations International.

In the United States, a nonprofit organization called TransFair USA places the Fair Trade Certified label on coffee, cocoa, tea, rice, sugar, bananas, and other fresh fruits currently available at over 40,000 retail locations. This label is product specific; its presence on one product doesn't mean that all of that company's products are certified fair trade. The relatively recent practice of labeling individual products allows any company that follows fair trade standards to seek certification of its products.

Also in the United States, the Fair Trade Federation is an association of businesses that follow fair trade principles across the board, so its presence on a product means that a company supports the highest level of commitment to fair trade in all of its products.

Great Britain's Fairtrade label and Europe's Max Havelaar label indicate that a product was created under fair trade standards.

We have seen Fair Trade Certified labels only on foods so far. On coffee, it's a beige and brown label that looks like a postage stamp. It says clearly, *Fair Trade Certified*, and nothing else. Many coffee packages bear fake labels that look like postage stamps but with different words, designed to imitate the fair trade stamp for inattentive consumers. This deceptive practice is annoying, but is a testament to the fact that shoppers are paying attention to the label. The certification has brought awareness of fair trade issues to mainstream consumers.

Sweatshop Watch Has a Useful List of Fair Trade Items

While no clothing is Fair Trade Certified as of yet, several organizations have created directories of clothing providers that meet various fair trade criteria. One useful list of labor-friendly clothing producers is from Sweatshop Watch. To qualify for this list, a company must employ unionized workers or be a worker-owned co-op. A staffer at Sweatshop Watch told us that she knew of only one company on the list that also uses organic

cotton: Maggie's Organics. As mentioned previously, all of Maggie's clothes are organic, and their shirts and camisoles are made by a worker-owned co-op in Nicaragua. See Maggie's website for details (www.organic clothes.com).

Fair Trade Helps Farmers in Forty-Eight Countries

The fair trade certification and labeling system benefits over 800,000 farmers organized into cooperatives and unions in forty-eight countries. Fair trade practices have helped farmers earn enough to provide for their families' basic needs and invest in community development. But unfortunately, these farmers are still selling most of their crops outside of the fair trade system because not enough companies are willing to pay the somewhat higher fair trade prices.

You can help increase the demand for fair trade products among companies, retailers, and consumers, and make a difference for small-scale producers. Pay a dollar more and buy the product with the fair trade label or the union label. Ask your retailers to carry fair trade and union products. When we support fair trade, we're using our consumer power to create a better world for everyone.

Notes
1. Global Exchange, www.globalexchange .org/campaigns/fairtrade/.
2. Ibid.

Community Voice
Lynda Grose: What Is a Consumer?

The following is a reflection from clothing-industry professional Lynda Grose. Grose is a designer and an educator in sustainable fashion design at California College of the Arts. She also serves as a consultant for the Sustainable Cotton Project.

"How do we feel about being 'consumers'? The word suggests that we are at the end of the supply line for products; that our sole function is to receive products and devour them. To consume.

"It suggests that we don't even think about what goes into the product before it reaches us. That we don't care where our food and fiber come from or what they go through to get to our table and onto our body.

"We've learned something by now about the impacts food and fiber production have on the environment and on the people in the supply chain. Knowing it makes us uncomfortable. We weren't looking for a chicken that's been cramped and miserable its whole life; we just wanted a healthy meal. We didn't want to buy into child labor and sweatshops; we just wanted a new T-shirt at a reasonable price.

"Now that we know, we feel powerless to do anything about it. The economic system and manufacturing are so big and complex, how can any one person do anything to influence it? The corporations are beyond our control. We prefer to block out the negative information so as not to spoil the pleasure of our shopping experience.

"The truth is, we are the *most powerful* link in the chain. Businesses spend millions of dollars to study us, our attitudes, the cultural influences, our desires, our behaviors. They spend millions more dollars on developing products that they feel we will aspire to buy and own, and millions more on advertising those products to *us*, the consumers.

"Can you imagine what would happen if we *didn't* buy their products? The business managers would go back to the drawing board to analyze why the product failed and how to correct or improve it.

"What if we sent the message that we prefer not to be part of a supply chain that causes child labor and environmental degradation? That we will take our business elsewhere, to more responsible providers? Businesses would take this feedback from their prospective customers and change the way they made the product. The U.S. market is the most populous in the world. We have the largest disposable income. The U.S. consumer is king.

"*We* have the greatest power in the world to influence business production practices to change. It's time for us to be active coproducers, instead of passive consumers.

"*We* have a significant part to play in making products ecologically benign. Let's flex our consumer muscle and redirect company policies."

What You Can Do

- Buy vintage clothing. Donate your old clothes to thrift shops.

- Avoid clothing brands that have been known to use sweatshops. According to Worldwatch, these include Wal-Mart, Gap (Old Navy, Banana Republic), and Target.[1]

- When you buy new clothing, choose at least some of it from companies that use organic fibers and worker-friendly practices, such as Maggie's Organics and American Apparel. Make a personal commitment to become educated about where you can find organic cotton and organic wool products.

- Write to companies that use sweatshops and conventional cotton telling them you won't buy their products until they change. Ask for organic cotton products at your favorite and local clothes stores. Drop a note in the suggestion box, or even chat with the manager or employees.

- Write a letter to the editor or an article in your local newspaper about your concern for cotton farmers and factory workers and your commitment to seeing organic cotton products in your community.

- Push for your organization, club, or university to commit themselves to organic and fairly made clothing.

- Connect your local screen printer or club with vendors that sell organic cotton clothes.

- Use organic cotton for event and fundraiser bags or T-shirts.

- Support the legalization of hemp cultivation. Write a letter to your legislators about it.
- Ask questions of vendors. Tell your friends and coworkers what you learn. When you make green and labor-friendly purchases, be vocal about it. Setting an example goes a long way in helping others to take that first step.

Note

1. Worldwatch, www.worldwatch.org/pubs/goodstuff/clothing.

(Some of the suggestions above are from the Sustainable Cotton Project, www.sustainablecotton.org/html/consumers/ten_things.html.)

Additonal Resources

Companies and Organizations

Behind the Label, www.behindthelabel.org.
Campaign for Labor Rights (grassroots mobilizing department of the United States anti-sweatshop movement), www.clrlabor.org.
Clean Clothes campaign, www.cleanclothes.org.
Cleaner Cotton campaign, Sustainable Cotton, www.sustainablecotton.org/html/manufacturers/manufacturers/html.
Co-Op America, www.coopamerica.org/programs/sweatshops/.
Environmental Justice Foundation, www.ejfoundation.org.
Ethical Sourcing Group, www.ethicalsourcinggroup.org.
Fair Labor Association, Workplace Code of Conduct, www.fairlabor.org/all/code/index.html.
Fairtrade Labelling Organizations International, www.fairtrade.net.
FINE (an informal umbrella of the four main fair trade networks: Fairtrade Labelling Organizations International, International Fair Trade Association, Network of European Worldshops, and European Fair Trade Association. These groups have developed a universally accepted definition of fair trade, an indication of the increasing harmony within the forty-year-old fair trade movement.), www.eftafairtrade.org/definition.asp.
Global Exchange, www.globalexchange.org.
Green Choices, www.greenchoices.org/clothes.html.
Human Rights Watch, www.hrw.org.
International Federation for Alternative Trade, www.ifat.org.
International Labor Rights Forum, www.laborrights.org.
North American Industrial Hemp Council, http://naihc.org.
Organic Consumers Association, www.organicconsumers.org.
Organic Cotton Facts, Organic Trade Association, www.ota.com/organic/mt/organic_cotton.html.
Organic Exchange, www.organicexchange.org.
Organic Trade Association, www.ota.com.
Pesticide Action Network North America, www.panna.org.
Pesticide Action Network Pesticides Database, www.pesticideinfo.org/Index.html.
Sustainable Cotton Project, www.sustainablecotton.org.
SweatFree Communities (a network for local action against sweatshops), www.sweatfree.org.
Transfair USA, www.transfairusa.org.
Fair Trade Certified, www.FairTradeCertified.org.
United Farm Workers, www.ufw.org.
UNITE (union of needletrades, industrial, and textile employees), www.unitehere.org.
United Students Against Sweatshops, www.studentsagainstsweatshops.org.
U.S. Department of Energy, Energy Efficiency and Renewable Energy, www.eere.energy.gov/consumer/tips/.
Worker Rights Consortium, www.workersrights.org.

Articles about Environmental, Health, and Labor Concerns within the Clothing Industry

Catherine Greene and Carolyn Dimitri, "Organic Agriculture: Gaining Ground," United States Department of Agriculture, Economic Research Service, Amber Waves, February 2003, www.ers.usda.gov/amberwaves/feb03/findings/organicagriculture.htm.
"Fields of Poison 2002," Pesticide Action Network North America, http://panna.org/campaigns/docsWorkers/newsrelease.pdf.
Geoffrey Skinner, "How 'Green' Is Your Gear? The Environmental Impact of Nylon," *The Trail Companion* (Spring 2000), www.trailcenter.org/newsletter/2000/spring2000/spring2000-06.htm.
Kim Erickson, "Greener Cleaners: Nontoxic Technology Throws Cold Water on Dry-Cleaning," *Sierra* magazine (September/October 1998), www.sierraclub.org/sierra/199809/hearth.asp.
Organic Trade Association's American Organic Standards for Fiber, www.ota.com/AmericanOrganicStandardsforFiber.html.
"The Price of Childhood: On the Link between Prices Paid to Farmers and the Use of Child Labour in Cottonseed Production in Andhra Pradesh, India," www.laborrights.org/projects/childlab/Price_of_Childhood_102105.pdf.
"White Gold: The True Cost of Cotton: Uzbekistan, Cotton, and the Crushing of a Nation," www.ejfoundation.org/pdf/white_gold_the_true_cost_of_cotton.pdf.

Vendors and Vendor Directories for Green and/or Worker-Friendly Clothing and Other Products

American Apparel, www.americanapparel.net.

bgreen (organic lifestyle apparel), http://natureusa.net/.

Co-Op America's National Green Pages, "The Nation's Only Directory of Screened and Approved Green Businesses," www.coopamerica.org/pubs/greenpages/.

Directory for organic cotton and organic cotton products, www.organiccottondirectory.net/.

Green People, www.organicconsumers.org/purelink.html.

Maggie's Organics, www.organicconsumers.org/sponsors/ maggies. (This is the only company Sweatshop Watch recommends that meets the maximum eco-friendly *and* worker-friendly standards. Garments are made of 100 percent organic cotton and produced by a worker-owned factory.)

Natural Selections & Organic Selections, http://organic selections.com/catalog/.

Organic Exchange, Consumer Marketplace, www.organic exchange.org/consumer_marketplace.php.

The Organic Trade Association, The Organic Pages Online, www.theorganicpages.com/topo/index.html.

Patagonia, www.patagonia.com/enviro/organic_cotton .shtml. (Their entire line of sportswear is made of 100 organic cotton.)

Spiritex, www.spiritex.net.

Chapter Six

Using Our Forests Responsibly

Choosing Paper and Wood Products

The story of the timber industry is a tale of unbridled destruction of forests and of quality of life for those who depend on the forests. It's also about the doublespeak of justification from the timber industry. But like every story in this book, our rendering includes a prescription for action. This section has very specific instructions for consumers. We can buy paper and wood products that promote sustainable use of forest resources and that protect laborers and wildlife into the future.

A Sand Hills Search

It took me six trips to the Carolina sand hills before I ever saw a red-cockaded woodpecker. The sand hills are a unique ecosystem whose keystone species is the longleaf pine, a startlingly beautiful tree with droopy green needles more than a foot long. This ecosystem at one time dominated the broad coastal plain of all the southeastern states, from Virginia through Florida and along the Gulf Coast from Florida through Mississipi. It now survives only in small fragments.

The red-cockaded woodpeckers are even more threatened than the longleaf pine ecosystem that supports them. These elusive birds excavate nest cavities from trees that have heartwood disease, an affliction of pines more than 100 years old that renders the wood soft enough to be carved by a woodpecker's bill.

The red-cockaded is endangered because pine trees are no longer allowed to mature. Almost all pine trees are cut these days long before they're old enough to have heartwood disease.

Will They Come?

I finally saw the woodpeckers on a trip with my husband and his biology students. After an hour's trek and maybe thirty minutes of awkward waiting with the antsy students, we got lucky. Whoosh! A bird suddenly appeared, clinging to the bark outside one of the holes. As we all watched, transfixed, the woodpecker ducked into the deep cavity in the longleaf and the faint sound of cheeping baby birds drifted back to us. After a minute, the parent emerged and flew off in search of more grubs to feed its young.

The longleaf preserves are exciting field trip destinations, not only because of the trees and the woodpeckers, but because of the unusual frog and bird diversity that persists, precariously, in the small fragments of forest. On spring evenings, as many as thirteen different species of frogs, toads, and tree frogs can be heard calling from the forests' wetlands, including the endangered pine barrens tree frog.

A Dubious Distinction

The red-cockaded woodpeckers and their fragmented ecosystem are just the tip of the iceberg in a much deeper story of forests lost to commercial exploitation. The longleaf ecosystem is one of *fourteen* southern forest community types between Virginia and Texas that have been reduced to 2 percent or less of their original range.[1]

Our old-growth trees are long gone, having been hauled out by lumber companies in the early 1900s. After the gold mine of southern old-growth was plundered, the industry turned its attention to the Midwest, gobbled their trees, and then moved on to the Pacific Northwest. Timber companies knocked out a hefty proportion of that region's old-growth forests before being chased back to the South in the 1980s, where forests were staggering to their feet with secondary growth. But the rug's been jerked out again. The industry is at present ripping through the South's small immature hardwoods as fast as possible. The younger and smaller southern hardwoods of today aren't big enough for high-quality lumber, so they're targeted by the wood-fiber industry instead. The trees are ground up by chip mills and pulp mills, operating like giant pencil sharpeners, to produce paper and building products such as oriented strand board and medium-density fiber board. Southern forests have earned the unhappy moniker "fiber basket of the world," as they provide 60 percent of the wood products used in the United States and 15 to 20 percent of the world's paper supply, more than any country other than the United States.

Community Voice

Alan Kneidel: Mystical Land of the Longleaf Pines

Even before dawn, life in the longleaf pine savanna is well underway. The clucking call of the chuck-wills-widow accompanies the raucous hoots of a barred owl as a constant murmur of insects backs them up. The sun rises and humid mists drift from the ground to the peaks of lofty pine trees. Kept open by frequent wildfires, the understory is a haven for rare wildflowers and orchids, some of which are found nowhere else than this habitat. Famous for their plant life, these savannas have been known to contain up to 124 plant species in 100 square feet, including carnivorous pitcher plants, sundews, and Venus flytraps.

From one of the pine trunks, white sap oozes from a small hole. This hole marks the home of the endangered red-cockaded woodpecker, indigenous to the pine savanna. Extended families of this species travel widely through the woods, but always make it back to their nest holes as dusk approaches. The longleaf pines provide food for a variety of animals, such as the brown-headed nuthatch, turkey, quail, and the giant eastern fox squirrel. As these forests have been cleared several species native to this habitat have suffered greatly. The indigo snake is now endangered, and gopher tortoises and eastern diamondback rattlesnakes are on the verge of being so. Today, more than thirty plant and animal species associated with longleaf pine ecosystems are listed as threatened or endangered.

This unique ecosystem used to spread from the Carolinas to Texas, but today there are only scattered patches left. This is due in part to the commercial conversion of the forests to faster-growing trees, such as loblolly pine, creating forests devoid of almost all wildlife.

Logging in the West

Recently, we visited Washington state. Part of the trip included driving out to Cape Flattery, the westernmost point of the Olympic Peninsula and of the continental United States. Our family loves that area because of its remote wild shore with its immense rocky sea caves and crashing surf. Oceanic birds nest on the offshore islands and smaller sea stacks. The area was once covered by vast temperate rainforests of evergreens—spruce, fir, and cedar. What remains of the forest is mostly in Olympic National Park, which includes Pacific shoreline as well as pieces of forest. But because Cape Flattery is a very long drive from the harbors of Puget Sound and the Seattle area, the forests there have lasted longer than most. As we drove across the northern edge of the peninsula toward the cape, we passed fewer and fewer towns. We did see forests, none of them virgin, but forests nonetheless. We also passed clear-cuts, a lot of them—ugly, bald, and barren slopes that had been wiped clean of trees, leaving behind a sea of stumps. Just before the road reaches Cape Flattery, it passes through Neah Bay, a small Native American community on a Macah reservation. The small coastal town sports a number of locally carved totem poles that bring home to passersby the residents' traditional connection to nature. The poles feature carvings of eagles, fish, and marine

A forest that has been clear-cut. Clear-cutting and replanting with faster-growing nonnative species are common practices by the timber industry that reduce biodiversity.

mammals that have historically been part of the Macah's livelihood and their culture.

As we drove, we passed a surprising number of logging trucks. The trucks headed toward the cape were all empty. The trucks headed from the cape back toward the ports of Puget Sound and Seattle were full. About every fifth vehicle we passed was a logging truck. We spent the night in the coastal town of Sekiu, a fishing village just east of Neah Bay. I spent an hour or so talking with the proprietor of the motel, who moved to the area twenty years ago from a cattle ranch in Kansas. We talked about logging and fishing. He told me that the great majority of the trees logged along the northern Olympic Peninsula leave the country. They're driven to Seattle and loaded onto ships for Japan, or other destinations across the Pacific. The logging trucks we passed are delivering the region's forests to international timber companies, and the profits are going into the bank accounts of executives who probably don't even live in the United States.

The proprietor of the Sekiu motel also told me that when he first moved to Sekiu, the logged trees were so big that a logging truck could only carry a single tree trunk. Now, he said, the trucks are loaded up with dozens of little "pecker poles." That's what's left, or what's regrown. The coastal enterprises such as logging, fishing, and hunting that depend on forests and other natural resources cannot persist very long with practices that diminish the region's natural capital. What happens when these resources are all gone?

The timber industry has done a number on Washington, but logging in the Northwest is more restricted than it once was. Activists have made a difference. Forests that are home to the endangered spotted owl have gained some protection. And the region has become an area of diminishing returns for loggers because the bulk of the virgin forests have been plundered. The overexploitation of the Pacific Northwest and the activist uproar sent many timber companies scurrying back to the Southeast. Now they're going through our forests lickety-split, feasting on our own pecker poles.

Southern Forests Are Rich in Biodiversity

We recently interviewed Scot Quaranda of the Dogwood Alliance, a nonprofit whose mission is to promote sustainable forestry practices. Southeastern forests need all the help they can get, he said, because "90 percent of the forests in the [Southeast] are privately owned and have no protection—there

are no laws keeping landowners from doing as they please to make money. Six million acres are cut every year in the South, mostly for paper."

Thirty-two million of the 200 million acres of southern forest have been replaced, after clear-cutting, with sterile plantations of loblolly pine. Loblollies are the tree of choice for plantations because they provide good fiber and grow fast—they can be harvested in only ten to sixteen years for paper. According to U.S. Forest Service projections, pine plantations will expand 60 percent by the year 2040 to occupy 54 to 58 million acres of southern forest.[2]

Earlier, I had spoken with an executive of a lumber company who declined to be quoted but who extolled the virtues of pine plantations to me, calling them "reforestation." Quaranda assured us that research does not support this perspective on pine plantations. E. O. Wilson, a Harvard biologist and Pulitzer Prize winner, agrees with Quaranda. Wilson told me that a pine plantation contains at least 90 percent fewer species than the forest that preceded it. He compared the effects of tree farms on biological diversity to "building a line of discount stores."[3] Pine plantations are heavily treated with herbicides and pesticides to kill the native plants and invertebrates that would normally feed birds and other vertebrates. For this reason, pine plantations are more aptly called monocultures or factory farms than forests.

Like the big meatpacking companies, the timber industry also abuses laborers and human communities. Quaranda told us that

Scot Quaranda of the Dogwood Alliance, a nonprofit that promotes sustainable forestry practices through education, certification of forest products, and activist campaigns.

many timber industry workers are employed by chip mills, which grind trees into bits before sending them along to a pulp mill to be made into paper. "If you look at the map of all the chip mills in the region," Quaranda said, "and you put a big circle around each mill to include the sourcing area for it, you can see that *every inch* of the South is covered in the sourcing area of one chip mill or another."

And yet, virtually no chip mill workers are unionized, said Quaranda. "When you look at rural communities whose main resource is a forest, the communities that are dependent on chip mills or pulp mills ... have the lowest levels of education, the lowest wages, the highest levels of poverty. Communities that produce higher quality wood products are somewhat better off. But by far, the healthiest forest-based communities are tourism- and recreation-based economies." Ironically, the survival of those healthy communities also requires healthy forests.

"What's it like to live in a chip mill community?" Sadie asked Quaranda.

"Chip mill communities have constant log-truck traffic, safety issues on the road, and noise problems because they're incredibly loud facilities," he replied. "In addition to that, all the forests within miles of the chip mill are destroyed, so all the places that you hiked or hunted as a child, streams you waded or fished in, are gone or fouled.

"Pulp mills are among the worst offenders in terms of energy consumption and release of greenhouse gases. They also dump chemicals like dioxin into surface waters as a result of the bleaching process. Pulp mills are considered to be one of the top five most toxic industries."

With that, we felt the problems were clear. We were anxious to hear Quaranda's ideas about solutions. How do consumers have any control over the loss and degradation of forests?

What Consumers Can Do

Environmentally friendly forest products are not as easy to find as green transportation or food. Asking at stores for sustainably produced lumber or paper often leaves retailers looking mystified. Unfortunately, that means it's all the more important to ask.

According to Quaranda, regulating timber production on private land is nearly impossible. Consequently, environmentalists have found that it's more productive to offer voluntary certification for producers interested in distinguishing themselves. There are two certifications for lumber products: SFI and FSC. One is bogus; one is not.

SFI, or the Sustainable Forestry Initiative, was created by and for the timber industry. "They created the SFI in the 1990s to paint themselves green," said Quaranda, "You can log endangered forests, do large-scale clearcutting, and convert native forests to plantations, and still get the SFI stamp of approval saying that your forest has been managed sustainably. Pretty much every timber company is SFI certified."

The Forest Stewardship Council, meanwhile, is a third-party system composed of community groups, first nations (Native American tribes), environmental groups, foresters, and wood producers. The FSC forest management system even includes a restoration component to reclaim areas that were degraded from destructive forestry practices in the past. "The FSC is a good program that we support," said Quaranda. "None of the most egregious timber companies are FSC certified, such as International Paper and Weyerhaueser. But a lot of other companies are."

Retailers of Certified Paper and Wood Products

If you go on the FSC website and click on Certificates in U.S., you'll find a long list of timber companies that are FSC certified (www.nffe-fsc.org/). You can also look in the store; FSC–certified products, from lumber to paper, have a certification label.

The Rainforest Alliance, one of the certifiers for FSC, says in their "Smart Wood Guide to Print & Paper Sources" that Office Max and Fed Ex/Kinkos carry FSC–certified paper.[4] I visited the Fed/Ex Kinkos closest to my home and asked; they had never heard of either FSC– or Smart Wood–certified paper, but I asked the manager to stock it, and got the phone number of the corporate office to call them too.

I also asked them for 100 percent post-consumer recycled paper. The manager at first knew nothing about it, but after I pressed, he came up with one package. For $13. That was an unhappy discovery. Staples carries partly recycled paper for much less— thanks to insistent consumer demand.

If you can't buy FSC– or Smart Wood–certified paper, you can find paper that's recycled. *Postconsumer recycled* means specifically that it has been used by consumers and then recycled, rather than trimmed off of rolls in the paper mill, fresh from the forest.

Next, I went to the Home Depot near my home. Home Depot is purportedly the largest marketer of FSC wood, but when I asked the lumber department about it, no one had heard of it. I came back the next day when the head of the lumber department was on duty and asked him. He said they do carry FSC, but it must be special ordered. The only FSC–certified lumber they had in stock was spruce two-by-fours and two-by-sixes.

I asked him why they don't stock more. He said, "The vendor won't sell me more unless I buy full units." And he can't buy full units because floor space is limited and there's little demand for FSC lumber. He said that I was only the second person in four months to ask about FSC products. FSC lumber, he said, costs 25 percent more than non–FSC certified wood because sustainable practices are more costly to the producers.

Home Depot Exec Takes Green Steps

The day after my visit to Home Depot, I called Home Depot headquarters in Atlanta and spoke with Ron Jarvis, an executive in charge of the whole company's environmental program. I asked him why the Home Depot stores don't promote FSC wood, or at least tell their workers what it is in case a customer asks. He said they did train workers for a while, but the training was expensive and the workers reported that no one ever asked for FSC products, so they stopped the training. He confirmed, though, that Home Depot sells more FSC wood than any other retailer—

more than $450 million in sales each year. But, said Jarvis, less than $1 million of that is to people who are *looking* for FSC wood. He said he gets only one to two calls per month for FSC wood from the 2,000 Home Depot stores in the United States.

Jarvis pointed out that Home Depot carries more than 8,000 different products that contain some wood, such as shelving boards, garden products, tools with wooden handles, doors, windows, and so on. Although the store near me doesn't stock FSC–certified lumber or construction plywood, he said that my particular neighborhood store does stock some of the other items made of FSC–certified wood.

He seemed very anxious to convince me that Home Depot is a green company that practices environmental stewardship, and I was impressed with some of what he told me. After he was appointed as the environmental executive for the company, he contacted the World Wildlife Fund and asked for a list of the ten most threatened forests in the world and the forty most endangered tree species in the world. He told all of Home Depot's vendors that Home Depot will no longer buy products from those forests or made from those endangered trees. The forests, he said, include threatened and heavily exploited areas in Ecuador, Indonesia, northern Brazil, Congo, and the Amazon. For a more thorough account of Jarvis's efforts to protect some of the world's most threatened forests, see *The Wall Street Journal* online article by Jim Carlton.[5]

Wanted: Consumer Demand

It's clear that customer demand will be key in bringing about change in the timber industry. Many retailers now have told us that no one asks for certified wood, or else the retailers seemed completely blank themselves about their company's green products. Maybe if they received frequent consumer requests, they'd know more and stock more and try to stock competitively priced green products. I now ask managers at every office-supply and home-supply store I visit to carry FSC products and postconsumer recycled paper.

Reduce, Reuse, Recycle

Quaranda says that it's important for consumers to reduce, reuse, and recycle. Use both sides of paper. At home and at work, we keep a stack of paper by the computer that's already been printed on one side, and we always use that unless the printout is for something special.

In the kitchen, we have a small shelf for paper scraps. Even paper that's partly printed on both sides can be trimmed for phone notes or grocery lists. We wrap presents in the Sunday comic pages when possible.

Quaranda told us about the Paper Calculator, a website that calculates the average energy and wood consumption and environmental releases for each of five major grades of paper and paperboard. For a given grade, it allows the user to compare the environmental impacts of papers made with different levels of postconsumer recycled content, ranging from 0 percent (virgin paper) to 100 percent postconsumer recycled.[6]

Be an Activist

Consider joining an activist group to put pressure on timber companies and retailers that sell wood products. Many companies, such as Lowes, Home Depot, Office Depot, and Staples, have already made some concessions to activist groups demanding more sustainable forest practices. But they still have a long way to go. And companies such as International Paper, Weyerhaueser, and Georgia Pacific haven't cooperated at all. The Dogwood Alliance website[7] offers accounts of their successful campaigns, as does Sadie's sidebar Chain-Saw Activists Get Powerful Results about her participation in Dogwood Alliance's campaign to pressure Staples (see pages 217–218). Activist tactics may work faster than legislation and regulation to force policy changes.

Woodpeckers Revisited

I haven't been back to the sand hills since our conversation with Quaranda and our investigation into sustainably produced forest products. But next time I go, I'll look at the birds and frogs differently. I won't feel so detached from their problems, so powerless to do anything about it. I have a new understanding of the challenges they face, who's to blame, and where the solutions lie. I know now that I can be a part of the solution, with a minimal amount of effort. We all can be. Once again, the most powerful and long-range solution is in educating ourselves as consumers and *buying selectively*. What if we, all of us, bought only FSC– or Smart Wood–certified wood products, or bought only 100 percent postconsumer recycled paper? I know that won't happen today because some of these products are more expensive and are hard to find. But we can move in that direction by asking, asking, asking, and choosing green products when we can. The more steps we take in that direction, the more widely available those products will be.

Notes

1. "Table 9: Ecosystem Communities That have Declined by 70 Percent or More in the South," Southern Forest Resource Assessment, www.srs.fs.usda.gov/sustain/draft/terra1/terra1-27.htm.
2. David N. Wear and John G. Greis, Southern Forest Resource Assessment Summary Report, Southern Research Station and Southern Region, U.S. Department of Agriculture Forest Service, www.srs.fs.usda.gov/sustain/report/summry/summary.htm.
3. Personal communication.
4. "A Smart Guide to Paper & Print Sources," Rainforest Alliance, www.rainforest-alliance.org/programs/forestry/pdf/smartguide.pdf.
5. Jim Carlton, "Once Targeted by Protesters, Home Depot Plays Green Role," *Wall Street Journal*, August 6, 2004, ForestEthics, www.forestethics.org/article.php?id=1036.
6. Paper Calculator, www.environmentaldefense.org/papercalculator/.
7. Dogwood Alliance, www.dogwoodalliance.org.

Additional resources

Southern Research Station Headquarters, www.srs.fs.usda.gov/.

Ted Williams, "False Forests," *Mother Jones* (May/June 2000), www.motherjones.com/news/feature/2000/05/false_forests.html.

U.S. Department of Agriculture Forest Service, www.fs.fed.us/.

Chain-Saw Activists
Get Powerful Results

My first protest involved a thirty-five-foot inflatable chain saw, a furious knife-wielding store manager, and several police cars.

My second protest involved soggy cardboard trees, a torrential thunderstorm, and a news crew.

We never meant them to be so dramatic. We were just a bunch of high school kids who were alarmed about the state of things and didn't know what else to do but go out on the street corner and make a fuss about it.

I'll admit, I had my doubts. When our high school's brand-new environmental action group teamed up with the Dogwood Alliance, I wasn't sure what we were getting ourselves into. The Dogwood Alliance, an organization focused on modifying the paper industry and slowing the destruction of southern forests, was eager to work with our group. They even sent down their communications director, Scot Quaranda, to teach us about chip mills and the alliance's campaign to mitigate the unnecessary consumption of paper and wood products.

Their approach consisted mostly of direct action—writing letters, calling politicians, and putting pressure on retail stores. They, along with ForestEthics, were in the midst of a great Paper Campaign, striving to protect forests by changing the way paper is sold. The principle targets were the country's largest retail paper sellers: Staples, Office Max, and Office Depot.

And that was why, one dismal spring afternoon, I found myself standing outside a Staples in Monroe, North Carolina, with a soggy paper tree tied to my chest and a thunderstorm raging overhead. It was a national day of action—a coordinated day in which groups all over the country held simultaneous demonstrations requiring the corporation to acknowledge our presence and demands.

I was somewhat mortified. We were certainly getting attention, but not in the way we'd intended. We had planned to do a die-in—that is, dressed up as trees, we would be "chopped down," and fall down in the parking lot, meanwhile shouting facts about deforestation. It would be theatrical, maybe even comical.

However, we had not taken into account the most fearsome thunderstorm of the season, which was currently lashing down upon us. Thunder roared above us, lightening splintered the sky, rain poured in torrents. The parking lot was a greasy lagoon of undrained water. Getting "chopped down" meant collapsing into a slurry of SUV drippings and chewed-up gum. Shivering, I glanced at my friend Dave, who stood clutching one end of a nearly illegible banner. He opened his mouth and screamed a wail of pure misery.

The reason we hadn't postponed the protest, as any sane person would do, is that we were on television. A news crew from the *Jim Lehrer News Hour* had come all the way out from Hollywood to film our demonstration, and we couldn't send them back with nothing. Initially, we had imagined glory: getting our cause on the air. Now we just looked like idiots. "Get outta my face, you stupid kids!" a woman in a Jeep shouted, her tires dousing us in a spray of icy water. *I bet they got that on film,* I thought bitterly.

Three hours later, finally safe and dry at home, my mood had not improved. What an idiotic waste of time. No one there was listening to us. We looked like fools, or worse. All my relatives were going to see me on television looking like a total lunatic. I was probably going to get pneumonia and die, and no one would even know what the point was.

As it turned out, I was completely wrong. Though our protests seemed to go unheard on the site, Staples was actually paying very close attention.

Just over a year later, as a direct result of the Dogwood Alliance and ForestEthics campaign, Staples released a landmark environmental policy. After more than 600 demonstrations, 15,000 postcards, and thousands of phone calls and letters, Staples committed to:

- Achieve an average of 30 percent postconsumer recycled content across all paper products;
- Phase out purchases of paper products from endangered forests, including key forests in the southern United States, U.S. national forests, and the world's last remaining ancient forests, such as the boreal forests of Canada;
- Report annually to the public on its progress toward reaching these goals; and
- Create an environmental affairs division headed by a senior executive reporting to the Staples CEO.[1]

By November 2003, one year after the campaign victory, the average postconsumer recycled content of Staples' paper products had leapt to 26.6 percent. Within that year, the corporation also "set benchmarks for its suppliers in Indonesia [and] identified the southern forest region as a priority area for the implementation of its policy due to the adverse impact caused by paper production and the important ecological values of these forests."[2] Staples estimated that in the first year after the new agreement, their policy changes saved 1,150,743 trees, 473,830,000 gallons of water, 34,480 barrels of oil, 20,688 tons of coal, and 68,964,053 kilowatt hours of electricity. They also reduced emissions of greenhouse gases carbon dioxide, sulfur dioxide, and nitrogen oxide by 298,296 tons.[3]

"This campaign victory is a testament to the power of citizens joining together to demand corporate environmental accountability," stressed the Dogwood Alliance.[4] After this victory, a similar campaign successfully targeted Office Depot, resulting in the revision of their environmental policy. An Office Max campaign began in late 2005. It has yet to see results, but I have faith that Office Max will capitulate before long. It's funny, but after witnessing the success of these campaigns I have a lot more faith in demonstrations than I did at the time I actually participated in them. I can't say for sure whether our miserable presence in the parking lot that day actually made a difference or not, but it seems to have. And that feels good.

—Sadie

Notes

1. "Staples Campaign Victory!," Dogwood Alliance, Campaigns, Office Supply Industry, www.dogwoodalliance.org/content/view/52/113/#staplevictory.
2. Ibid.
3. Ibid.
4. Ibid.

Chapter Seven
The Power of Your Investments

The direct purchases you make are only one way your money finances the business world. Your investment in companies by buying their stocks is another way of making a statement. A stock is, after all, a share of ownership in a company. The company uses the money you spend on its stocks to fund their growth and expansion into new markets. If they're building factory farms in China, or a refrigerator factory in Mexico, and you're a shareholder, then you're financing it.

Owning stock is particularly influential because, as owners in the business, stockholders get to vote in the election of the company's board of directors. These directors make the hugely important decisions of how the company spends its profits—and how environmentally and socially responsible these choices are.

A bond, meanwhile, is an IOU from a corporation or the government. Unlike a stock, the amount of return from a bond is fixed when you buy it, no matter what the economy does. In essence, the government or company is paying you more than you paid them for the use of your money.

In a mutual fund, a financial advisor divides your money between a variety of stocks and bonds.

A money market is a kind of mutual fund specializing in short-term bonds.

Shareholder Advocacy

Socially Responsible Investing, or SRI, is a method of investing both for personal gain and for benefits to society as a whole. You can choose an SRI mutual fund that will invest your money in a variety of companies with certain standards of worker rights, environmental protection, community involvement, and ethical products. A factory with labor abuses would be screened out, as would a company producing defense weapons. Animal exploitation could be grounds for exclusion, as could environmental pollution.

Sometimes SRI funds intentionally invest in companies with questionable practices so that ethical shareholders can alter company policies. This can be accomplished when shareholders either propose changes to company management or elect more responsible directors.[1]

Shareholders can also resort to a divestment campaign, in which they sell off their shares in massive groups in protest. This is a potentially huge disaster for the company and can be a very effective technique. The precedent of divestment was established in the 1980s, when American investors targeted U.S. university endowments and pension plans, convincing them to withdraw from South Africa as a means of pressuring that government to end apartheid. While international diplomacy, sanctions, and public outcry had failed, financial influence prevailed.

Campaigns for massive divestment in Sudan (due to genocide) and Israel (due to the occupation of Palestine) are currently underway.[2]

Many skeptical potential investors worry that SRI is not as lucrative as traditional investing. However, this is not the case. In fact, the Social Investment Forum reports that SRI funds grew faster than the rest of the investment world in the last decade. Since 1995, SRI has increased 260 percent; mutual funds alone increased fifteenfold in that time.[3] Given rising awareness of social and environmental concerns, this isn't too surprising. But it is encouraging.

Just as in traditional investing, a wide array of funds are available, from domestic to international, large to small. There are socially responsible index funds designed to follow the market as a whole. As long as the market gains, they will too. You can also invest in individual stocks and bonds, just as in traditional investing. Before choosing any investment fund, it's important to read the prospectus, or financial report, and understand its past performance.

For more information, see the Social Investment Forum[4] and Co-Op America.[5]

Community Investing

Keeping your financial resources in your own community is another option. Rather than investing in businesses, you can devote your resources to community development by placing your money in a community bank or credit union. While you earn interest, these institutions lend your money to local organizations that fund education, jobs, and environmental conservation. Just as in a traditional bank or credit union, you can have a checking or savings account, buy a certificate of deposit or invest in a money market. The only difference is that, as with SRI, your money is carefully directed to positive forces for social change.

Rates are generally very competitive. We found that in our state, the locally run Self-Help Credit Union has the highest rates of any institution except the state employees credit union. You can earn interest at rates higher than 5 percent while your money funds a variety of community and environmental programs. These range from community development loan funds, which finance co-ops, nonprofits, and housing projects in economically depressed communities, to microenterprise loan funds, which lend money to grassroots entrepreneurs working to develop businesses and jobs.[6]

Through the Community Investing Center online, you can search for banks, credit unions, and other organizations that are in your area or that fund projects you're interested in.[7] Organizations range from COOCAFE, a co-op representing more than 3,500 small Costa Rican farmers in environmentally sustainable coffee production, to the New Mexico Community Development Loan Fund, which provides loans and assistance to nonprofits and small businesses in New Mexico that can't get loans through traditional sources.[8]

Whether through consumer spending or through investing, our dollars are powerful tools for change. Unless we are politicians or media pundits or corporate executives ourselves, our dollars are our most effective means of directing the course of future events, of protecting the environment and laborers. Think carefully about how you spend yours.

Notes

1. Co-op America, Social Investing, www.coopamerica .org/socialinvesting.
2. The South Africa Model, Empowering Americans to Defeat Terrorism, www.divestterror.org.
3. Social Investment Forum, www.socialinvest.org.
4. Ibid.
5. Co-Op America, Social Investing.
6. Self-Help Credit Union, www.self-help.org.
7. Community Investing Center, www.communityinvest.org.
8. Ibid.

Conclusion

Awareness is the first step. Researching this book opened our eyes to choices we didn't know we had. What we've learned has changed the way we buy clothes; we buy vintage-wear now, and organic cotton. We look for postconsumer recycled paper, and ask for FSC—certified wood—even when we know a store doesn't carry it. We ask just to increase *their* awareness. We reduced our home energy consumption by 36 percent by changing our lightbulbs and changing our thermostat settings. We're biking more and looking for a car that will burn biodiesel. We try to buy local and organic food, we don't eat meat or eggs, and eat few dairy products; the environmental impact of densely concentrated farm animals is too great.

We realize now that most of the things we buy have environmental costs, and very few of the manufactured goods on the market are made with transparency. We often have to dig to find the true costs. These costs—the smokestack emissions, the chemicals flowing into rivers, the conversion of forests to cotton fields and feedlots and pine plantations—were tolerable as long as the human population was small. Ecosystems healed themselves and rebounded. But now our numbers are huge and mushrooming; the effects of our careless ways exceed the planet's ability to absorb and overcome the blows.

In some ways, we're too late. Our planet has warmed and will continue warming, even if we stop burning all fossil fuels today. The rain forests we've cut for timber will never be as they were. We've already extinguished many species of animals by overharvesting or destroying habitats. Millions of acres of fertile cropland have already been degraded beyond recovery.

But in other ways, we're not too late. For the time being, we're still at a threshold. Two doors lie before us. We're probably the last generation that will have much choice, but we still do. We can carry on with business as usual, or we can change our ways. We can still save what remains of our forests and fertile farmland. We can use fewer fossil fuels to slow global climate change, to clean up the air, and to give our scientists and our government a chance to develop greener sources of energy. We can decide to protect needy populations that are routinely exploited—children and impoverished women. We can protect the health of babies who are so vulnerable to mercury and nitrate pollution. We can do all this by changing our buying patterns.

Reviewing Our Recommendations

To slow the warming of our planet, consider buying a more fuel-efficient car, drive less, and look for opportunities to use other ways of getting around, such as biking, walking, and mass transit.

Make your home more energy efficient by repairing air leaks and using energy-saving appliances and compact fluorescent lightbulbs. For new construction, consider adopting a passive solar design that saves heating and cooling expenses while reducing your consumption of fossil fuels.

The choices we make in landscaping our yards can have a tremendous impact on our streams and on local wildlife populations. Options range from choosing native plants that provide food for birds to converting entire lawns to native meadows or woodlands. Using paving stones for driveways can protect our streams. Supporting local land conservancies can protect your community's remaining green spaces.

For meals, shop for organic and locally grown foods. Ask your grocer to clearly label local produce. When buying animal products, look for providers who raise the animals at pasture. You may find local, pastured animal products through your nearby farmers market. If not, look on Local Harvest[1] or Eat Wild[2] for local providers. If local products are not available, you can order beef and pork online from Niman Ranch,[3] a national company that uses humane and environmentally sustainable practices and has ethical labor standards. Buy Fair Trade Certified coffee, and other fair trade products as they become increasingly available. Consider eating fewer animal products in general for a cleaner environment and more efficient use of agricultural lands.

When choosing paper products, look for postconsumer recycled paper—100 percent postconsumer recycled (PCR) is best. Ask your local office-supply stores to carry PCR and Smart Wood–certified papers. For wood products, look for Forest Stewardship Council (FSC) certified products. If they're not available, ask your home-supply store to carry them. Many stores, such as Home Depot, can order them even if they are not routinely stocked. Even if you choose not to order FSC products, tell the managers of your local stores that you want them to carry Smart Wood– and FSC–certified products at competitive prices. Ask them to label clearly the certified and postconsumer recycled products that they do carry.

Clothing choices are more complex because clothes are made from so many different fibers, and the processing issues are completely separate from the cultivation issues. Our clothing section offers specific guidance. In general, buy organic cotton and organic wool. Ask stores to carry these products, and to carry Organic Trade Association (OTA) certified fabrics. OTA certification refers to processing. Avoid Kelly green and turquoise clothing, which is sometimes dyed with heavy metals, unless you check with the manufacturer. To protect labor, buy union-made goods or garments from worker-owned factories. The greenest choice for clothing is to buy secondhand.

To protect wildlife, check the online resources we provide in our wildlife section before you buy any products made from wildlife body parts, including gifts, trinkets, purses, shoes, or traditional medicines—especially while traveling, but here in the United States as well. Support the efforts of organizations such as World Wildlife Fund to protect wildlife from commercial trade, whether legal or illegal. Educate yourself and let your voice be heard.

Finally, consider investing in responsible companies. Socially responsible mutual funds, shareholder advocacy, and community investing are powerful tools for putting your dollars to work toward social change.

General Tools for Green Consumers— Buy Secondhand and Recycle

Buying used goods is usually more earth friendly than buying new. This is particularly true of items that are labor and chemical intensive, such as nonfood agricultural products like clothing, paper, and wood. Using secondhand paper means reusing your own paper, front and back, in your computer printer. Ask your coworkers to save their discarded paper for you—or better yet, start a recycling program at your workplace. It also means buying postconsumer recycled papers. For wood, it means buying used furniture. Almost every piece of wood furniture in our house is secondhand. We shop at yard sales; we tell our family and friends to think of us when they're remodeling and discarding furniture. We buy from newspaper ads. We even pick up furniture such as desks or chairs that have been set out by the side of the road for trash.

Many thrift stores offer a wide variety of secondhand goods in addition to clothing. Most of our bedding and dishes have come from thrift stores too. We often shop at a used appliance and furniture store operated by Habitat for Humanity that has a good selection. Used appliances can be much cheaper than new ones. Pawnshops can be a great source for used electronics, such as televisions and stereos. With careful shopping, you can even find used appliances that are energy-efficient and have the Energy Star label.

Used cars can be a huge savings, although very old cars tend to lack the emissions controls that newer models have. An auto mechanic can help you evaluate a potential used-car purchase in terms of its energy efficiency and its emissions control system. The manufacturing of a new car uses a tremendous amount of energy and materials, and the disposal of an old car takes up a lot of landfill space. So if your car is energy efficient and does have up-to-date emissions controls, drive it until it wears out, rather than trading it in on a new one every three to five years.

Recycling old houses is perhaps the ultimate in recycling. Moving and restoring an old house slated for demolition saves all the materials and energy that would go into building a new one, and keeps the old one out of the waste stream.

Tolerate Wear, and Reuse

In the tried-and-true environmental mantra of "reduce, reuse, recycle," keep *reusing* in mind. In the United States, we have become accustomed to replacing things at the slightest sign of wear. If a shirt is a little frayed at the collar, the temptation is to toss it out. If a sofa shows a little wear on the arm, we think of replacing it. If the toaster oven needs a paper clip to hold the door shut, we feel we need a new one. People around the world don't live that way; they can't afford to. Environmentally speaking, we Americans can't afford to either.

Reduce Consumption and Choose Long-Lasting Goods

When you choose goods with high durability, products that will last for a long time, you're reducing your consumption over time. Durability is a huge issue in housing because building a house uses so many materials. Shingles and carpets have extremely low durability and require replacement every few years. These two items are among the very biggest contributors to our landfills. Both also require a tremendous amount of energy to manufacture and use large amounts of fossil fuels. We go through them like paper plates, without a thought to the environmental costs, so we've explored better options. A steel roof and a tinted concrete floor, scored to look like polished stone, can both last for more than 100 years with no maintenance whatsoever. These two choices are probably the biggest durability improvements we discovered.

Use Online Resources, and Learn More

Co-Op America provides a comprehensive and extremely useful online compendium of screened and approved companies and organizations that offer green products, fair trade products, and various certifications. The Co-Op America website includes a search engine to help you locate any particular item.[4]

Great Green Goods[5] is a shopping blog whose creators search the Internet for the best in recycled or low-environmental-impact goods and gifts.

Buy Union Made

Look for union-made labels on products. Unions protect worker rights and unite workers to improve their bargaining power with their employees. Unionized workers are less vulnerable to being fired or mistreated for demanding safety, fair wages, and other rights from their employees. *Union made* doesn't guarantee anything, however, about environmental standards. Nonetheless, we can assume that companies employing unionized workers have a higher standard of working conditions than their nonunion counterparts.

Among their many useful tools, Co-Op America provides a list from the American Federation of Labor and Congress of Industrial Organizations (AFL-CIO) of companies whose products are made with unionized labor.[6] The AFL-CIO is the largest federation of unions in the United States.

Buy American

Supporting the American economy is one issue that seems to transcend party lines. From a conservative perspective, buying American supports freedom, democracy, and small-town America. From a liberal perspective, it takes a stand on human rights and environmental issues. But whatever your motivations, most of us can agree that bringing production home would help us all.

Bug Retailers and Manufacturers

Communicate with companies directly and let them know what you want. Every retailer we've spoken to has stressed that their product selection is strictly consumer driven. They carry what consumers ask for and especially what consumers buy. Period.

Pick up the phone, write a letter, or have

a word in person. Ask retailers and manufacturers about production practices. Ask for guarantees on environmental and labor standards. When writing, it helps to include a tag or label from one of their products to show that you're a customer and that you're paying specific attention to their company.

If you don't have time to write letters and can't get through on the phone, try filling out comment cards when you're in stores, or send feedback on websites. A simple note will do, such as, "I'm a long-time customer of your store. I sure love your product, but I have some questions I hope you can answer. Do you know where or how this product was made? Does your company offer any guarantee that its products are made in accordance with human rights and environmental standards? How are your factories monitored, and according to what standards? I am concerned about being a responsible consumer and I hope your company cares about these issues too."

Be an Activist

Join forces with other activists and work for change within your own community and beyond. Contact advocacy organizations such as the Sierra Club for information about local chapters in your area. The Nature Conservancy can direct you to a land conservancy near you. Write letters to your government representatives, to newspapers, to magazines. Call your county agencies and demand they take action on that polluted stream or stinky smokestack.

Go Forth; Do Good

If you've read and absorbed all this, you're ready. You don't have to do all of it to make a difference. Pick one thing. Look for locally grown apples at the grocery store this week. Next time you buy underwear, buy one pack from one of the organic cotton online vendors referenced in our clothing section. Next time you're at Home Depot, buy a couple of compact fluorescent lightbulbs. Tell your friends what you did.

If we all do just a few things, we will make a difference. Every little effort is a note in a bottle to the future, a little note saying, "I cared enough to do something."

Notes

1. Local Harvest, www.localharvest.org.
2. Eat Wild, www.eatwild.com.
3. Niman Ranch, nimanranch.com.
4. Co-Op America, National Green Pages, www.coop america.org/pubs/greenpages/.
5. Great Green Goods, www.greatgreengoods.com.
6. Co-Op America, Sweatshops, Union-Made Products, www.coopamerica.org/programs/sweatshops/sweatfree products.cfm.

Appendix

Things to Consider While Shopping

Safety and Health

- Does the item contain toxic ingredients or residues?
- Is it independently tested or certified? (Are there any third-party symbols or logos?)
- Is the item certified organic?
- Was this item made with dyes, pesticides, antibiotics, or hormones?

Value for Money

- Can I buy it more cheaply in bulk?
- Will I use this item enough for it to be worth the time I spent earning the money to pay for it?
- Equipment: Can I rent it, borrow it, or buy it secondhand, instead of buying new?

Resource Efficiency

- Is it made with the maximum amount of renewable and recyclable materials?
- Plastic items: Is there a "potato plastic" or starch alternative?
- Does this item require refrigerated or fast shipping?
- Is the item made to be repaired rather than replaced?
- Appliances: Is the item Energy Star certified?

Ethical Issues

- How was this item made, and in what conditions?
- Was this item produced by a small business or farm, or by a corporation? (See diagram.)
- Was this item fairly traded?
- Are any of the ingredients/materials genetically modified organisms (cotton, corn, soybean, canola, or wheat)?
- Was this product tested on animals?
- Any animal product: Is the item free range, grass finished, pastured, or cage free? Where did it come from?

Environmental Impact

- Where was this product made? Is there a more-local alternative?
- Food: Is this item in season?
- Can this be recycled or passed on to another owner?
- Will the item be toxic to nature when thrown away?
- Is the item overpackaged? Can the package be recycled?
- Detergents and soaps: Does it contain phosphates (Phosphate-free brands: All Temperature Cheer, Liquid Tide, Wisk, All)
- Clothes: Does the item have to be dry-cleaned?

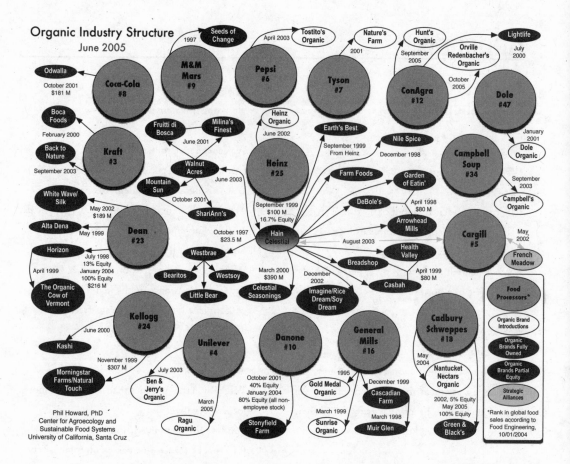

Organic Industry Structure
June 2005

Phil Howard, PhD
Center for Agroecology and
Sustainable Food Systems
University of California, Santa Cruz

Many organic brands (represented by white and black ovals) that consumers may think of as small, family-owned or green companies are actually owned or partially controlled by large corporations or conglomerates (represented by gray circles). Rather than ignoring these connections, we can maximize our consumer power by supporting companies or providers that use sustainable methods for *all* of their products.

Index